America's Future
Biden and the Progressives

America's Future
Biden and the Progressives

Daniel Quinn Mills
Harvard Business School, USA

Steven Rosefielde
University of North Carolina at Chapel Hill, USA

Published by

World Scientific Publishing Co. Pte. Ltd.
5 Toh Tuck Link, Singapore 596224
USA office: 27 Warren Street, Suite 401-402, Hackensack, NJ 07601
UK office: 57 Shelton Street, Covent Garden, London WC2H 9HE

Library of Congress Cataloging-in-Publication Data
Names: Mills, Daniel Quinn, author. | Rosefielde, Steven, author.
Title: America's future : Biden and the progressives /
   Daniel Quinn Mills, Harvard Business School, USA,
   Steven Rosefielde, University of North Carolina at Chapel Hill, USA.
Other titles: Biden and the progressives
Description: New Jersey : World Scientific, [2022]
Identifiers: LCCN 2022009988 | ISBN 9789811252440 (hardcover) |
   ISBN 9789811253348 (paperback) | ISBN 9789811252457 (ebook) |
   ISBN 9789811252464 (ebook other)
Subjects: LCSH: Biden, Joseph R., Jr. | Presidents--United States--History. |
   United States--Politics and government--2021– |
   Progressivism (United States politics) | Democratic Party (U.S.)
Classification: LCC E916 .M55 2022 | DDC 320.97309/05--dc23/eng/20220304
LC record available at https://lccn.loc.gov/2022009988

British Library Cataloguing-in-Publication Data
A catalogue record for this book is available from the British Library.

Copyright © 2022 by World Scientific Publishing Co. Pte. Ltd.

All rights reserved. This book, or parts thereof, may not be reproduced in any form or by any means, electronic or mechanical, including photocopying, recording or any information storage and retrieval system now known or to be invented, without written permission from the publisher.

For photocopying of material in this volume, please pay a copying fee through the Copyright Clearance Center, Inc., 222 Rosewood Drive, Danvers, MA 01923, USA. In this case permission to photocopy is not required from the publisher.

For any available supplementary material, please visit
https://www.worldscientific.com/worldscibooks/10.1142/12729#t=suppl

Desk Editor: Nimal Koliyat

Typeset by Stallion Press
Email: enquiries@stallionpress.com

Dedicated to Elizabeth Mills and Susan Rosefielde

Foreword

This book is about a choice President Biden must make that will determine the future of America. He can make the choice decisively and announce his choice to the world and he can seek support as he implements his choice. Alternatively, he can slip into a choice day-by-day without careful consideration. He can leave the pundits to explain to the world what is happening.

His choice is between being a partisan politician or a non-partisan statesman. He cannot be a partisan statesman, as he appears to think that he can. This is because partisanship in its form in America today prevents statesmanship. The political party's interests always precede those of the nation. That Biden recognizes the difference is shown by frequent contradictory statements from the White House. At one moment the President calls for the full enactment of his political party's program. At another moment he asks his opponents to join him to accomplish important things for the nation. At one moment he is the leader of the Democrat Party. At another he tries to rise above partisan political maneuvering in the national interest. He can be politician or statesman. He cannot be both. His role as top Democrat requires that he crush his opponents, not embrace them for the national good.

In this book, we examine Biden's dilemma in deciding between these two roles. We urge him to be a statesman in the nation's interest.

Biden might be so inclined. However, to be a statesman he must contend with the progressive wing of his party. Today's progressives have become revolutionaries whose purpose is to remake America by canceling their opponents and imposing one-party government. In his effort to satisfy the demands of the progressives Biden has endorsed their policies and isolated himself from political friends and opponents. He has marginalized his moderate Democrat friends and expelled all Republicans he can reach from the federal government. He has rejected efforts by the moderates in his party to include some Republicans and independents in his Administration.

Biden has a tiger by tail. As in all such situations the problem is how to let go. In this book, we suggest a way that Biden can free himself from the danger posed by the revolutionary progressives and simultaneously benefit America dramatically.

This book is not a call for bipartisanship. It is not a call for cooperation between the Democrats and Republicans. It is a call for much more. It is a call for Biden to rise above the partisanship that is making America unable to reverse its domestic decay and unable to continue its high status in the world. Partisan bickering is undermining American economic and social effectiveness. Biden will not be able to fashion a legacy of accomplishment by playing the partisan game. He must do more. He must resolve the partisan tangle by championing a higher vision of the nation's governance. He should do so by deciding to espouse non-partisanship, announcing his decision to the world, and beginning to act in that way while eschewing his role as champion of a single political party.

Preface

In this book, we attempt to distinguish today's progressives' revolutionary idealism from a practical pragmatism. Joe Biden declares that he wishes to model his presidency on that of Franklin Roosevelt. Franklin Roosevelt was a progressive — he ran on the progressive ticket in New York — but a very different type of progressive than Biden is now endorsing. Today's progressives are intoxicated with street justice idealism. We use the term "revolutionary progressive" to distinguish today's revolutionary anti-working-class progressivism from Franklin Roosevelt's reformist progressivism. FDR sponsored a soft form of socialism. Today's Democrat version of progressivism is not socialist because it cares nothing for working people. Instead, today's progressives focus on demographic groups. Unlike FDR's political philosophy today's progressives are revolutionary, not reformist. When Biden espouses today's progressives' policies, he is taking a very different direction than that taken by FDR.

We have no objection to progressive sentiments, but we reject revolutionary progressive totalitarianism. The American and British traditions have been pragmatically libertarian. Robert Owen was the originator of English socialist pragmatic, individualist libertarianism. We suggest that President Biden should shun European continental idealism for can-do American pragmatism.

About the Authors

 **Daniel Quinn Mills** provides thought leadership in several fields including leadership, strategy, economics, and geopolitics. He has been a director of publicly listed firms and is currently a director of several closely held private corporations. He has published books about business activities, the media, American foreign policy, economic policy, and political processes. During the Vietnam War, Mills spent several years in Washington, D.C. helping to control inflation. For several years, he was in charge of all wages, prices, and profits in the construction industry (then 14% of GDP). Simultaneously he taught at MIT's Sloan School of Management. Thereafter he taught at the Harvard Business School. He has done consulting and speaking in the following countries: United States, Canada, the United Kingdom, Indonesia, Ireland, France, the Netherlands, Germany, Switzerland, Italy, Russia, Israel, China, Japan, Malaysia, Brazil, Columbia, Mexico, Singapore, South Africa, Kuwait, the United Arab Emirates, Saudi Arabia, Vietnam, and Australia.

Mills earned his MA and PhD from Harvard, both in economics. He received his undergraduate degree from Ohio Wesleyan. Throughout his career, Mills has been an influential author. His recent books are *Beleaguered Superpower: Biden's America Adrift* (Steven Rosefielde), World Scientific, 2021.

Progressive and Populists, World Scientific, 2020 (with Steven Rosefielde), *The Trump Phenomenon and the Future of U.S. Foreign*

Policy (with Steven Rosefielde), 2016; *Global Economic Turmoil and the Public Good* (with Steven Rosefielde), 2015; *Shadows of the Civil War*, 2014; *The Leader's Guide to Past and Future*, 2013; *Democracy and Its Elected Enemies* (with Steven Rosefielde), 2013; *The Financial Crisis of 2008–10*, 2010; and *Rising Nations* (with Steven Rosefielde), 2009. Previously he published *Masters of Illusion: Presidential Leadership, Strategic Independence and America's Public Culture* (with Steven Rosefielde), 2007.

Steven Rosefielde, Professor of Economics, University of North Carolina, Chapel Hill. He received his PhD from Harvard University, and is a Member of Russian Academy of Natural Sciences (RAEN).

His books include: *Democracy and Its Elected Enemies: The West's Paralysis, Crisis and Decline*, Cambridge University Press, 2013; *Inclusive Economic Theory* (with Ralph W. Pfouts), World Scientific, 2014; *Global Economic Turmoil and the Public Good* (with Quinn Mills), World Scientific, 2015; *Transformation and Crisis in Central and Eastern Europe: Challenges and Prospects* (with Bruno Dallago), Routledge, 2016; *The Kremlin Strikes Back: Russia and the West After Crimea's Annexation*, Cambridge University Press, 2016; *The Trump Phenomenon and Future of US Foreign Policy* (with Quinn Mills), World Scientific, 2016; *Trump's Populist America*, World Scientific, 2017; *China's Market Communism: Challenges, Dilemmas, Solutions* (with Jonathan Leightner), Routledge, 2017; *The Unwinding of the Globalist Dream: EU, Russia and China* (with Masaaki Kuboniwa, Kumiko Haba, and Satoshi Mizobata, eds.), World Scientific, 2017; *Putin's Russia: Economic, Political and Military Foundations*, World Scientific, 2020, *Progressive and Populists* (with Quinn Mills), World Scientific, 2020; *Beleaguered Superpower: Biden's America Adrift*, (with Quinn Mills), World Scientific, 2021.

Executive Summary

We are writing about American politics. Not about which party should win, but about what the excessive partisan struggle between the parties is doing to our country — what it is doing to our economy, to our position abroad, and to our military preparedness. We believe that the damage to America is very substantial and increasing. We believe the President is on a course to make it much worse. We believe there is a better course and hope that he will embrace it.

The Biden Administration's course is of more importance than just to America. The revolutionary progressive element of the Democrat Party, of which Biden is the titular head, is exporting its ideology. French leaders have recently expressed the fear that American revolutionary progressive ideas imported to France from America will undermine the stability of the French Republic. The ideas of the revolutionary progressives are feared to encourage divisiveness, embolden Islamists in France, and stimulate public disorder. "Prominent intellectuals have banded together against what they regard as contamination by the out-of-control woke leftism of American campuses and its attendant cancel culture" (https://www.nytimes.com/2021/02/09/world/europe/france-threat-american-universities.html?action=click&module=Top%20Stories&pgtype=Homepage by Norimitsu Onishi).

Beneath most bitter political controversies between the two major political parties in America lie real problems that could be solved with goodwill but are allowed to fester so that each party can make political advantage out of it. We will identify many of those controversies, describe the underlying problems, and propose possible solutions. Among the issues are immigration, crime, climate change, relations with Russia and Iran, and combating the pandemic. There are also many lesser general problems that need to be addressed.

There are currently irreconcilable differences over policy toward China, educational policy, voting rights and procedures, the status of the Supreme Court, preferences for certain demographic groups, and extended limitations on free speech.

The American people want action on underlying problems which confront the nation. Political activists on both sides do not. Biden entered office promising such action. He immediately began to act as a partisan Democrat. Partisanship means that for every issue on which Biden has made a promise to the American people he has only to claim credit if anything good happens and assign blame to his opponents (the Republicans) if anything goes wrong. He doesn't have to accomplish anything to be a successful partisan president.

To be president for the people Biden does not have to cooperate with the Republican Party. He does not have to act in a bipartisan manner. The American people do not favor the parties — they favor the national interest.

Biden could act in a non-partisan manner. He could stay above the partisan controversies. But he is choosing not to. He is choosing to be a partisan Democrat who leans to the revolutionary progressive wing of the party. The desire of the American people for a government committed to getting things done for the people is still unfulfilled. Biden can reverse his course; he can choose to get above the partisan infighting that is crippling America. Will he do so?

Contents

Foreword		vii
Preface		ix
About the Authors		xi
Executive Summary		xiii
Part I	**Biden as President: Joe Biden, the Man and the Politician**	**1**
Chapter 1	The Joe Biden Who is President	3
Chapter 2	Biden as President	11
Chapter 3	Biden as a Modern Propagandist	19
Part II	**The Biden Administration**	**29**
Chapter 4	A Mandate to Govern or Not?	31
Chapter 5	Off on a Wrong Foot	37
Chapter 6	The Electoral Significance of Women	43
Part III	**Bidenomics**	**51**
Chapter 7	Biden Economics and the World	53

Chapter 8	Biden Economics and the United States	59
Chapter 9	Biden's Political Economics	69

Part IV　Biden's Domestic Policies　75

Chapter 10	Biden's Complex Game: Immigration	77
Chapter 11	Demographics is Destiny	85
Chapter 12	President Biden Confronts the Pandemic	91
Chapter 13	Mishandling the Pandemic	97

Part V　Biden and the Post-American World　103

Chapter 14	Biden and the World: A World Order Disintegrating	105
Chapter 15	End a War by Losing It: Afghanistan	115
Chapter 16	Sovereign Democracy: Russia	123

Part VI　The Rise of Global Military Insecurity　131

Chapter 17	Is the U.S. Ready for Armed Conflict?	133
Chapter 18	The Loss of a Major War	141
Chapter 19	The Decline of American and the Rise of Chinese Globalization	147

Part VII　Biden and China　155

Chapter 20	An Ideological Contest with China	157
Chapter 21	China and COVID-19	163
Chapter 22	The World's Flash-Point — Taiwan	169
Chapter 23	The Initiative Lies with China	177

Part VIII　Biden's America: The Perils of Biden's Democracy　185

Chapter 24	The Bastion of Democracy	187
Chapter 25	The Paradox of American Democracy	195

Chapter 26	How the U.S. is Governed	201
Chapter 27	Money and Power in American Politics	205
Chapter 28	The Challenge to Democracy	211

Part IX Too Much Partisanship 217

Chapter 29	The Bane of American Democracy	219
Chapter 30	The Democrat Party and Democracy	227
Chapter 31	The Partisan Battle	233
Chapter 32	The Critical Fight over Election Practices	241
Chapter 33	African Americans' Role in American Politics	247
Chapter 34	Coup and Coup Again	253

Part X The Progressives 259

Chapter 35	The Challenge of Progressivism	261
Chapter 36	The Danger of Revolutionary Progressivism	269
Chapter 37	Biden is a Liberal Who Struggles with Revolutionary Progressivism	275
Chapter 38	Canceling in the Name of Justice	283
Chapter 39	Radical Progressivism in the Democratic Party	289

Part XI How Biden Might Save America 301

Chapter 40	Putting America Back Together: What Our President Should Do	303
Chapter 41	Statesmanship as a Route to Unity	307
Chapter 42	A Program for America's President	315
Chapter 43	Biden Persists in Partisanship	321
Chapter 44	Progress and Biden's Destiny	337

Part I

Biden as President: Joe Biden, the Man and the Politician

Chapter 1

The Joe Biden Who is President

Joe Biden is now President of the United States. What kind of man is he?

"… Joe Biden is both an ordinary and an extraordinary man. He's decent, friendly, empathetic and approachable, while at the same time brilliant of mind, with deep-seated convictions and a stalwart determination to do what is right." (Lois Pope, "Joe Biden is a good man …," *Palm Beach Daily News*, February 7, 2021, p. 16A.) This is Lois Pope's assessment of Joe Biden. She has known Joe Biden for many years working with him on social betterment projects.

Biden has been a politician almost all his adult life. He has done nothing else. He has a politician's instinct for the appearance rather than the reality. He focuses on the short-term impact on the voter of any event. He drives his own activity — it can't really be called policy — by public opinion polls. These characteristics of the President were on display in his handling of the American withdrawal from Afghanistan in the summer of 2021. A *Reuters* report published on September 1, 2021, revealed that in a telephone conversation on July 23, 2021, President Biden said to President Ghani of Afghanistan, "There is a need, whether it is true or not, there is a need to project a different picture," of the situation in Afghanistan. "Whether it is true or not," is the American politician speaking. When American public opinion polls continued to show that a large majority of the American people favored an end to the American military presence in Afghanistan, Biden crafted a withdrawal to coincide with the 20th anniversary of the Al Qaeda attack on the World Trade Center in New York City. Biden apparently intended a public relations celebration for the end of the conflict in Afghanistan. The American withdrawal from

Afghanistan was a major shift in policy, but it was designed on primarily political grounds. This should not be a surprise to anyone. It is how democracies work — what the electorate wants and will welcome, daily, is a continuing concern of politicians. Biden is of that breed.

Until Biden became Vice-President of the United States, he had accumulated almost no wealth and was one of the poorest members of the Senate. He was admired as one of the few members of the Senate who could be considered aloof from the corruption that is common in American political life.

Biden served as Barak Obama's Vice-President. After leaving office with Barak Obama, he found ways to increase his net worth. His methods are not well documented, but he now owns some 4 million dollars' worth of homes; has some 4 million dollars in financial investments; and an estimated additional million dollars in various other items. His net worth is estimated at 9 million dollars. These are official figures. He seems to have had business dealings with members of his family, especially his son Hunter and his brother. Unofficially, Biden's family is thought to have accumulated much more wealth peddling his influence, and his own net worth is thought to be significantly understated.

Joe Biden has a family of brothers, sisters, and his own children. Several of his family have done business employing the support of his name, and possibly with his active involvement. Combined with the general corruption of the U.S. government process, this leads to concerns that the American President can be bought.

What Is Biden Like?

Biden's personality has an important impact on his political success in becoming President of the United States.

The last few years of American politics suggest that the messenger is as important as the message. This is why Biden is President. This is also key to the Biden presidency.

Millions of people voted against Donald Trump for a second term in the presidency because they didn't like or approve of his personality and behavior. Biden ran as the anti-Trump. To Trump's bluster Biden opposed a quiet and dignified personality. It was effective.

We must be careful not to be misled by political propaganda. In fact, when we consider Trump's foreign policies, we may consider him a sheep in wolf's clothing. He had a loud bark, but almost never bit.

Biden appears to be the opposite. He is a wolf in sheep's clothing. He speaks softly and takes both sides of each issue. But his actions are often in support of the progressive wing of the Democrat Party and are biting in their impact.

Biden once said, "If you don't vote for me, you're not black." That is, a person who doesn't share the same political views as others is not really of the same identity group. He was widely criticized for typing all blacks as alike in their opinions.

It is worth noting that the Republican, who has been criticized as a racist since his first steps into politics, did not respond, as he could have, "If you do vote for Biden, then you are black, not white." Implying that all white people, a strong majority in the U.S., to confirm their whiteness must vote for the Republicans. Such an undoubtedly racist comment the Republican chose not to make.

This incident, Biden's comment, and the Republican's silence, have been used by Biden's opponents to assert that Biden is a racist. This is almost certainly untrue — in the political sphere Biden supports and is supported by the large majority of African Americans.

At a somewhat typical meeting during the 2020 presidential campaign via Zoom, Biden presented himself in the following manner. Biden was scheduled for 20 minutes; he stayed an hour appearing from his home. He would have stayed longer if someone hadn't ended the session to meet another engagement. Biden looked healthy and very comfortable. Biden addressed racism and criminal justice — but said nothing about the looting and violence occurring in concurrent demonstrations by progressives in major American cities. He attacked the Republicans implicitly. His answer to every question about a significant national issue was that as President he would spend more money on it. He stuttered a bit, but with no significant misspeaking. He seemed to live in a world of illusion. In his world there was no rioting, no violence, only peaceful demonstrations. It was this behavior that gave rise to the suspicion that Biden was a closet progressive. Biden slid from one topic to another without transition. He seemed to love to talk. He seemed to enjoy listening to himself. He was interrupted many times and he complained about it. He was grandfatherly; non-threatening.

In human affairs there are always two elements: what is done and how it is done. Trump is very weak on the how. Much of the bitterness directed at Trump is about how he does things. Biden emphasized this in his campaign ads during the 2020 election. He called for politeness and civility. Biden usually expresses these values.

Biden identifies himself as a problem-solver. He said in his first press conference that his job is to solve the problems of the American people. Yet he has never had a managerial job, or even an administrative job of any significance. He has always addressed problems as a legislator. His concept of solving a problem has always been to make a rule about it, and to believe that if there were a rule, it would be obeyed, and the problem solved. Now, as President, he must get problems resolved by other means. It should not be a surprise if it takes this old dog a while to learn new tricks.

He has a keen sense of humor which makes him likeable. For example, he once commented that "When I entered the Senate — one hundred and twenty years ago …." In this way he made fun of the concern that surrounds his age. Of course, he entered the Senate many fewer years ago than 120.

Biden is likeable, but he has inherited a damaged position. For years the Democrats have attacked the previous holder of the presidency. They continued this after Biden was elected. For example, on December 6, 2020, CNN reported that the Republican President had flown to Valdosta, Georgia on the previous evening for a rally in which he told multiple "lies." This was simply part of a pattern of vilification of President Trump.

There is no way to vilify the office holder without damaging the reputation of the office. Yet most media supported Biden for President and were delighted when Biden gained the office and seemed to think that the office and its reputation and aura were undamaged by five years of attacks on its previous holder. It wasn't. The reputation of the office of the President of the United States is badly damaged by attacks (whatever their merit) on everyone who has held the office since George H. W. Bush. By now it needs someone of outstanding stature to begin to restore it. Joe Biden is not that person. During the withdrawal from Afghanistan which took place during the summer of 2021 many people and media outlets which opposed the way the withdrawal was conducted condemned Biden angrily. Again, the office of the President was damaged significantly.

Biden as President

Biden is said to have met early in his presidency with historians to discuss how he could become a transformational President in the image of Franklin D. Roosevelt. This is a very high ambition. It is a political ambition and a personal one. It is not an ambition for the country, except indirectly through his own self-satisfaction.

Biden is a big spender. He was no sooner inaugurated President than he supported an almost 2 trillion dollar economic stimulus package that passed Congress and he signed about six months into his presidency.

Immediately after the passage of that measure, Biden called for a roughly 3 trillion dollar spending bill. He also called for passage of a roughly 1 trillion dollar infrastructure spending bill.

Democrat-sponsored and enacted spending might break a log-jam that has tied up comprehensive bills on many major needs in the United States. An infrastructure building bill is one of them. Another is a bill mandating cooperation between the government and the private sector in dealing with certain national problems. Bills building infrastructure and mandating cooperation have languished in partisan bickering for a decade or more. What partisanship prevents from occurring on a bipartisan basis might occur by one-party domination.

This would turn some of Biden's spending proclivity into a good result for the country.

But the rules of the Senate make it unlikely to happen. The stimulus bill was passed in the Senate by a simple majority composed solely of Democrats because of a particular rule in the Senate. But other spending bills require a majority of 60 votes out of the 100 senators. This the Democrats do not have on a party-line vote.

It is possible that the Democrats will change that rule to one requiring a simple majority vote in the Senate for most bills. Such a rule change is possible but not likely. If it were to be made, the Democrats might pass major spending bills on many topics which have long lain in contentious stalemate in America — if the Democrats could resist spending on partisan advantages, instead of national needs. The stimulus bill was, of course, a combination of both.

Biden and Religion

Biden identifies himself as a man of faith. He is a life-long Catholic. There is no reason to doubt his faith.

His predecessor supported religion strongly and had the political support of major Christian denominations on a variety of issues but did not really walk the talk.

Biden worships publicly but is the leader of a political party that is increasingly anti-religion, and which denigrates people of faith.

"We all know," said one prominent Democrat TV news anchor, "that people who believe in a personal god and traditional morality are culturally backward."

The paradoxes of American politics place a man of religious faith into the top leadership position in the most anti-religious of American political parties.

The likely outcome is that Biden will keep his personal faith under control and support the anti-religious elements in his party.

But there is more to Biden's religion than its reality. Whether sincere or not, it also plays a subtle political role. One of the key elements of modern propaganda is to confuse your opponent about your commitments. Biden presents himself as a religious person when his political party is not. Whatever Biden's sincerity or not, he confuses his opponents about what role religion plays in his political thinking. While supporting the anti-religion movement which is very important among his activist supporters, he bewilders his opponents by espousing his own and his wife's religious faith. What will he do? Will he abide by his faith and adhere to it in his decisions as President, or will it play no role in his politics? Given the strength of the progressives' anti-religious orientation, Biden is most likely to be employing his faith only as a decoy to confuse his opponents.

Biden's Ethnicity: The Interplay of Demographic Groups in the Democrat Party in the Search for the Presidency

It may seem ironic that Biden is exactly of the ethnicity which the progressives of his party denounce as the oppressors and exploiters of all other demographic groups in the United States. The bitterness of their denunciations is remarkable. But there is Biden, a white male who is now, as the leader of their political party, the Democrat Party, President of the United States. How did this happen?

The Democrat Party is composed of demographic identity groups which jostle for power in the Party. The groups also jostle for the opportunity to run candidates for office. The most important of those offices is the presidency. Others include the Speaker of the House when the

Democrats control the House of Representatives, and the majority leader of the Senate when the Democrats have a majority in the Senate.

It is ironic that now, when the Democrats control all these offices, two white men and one white woman are their occupants, not a single person of color.

In the demographic accounting of identity politics Biden, a white man of English, Scotch, and Irish extraction, was due to receive the Democrat nomination for President in 2016. This was because he had been Vice-President in the outgoing Obama Administration. But a man — an African American man — had been in the White House for 8 years. Thus, men and African Americans, two of the Democrat Party's major demographic identity groups, had recently been in office. Now the women wanted their turn. Mrs. Clinton pushed Biden aside and obtained the nomination to be President. She ran for the presidency. She expected to be elected. She unexpectedly lost. So, the women in the Democrat Party missed their turn in the White House.

They sought another opportunity. In 2020 all the elements of the Democrat Party sought the Presidency. In the primaries there were candidates who were women, African Americans, gays, Hispanics, black women, and white males. By some unrevealed process the white male won the nomination, and the other demographic groups accepted the result. Biden's nomination represented a return to a tradition that a former Vice-President is entitled to run for the presidency. It was surprising that Biden, a moderate liberal, was selected in the primaries by an increasingly radical party electorate.

Biden's Preparation for the Presidency

Joe Biden has years of political experience in Washington, and almost no other experiences. As such, he is a life-long participant in an increasingly corrupt political system.

A valuable book about American politics is titled *The Best Democracy Money Can Buy* (Greg Palast, London: Pluto Press, 2002). It is now almost 20 years since this expose' was published. It has been followed by many more exposes. Despite them, corruption has gotten much worse. Biden is a successful player in this game and though he may occasionally criticize it, it is unlikely that he will make any serious effort to reform it.

Chapter 2

Biden as President

Biden versus the Republicans in Temper and in the Exercise of Authority

At the time of the establishment of the United States an influential Pennsylvania politician wrote to George Washington urging him to accept the Presidency of the new nation. "The exercise of authority depends on personal character," he wrote. "Your cool, steady temper is indispensably necessary…"

Joe Biden has a cool, steady temper. This is one of his major qualifications for the presidency. It may fit him well to exercise presidential authority. In addition, he has a lifetime of experience in American politics. He knows the principal office holders of each party, and the most influential supporters of the Democrat Party. This should enable him to work closely with the powerful people in Washington, and to avoid problems that might arise from interactions with persons he does not know personally.

Biden's cool, steady temper seems to fit him well to exercise leadership. People are willing to listen to him without a strong negative reaction to his personality. This is to his advantage.

However, whatever he may have been like in the past, at his current advanced age Biden does not appear to be a strong leader. His personality now does not fit him well to exercise presidential authority. Whatever leadership he exercises flows from his position as president; it does not flow from his personality, character, or objectives. He appears to endorse the directions and policies initiated by others in his party. It is frequently asserted that at a time when the United States needs a strong chief executive we have instead Biden — who appears to be one of the weakest American chief executives in the past century.

The danger in Biden's weakness is that he is joined in Congress by leaders of his own party who lack the qualifications of temper that Biden has but who may overtake Biden's exercise of authority. He is president, but his weakness forces him to accept as equals in national authority the leaders of both the House of Representatives and the Senate. His weakness forces him to accept the demands of progressives in his party. This is a weakness he shares with the other leaders of his party who run the House of Representatives and the Senate.

Biden's weakness is offset to a degree by his close relationship with former President Barak Obama. Obama is one of the most popular leaders of the Democrat Party and is a strong personality. Biden leans on him for support in dealing with other Democrats. So close are the two men that some observers question who is in charge in the Biden presidency. Some of Obama's comments in the past have given currency to this question.

Barak Obama in a TV interview in November 2020, was asked if he would want to serve a third term as president if the Constitution permitted. He replied, "If I could just stay in my basement in sweats and let someone else do all the talking and the work, I'd be okay with that."

In spring, 2021, Biden's press secretary revealed that President Biden spoke to former President Obama several times a week.

Whether or not Obama is in charge during the Biden presidency, he is undoubtedly very influential with the President. Obama is considered a moderate Democrat, but he is respected by the progressives. He serves to calm the troubled waters of division within the Democrat Party.

On April 8, 2021, in a speech accompanying his announcement of executive orders restricting gun ownership, Biden offered his opinion that "No amendment to the Constitution is absolute." He was speaking of the Second Amendment but there are some 26 others. One of them is the Thirteenth Amendment which abolished slavery and involuntary servitude, except as punishment for a crime. Did the President mean that in his view this amendment is not absolute? Was the President implying that in order to restrict gun ownership in America despite the strictures of the Second Amendment, he would accept modifications to the Thirteen Amendment? It can't be thought that that was his intention. But this sort of confusion in his leadership is continual.

Biden is believed to be a moderate, but he is recognized to have to placate the progressives in his party with offices and policies. He is torn between his own moderation and the energy of the Democrat progressives. The result of his attempt to balance between the two wings of his party is a set of inconsistent pronouncements and policies leading to unfavorable outcomes. The consequence is an increasingly radical and ineffective American government.

The Strength of Biden's Presidency

The argument is often made that the Congress has been seriously weakened by the growing strength of the Presidency. The Congress is now said to be dependent on the Executive branch for much of its facts and research; and to have surrendered much of its constitutional power — especially the power to make war — to the Presidency.

This ignores two major considerations. First, the Congress through the power of the purse controls many executive agencies so that the president really has little direction of them. Much of the executive branch is an extension of the control of the Congress and is mislabeled as belonging to the president. Second, the president is increasingly isolated in the White House without control of the agencies of the executive branch — partly because of Congressional control of those agencies, and partly because of partisan political resistance to a president's legal authority.

The war-making power has been surrendered inappropriately by Congress. When the Republican came to office, he was promising to demand that Congress formally make declaration of the Middle Eastern wars which were being waged by the executive branch or he would end them. Congressional declaration of war was the Constitutional requirement. The Republican in the White House was unable to do either — to get Congress to accept responsibility for the wars by declaring them, or to end them — largely due to Congressional opposition. These lengthy military conflicts are arguably the most important scandal of American Constitutional behavior today and are the result not of presidential power but of presidential weakness. Yet, as we shall see in a later chapter, strong arguments for the continuation of the conflicts in the Middle East and Central Asia are made. The failure of Congress to authorize the conflicts in Iraq, Syria, and Afghanistan possibly should not have contributed to persuading President Biden to end American military involvement in Afghanistan.

Biden's Promise to Unify the American People

Biden entered his presidency promising the American people that he would work to unify the nation. "I have my whole heart and soul in this," he said at his inauguration.

Many observers, especially Republicans, jumped to the conclusion that Biden meant that he would work in a bipartisan fashion with his political opponents. This had been done often in the past when Biden was in the Congress by previous presidents.

But he didn't mean that at all. From the first moments of his administration, Biden ignored Republicans in Congress and pushed a Democrat agenda by party-line votes. The Democrat Party is complex.

The Democrat Party is largely made up of and financed by special interest groups which press for presidential policies in their favor, not that of the public. It is not easy for Biden to govern in the interest of his party, because his party is so complex.

For example, the teachers' unions gave about 43 million dollar in campaign contributions to Democrat candidates in the 2020 election. President Biden got caught in a battle between parents and the teachers' unions over the reopening of schools during the pandemic. Parents and school boards wanted the schools reopened; teachers unions resisted, saying that the schools were not safe from the virus, and wanting more money. In effect, Biden was caught in a conflict between the public and a special interest group which was a key element of the Democrat Party. Would Biden stand for reopening schools, as he had promised to do, or would he support the teachers' concerns? He tried to temporize, and many major school districts stayed closed. Because of the composition of the Democrat Party, Biden faces situations of this nature continually. He has to choose between special interest groups and the public as a whole, with Republicans watching to criticize whenever he chooses against the public or hesitates to choose on the public's behalf.

A similar dynamic exists with Biden's legislative proposals. To every legislative bill which benefits the public generally, the Democrats attach money for their special interest groups. For example, to the 1.9 trillion dollar stimulus bill with payments to the public to help with the pressures of the pandemic on people's lives, the Democrats attached money for their feminists' organizations to finance abortions; they attached money to cover revenue problems for the big cities run by Democrat mayors. Without these benefits for special interests, the Republicans would have joined to support passage of the bill. But because the legislation contained special payments to Democrat interest groups, the Republicans opposed the bill.

If the Democrats approach most issues as problems of allocation — providing benefits to Democrats and not Republicans — then "we together" is precluded because Republicans will be taxed to pay for the Democrats' gains. Because of the Biden Administration allocating so much public money to the elements of the Democrat party, it is seen by many people as being primarily concerned with handouts to insiders. Its "public" policy positions then appear as just a smoke screen for feathering insiders' nests.

What does Biden mean by his promise to unify the country? He doesn't mean bipartisanship. He means that he will try to gain universal support for the Democrat Party. Americans are to be unified as Democrats. He is trying to unify America on his terms — on the agenda of the Democrat Party. He appears to believe that the Democrat Party's policies can be so persuasive that all Americans will come to support them. The nation will be unified in the single political party of which Biden is the head.

The Importance of Women in Biden's Presidency

American political offices are still strongly dominated by men. But women make up most of the American electorate and play an increasing role in American politics. They are far more important in the Biden Administration than their numbers as office holders suggest.

Joe Biden and His Wife

Jill Biden is a formidable woman. She is well-educated. She has a career as a teacher. She is a decade younger than her husband and is in vigorous health. She is informed and experienced about American politics. Jill Biden is a smart and well-informed woman whose influence on her husband with respect to policy and politics (which are very closely related in the Biden Administration) should not be underestimated. Her influence is generally concealed behind the marriage framework and is often hard to perceive.

Jill Biden is with her husband continually. She is there to help see that he will serve his entire term. She is said to enjoy being First Lady of the

United States and the White House hostess. She would lose those roles should her husband leave the presidency before his term ends. This she does not want him to do. She wants to remain First Lady and hostess. She supports him vigorously every day of his presidency. She intends that he remain in office.

Vice President Kamala Harris is another woman who is very close to Joe Biden. She is with him almost every day as he conducts his term as president. When TV cameras watch the President, Harris is often picked up in a corner of the room. When she realizes that she is on camera, she often steps out of the way.

Mrs. Harris is virtually certain to run for president in 2024, presuming that President Biden, who will then be in his 80s and is already somewhat feeble, will not seek a second term. Mrs. Harris is the champion of the progressives. She is younger than President Biden and she is vigorous. She is being trained for the office of president by Biden.

Mrs. Harris's chances of being elected president are far greater should she be able to run in 2024 as an incumbent president rather than as vice president. If Biden serves out his term as president, then Mrs. Harris is almost certain to have to run in the Democrat primaries to seek the nomination for president. She was not a popular candidate for president in the 2020 Democrat primaries and she did not come close to winning the nomination. She might not do better in the 2024 primaries and might not win the nomination. If she has replaced Biden as president before the primaries, then she is likely to receive the Democrat nomination for president without primary contests. She would be running as an incumbent president for reelection.

She has, therefore, a strong interest in Mr. Biden not serving out his term. Americans are discussing this situation. Some are saying that Mrs. Harris would prefer to replace Mr. Biden as president in the second half of his term, because then she could run twice (in 2024 and 2028) to serve a total of 10 years as president. However, if she were to replace Mr. Biden before his term is half over, she could herself if elected in 2024 serve only that term, the provisions of the American Constitution providing thus. But, regardless of this calculation, Mrs. Harris would benefit enormously politically from replacing Mr. Biden as president whenever possible.

Jill Biden knows of Mrs. Harris's interest in displacing her husband as president. She apparently wishes to thwart it. Jill stays close to Joe always to prevent Vice President Kamala Harris from gaining too much influence over her husband. Other women point out that women often have a refined sense of their own territory and of when other women invade it — particularly with respect to their husbands. It appears that Jill Biden sees an invasion of Jill's territory — which is Joe Biden — by Kamala Harris and is actively repelling it.

There is thus a contest between Jill and Kamala over Joe. Jill is trying to keep her husband in office. Kamala is trying to displace him. Both women are subtle, clever, determined contestants and it is not possible to ascertain who will prevail. As Biden's term lengthens, the struggle will become more intense.

How Biden Weakened His Own Position

The Biden Administration governs the United States on an almost solely political basis. Decisions are made in conjunction with public opinion polls. Polls indicate what the American people favor. The President tries to satisfy their preferences. Democrat influence groups make their objectives known to the White House and the President does what he can to gain their financial and electoral support. There seem to be very little, if any, objectives for the nation from President Biden other than politically driven objectives. Biden administers a political party agenda; there is no leadership beyond this.

For example, almost immediately in his presidency Biden reversed the Republican's policies which limited immigration across the southern border of the United States. Soon large numbers of people came across legally and illegally. There was human tragedy day-after-day at the southern border of the United States, but the Biden Administration was unable to view it as anything other than a political problem. This told impartial observers a great deal about the administration and Biden himself.

The border fiasco forecasted the fiasco of the Afghanistan withdrawal, to which we will return in a later chapter. Observers debated whether the situation at the border and the withdrawal from Afghanistan were incompetence or intention — was it possible that the Biden Administration wanted more illegal immigrants, or that it wanted a militant Islam takeover in Afghanistan? But in both instances polls of American voters indicated that at the outset of Biden's presidency majorities wanted a change in Republicans' policies on the border and withdrawal from Afghanistan. When the policies turned into fiascos, public opinion turned dramatically. But probably the key element to the

Biden policies was to try to satisfy public opinion. So empty seemed the decision-making of the Biden Administration that a parallel was seen to George Orwell's *1984*, in which the narrator suggests the possibility that there is no Big Brother — no government leadership. Instead, Big Brother is a hologram.

Biden's failure in Afghanistan undermined his presidential leadership. After the Afghan fiasco Biden remained president of the U.S. with all the authority that entailed, though his leadership was compromised considerably. But he had removed himself as leader of the free world — there had never been formal authority there, and his allies were so infuriated by his failure to consult or notify them about what the U.S. was going to do in Afghanistan that they no longer accepted his leadership.

Chapter 3

Biden as a Modern Propagandist

Propaganda is the central element of modern politics. Many democracies, including the U.S., have large populations. People cannot be reached except by large-scale communications — mass media of some sort (television, internet, or social media). It is critical for any political candidate, official or party to reach the population. Failure to have mass media access to an electorate normally means political disaster.

In the United States prior to the presidential election of 1964 presidential campaigns were carried out largely by local offices of each party. In 1964 Lyndon Johnson, the Democrat candidate for president, abandoned local party members and ran his election by appeals to the voters via mass media. Local offices of the Democrat Party turned away people volunteering to work in Johnson's campaign. Eventually the offices closed. There was nothing for them to do. Johnson won reelection by a very large majority and messages carried on mass media became the dominant form of presidential politics in the U.S.

In the 2020 presidential campaign the Republicans lacked access to most mass media. They made effective use of Twitter, a social media platform, until in the president's reelection campaign he was barred from the site. Mass media was in the hands of the Republicans' opponents. The President was, however, expert at speeches to large audiences. By the end of the presidential campaign in 2020 he was giving several speeches a day to audiences in the tens of thousands. No other American politician could attract audiences anywhere near that large. But if he gave five speeches a day to audiences of 40,000 people each time, for the last three weeks (seven days a week, which would exhaust him) of the presidential campaign (when voters were focusing on the campaign), he would still reach only about 4 million voters — some 3% of the American electorate. If no national media covered his speeches, then that was the end of the reach of his speech, while his Democrat opponent was reaching many more with messages over mass media. The failure of the Republican incumbent to have wide access to the American electorate was a key reason for his loss of the election. National media access to the electorate remains today a serious limitation on the Republicans political effectiveness.

Since mass media is central to modern politics, it follows that the message put on mass media by a political candidate or party is key to success. This message is a form of propaganda, and it is central to modern politics.

Modern techniques of propaganda were developed by Joseph Goebbels and the Nazi Party in Germany in the early twentieth century and have been copied by others since. The Nazis gained power by election but held power without regard to elections, of course, but they remained very sensitive to public opinion. They developed the modern techniques of widespread communications to the public. These techniques were remarkably effective. In our time, with improved methods of communication, the tactics are more effective than ever. This is very unfortunate. It may be almost fatal for democracies. Goebbels' techniques were developed for totalitarian systems and their use in democracies drives democracies toward totalitarianism and away from freedom.

To use these techniques a political movement must have no regard for truth. Liberals historically have a regard for truth. Progressives, by their own description of themselves, have none. Progressives have brought these techniques into wide use within the Democrat Party — not because they are from Goebbels, but despite it. They have adopted the methods because they are effective, just as Stalin's Soviet Union adopted them. It is likely that most progressives who employ the techniques have no knowledge that they originated in Hitler's Germany.

In this chapter we will give examples from the Democrats' use of these techniques, because the Democrats are now in power in the United States. Democrats will undoubtedly charge that the Republicans make use of the same tactics. This is likely true — if it is not, the Republicans must confront, as I (Mills) have heard some of their leaders discuss, the difficult challenge of confronting an opponent who uses these tactics while distaining Goebbels' tactics themselves. Can an opponent who adopts the tactics below be beaten by one who does not? Probably not, and from a Republican perspective that is a key challenge.

Once a reader is aware of these techniques, she or he will see them in use all the time in American political mass communication.

Below are listed the key elements of Hitlerite propaganda as developed by Joseph Goebbels, each with an example or two of their use in America today.

- A simple lie repeated over and over will eventually be believed. A simple untruth that is repeated endlessly becomes accepted generally in the population.

  The first example is of a lie that is simple and told so often that it is generally accepted as fact. It is confirmed continually by both our political parties. It is that the president is in charge of domestic matters.

  The American Constitution does not provide that. The Constitution rests domestic power in the Congress, and control of foreign affairs — except declarations of war — in the hands of the president. Presidential claims to control domestic matters are simply a presidential pretension. It is a very useful pretension in presidential election campaigning, since Americans generally do not care enough about foreign affairs to vote on that basis.

  Here are two more examples of lies repeated over and over so that they have come to be widely believed. They are both Democrat lies and both originated in or just before the Biden Administration. Examples could be chosen from the Republican side of American politics, but this book is about the Biden Administration.

  Brian Sicknick was a security officer at the Capitol in Washington on January 6, 2021, the day that the Capitol was invaded by a mob. He died the next day. Immediately major news outlets — led by *The New York Times* — reported that he had been killed by participants in the invasion who had hit him with a fire extinguisher. This has been repeated continually for months in multiple media outlets. It is generally believed by the American population. It is central to the narrative by the mass media about a violent attack on the Capitol by proponents of the Republican president. It is not true. The officer was hit by pepper spray and died the next day of natural causes. The public record about the use of a fire extinguisher has not yet been corrected.

  The Republican president "voted in the recent election in Florida by mail-in ballot," reported a CNN anchor. "This is astonishing. We all know how much the Republican hates mail-in ballots." In this so-called news report the Republican president is said to condemn mail ballots generally — which he has never done. He thus is made to appear a hypocrite and liar when he uses a mail-in absentee ballot. Yet Trump has always made a clear distinction between two types of mail-in ballots. One type is the absentee ballot which he endorses. The other is the mail-in ballot which he opposes. He views the absentee ballot as having security provisions to make sure the ballot is legitimate — including assurance that the voter is registered and has signed the ballot. General write-in ballots lack these security provisions. The President used an absentee ballot and was true to his principles, but the media outlet intentionally obscured this.

- The bigger the lie, the more likely it is to be believed.

Apparently, people can be persuaded to believe almost anything.

During Enver Hoxa's reign as Communist dictator of Albania, propaganda convinced ordinary workers that Albania's communist life was sublime and that workers in the West were starving. This lie prompted impoverished Albanians to send their European comrades subsistence money.

There could be no bigger lie in the United States than that a successful American presidential candidate obtained his office by virtue of collaboration with a foreign dictator who was a major opponent of the United States. It follows from this assertion that the candidate was a traitor, his campaign was involved in treason, and that he should be removed from office. That the Republicans colluded with the Russians to win the 2016 presidential campaign was loudly and continually proclaimed by the Democrats and their associates in the mass media. This assertion remains widely believed in the U.S. today. Yet an expensive, multi-year investigation of the allegation by the Mueller Commission found it to be unsubstantiated.

- Lies packaged with truth are very believable.

A report in American mass media is often viewed as "thoughtful." It can be well-done in an exact Soviet format, a propaganda piece — well thought-out for publication. It will be full of truths, which give credibility to the whole piece, and it will also contain key untruths which support the party line. We (Rosefielde and Mills) have read hundreds of pieces in this model from the U.S.S.R. and then China and now the U.S. over the past 70 years. The American public will read articles published by American officials — so when articles are

carefully crafted to create plausibility for untruths by being imbedded in truths, a propaganda advantage is gained.
- A half-truth is a complete and often effective lie.

The truth part provides credibility; the non-truth part is the desired deception. In Biden's inaugural speech he said, "now, a rise in political extremism, white supremacy, domestic terrorism that we must confront and we will defeat." He made no mention of leftist violence including rioting and other political extremism. If there is a justification for the omission, it is that Biden doesn't consider leftist violence to be political extremism. In which case his comment is still a half-truth, but he doesn't recognize that. His half-truth may be an error, not a lie — the motivation is key.

Here is another example. A report released March 16, 2021, by the Office of the Director of National Intelligence reported that Russia attempted to intervene in the 2020 presidential election in support of the Republicans. The report concluded that there was no evidence that the Russians impacted the election in any way.

Most American media reported only the first sentence above, that the Russians had supported the Republicans in the 2020 election and gave little or no mention of the conclusion that there was no impact on the election. The reader is expected to conclude that since the Russians attempted to intervene, they were successful.

This is reporting half a truth, and it results in so misleading a conclusion for the reader or listener that it is the equivalent of a full lie.

Half-truths which amount to lies are so important and so common that we provide another example.

On December 30, 2020, *The New York Times* ran a story under the headline, "A Violent Year in New York and Across the U.S. as Pandemic Fuels Crime Spike." This was true, but it was not the entire truth, and what was intentionally left out made the story a lie. Much more than the pandemic fueled the spike in crime. Efforts to defund the police and denunciations of police, including mayors refusing to let police act against people violating the law, lack of prosecution of criminal actions, political turmoil, each contributed to the spike in crime. The newspaper made no mention of any of these factors.

What the paper was doing was to provide in the guise of a news story a line for progressive activists — the increase in crime is due to the pandemic alone, nothing else.

The half-truth is a very effective form of lie.

- Accuse your enemies of what you are doing: if you employ thugs, accuse your opponent of causing violence; if you attack someone, blame the person attacked for inciting the violence. This is a very effective device of propaganda. It shifts the controversy over what has been done to the other side. It makes what you have done seem ordinary — the other side is said to be doing it.

    For example, in mid-2020 the Republicans deployed some troops to counter demonstrations (violence, church burning, and looting are the reasons given). Immediately, Don Lemon, a very articulate black news anchor on CNN, called for the demonstrators to resist, saying that if they gave in, all their freedoms will be lost, and the Republican President will be a dictator.

    This seemed the culmination of the "resistance" campaign that had begun with the Republican President's election. The political purpose of the violence was to get the Republican out of office. It was hoped that he would use the military to suppress the violence, and he would be hounded to resign because of it. The slogan would be that there could be no peace with the Republican in office. But the Republican didn't take the bait; he didn't call out the troops, and until the election of 2020 was settled in Biden's favor, he remained in office.

    Thus, violence would be used to incite violence, and the person who replied in kind would be blamed for the violence.

- Always take both sides of each issue. This confuses your opponents and allows each person in the population to pick which position of yours it prefers.

    Are you destroying jobs by your policy? Announce that full employment is the top priority of your administration.

    In the first days of his administration, Biden canceled construction projects that terminated thousands of jobs. To accompany these acts, he announced that creating jobs was the top priority of his administration.

    Had this promise been accompanied by job creation, it would have been a statement of fact, not a piece of propaganda. But it wasn't accompanied by jobs.

- When you do one thing, say you are doing its opposite.

    Seeking partisan domination, declare yourself seeking bipartisanship. Biden has done this since the first day of his administration.

    He has done more. From Biden's inauguration speech: "The right to dissent peaceably, within the guardrails of our Republic, is perhaps our nation's greatest strength." But the progressives he embraces are sponsoring cancel culture — the silencing now and in the past of any dissent.

When the Biden Administration was denying the media access to American facilities on the nation's southern border, its spokespersons including the President, continually insisted that Biden was determined to be fully transparent with the media about what was occurring on the southern border. The Administration's position was you can have access to any facility, but you can't have it. That is, its position was a contradiction. Denying access week after week, the Administration insisted every moment that it was doing the opposite.

- Misrepresent yourself: if you want war, say you are seeking peace. If you prize division, declare yourself for unity.

Biden supported an impeachment effort against the former President, while being warned that it would divide the country dramatically. Perhaps Biden couldn't prevent the Congressional leadership of the Democrats from doing this. But they were his party, and he was necessarily involved. And he did not explicitly ask the Democrat leadership not to do it.

- Always shift blame away from yourself or your political party. All modern politicians are blame shifters, and all deny it. For example, when Biden moved too quickly on changing his predecessor's policies at the southern border of the U.S. and a crisis of humanity was the result, he and his administration promptly and very publicly, using the mass media as a conduit, tried to shift the blame entirely to the previous Republican Administration. Biden claimed that the Republican Administration had dismantled all the systems by which floods of immigrants had been handled in the past, and so chaos resulted. Even if true, this shift of the blame begged the question why the Biden Administration had not restored the systems the Republicans had supposedly dismantled before Biden invited a rush of new immigrants. Blame shifting is a continual part of modern propaganda and is used by all politicians, Joe Biden included.

Modern propaganda is highly effective. Pursued with persistence and a common theme it provides a broad narrative so consistent and persuasive that it creates for its victims an alternative reality. The Republican

President was accused of doing this. If he tried, he wasn't very good at it. But this is an example of the Democrats accusing their opponent of what they themselves do very effectively.

Finally, modern sophisticated propaganda has not pushed out the old style of propaganda which is exemplified by the puff piece. A puff piece involves exaggerated praise for a politician, a political party or a political policy. Biden's Administration uses puff pieces effectively. Of many possible examples we pick one.

In its February 2021, issue, as the Biden Administration took hold, *Town and Country* magazine published an article with many endearing photos of Vice President Kamala Harris and her husband Douglas Emhoff. It told its readers that "Not only are Kamala Harris and Douglas Emhoff shredding political stereotypes, they are also — publicly and unabashedly — showing what a successful marriage can look like. Welcome to the new iconography of power and affection in America."

Indoctrination

The use of modern techniques of propaganda is not limited to mass media. It can be packaged into forms of delivery in what are termed educational settings — or as was done in China during the Cultural Revolution, into re-education sessions.

Similar indoctrination is now gaining ground in the United States. The *Harvard Gazette* on January 8, 2021, carried an article entitled "Unlearning Racial Bias." Miao Qian, a postdoctoral research fellow was said to envision "a future in which children are able to 'unlearn unconscious bias' through training and education starting early in their lives."

As is common with progressive proposals, this sounds fine. But since children are not able to identify their own biases and confront them rationally, it is merely a call for indoctrination at an early age. Progressives are today's experts at this.

Already there are extensive programs that are indoctrination about political issues, usually proceeding from doctrines about race, that are offered, usually required, in American institutions, including government agencies.

The Republican White House issued an executive order preventing federal agencies and organizations receiving federal funding from offering diversity training courses. That order dealt specifically with any form of race or sex stereotyping or any form of race or sex scapegoating. The order homed in on critical race theory — the notion that American society systematically favors white people and disadvantages non- whites. Teaching this was prohibited in government agencies or schools receiving federal money.

Senator John Kennedy of Louisiana, a Republican, described critical race theory thus, (Fox News 7/6/21) "Critical Race Theory is a fairy tale promoted by many — not all, but many — of my Democratic colleagues, including the Biden White House. Critical Race Theory teaches that America is totally screwed; we need to just tear it down and start over. Critical Race Theory teaches that the primary reason that America was founded was to maintain white supremacy — not freedom, not the rule of law, not equal opportunity, not personal responsibility, but white supremacy. Critical Race Theory also teaches that non-black Americans are racist; that they don't much like black people — whether those non-black Americans realize it or not. That is why Critical Race Theory also teaches that white children are born bad. It teaches that black children are born trapped; there's almost no hope for them. It's a very fatalistic point of view … In my judgment, Critical Race Theory is cynical, ahistorical, sophomoric, insipid and dumb as a bag of hair."

In his early days in office Biden revoked the Republican President's order and federal agencies, contractors and grantees were free to resume diversity indoctrination including Critical Race Theory.

Biden and the Techniques of Propaganda

Biden is not necessarily an expert on these techniques of propaganda, but he is a contributor to them, just as he is a contributor to the financial corruption of American politics. The Democrats seem to use them better than the Republicans. Their victory in the 2020 election is evidence of that. The Republicans will have to master the techniques and their dissemination (that is, obtain much better access to mass media) if they are to win another presidential election.

It is frequently recommended that young people be taught to think critically so that they can recognize disinformation. A key part of this reform would be to teach people to recognize propaganda and not be misled by it. Propaganda is not difficult to recognize once one is aware of how it works. When a piece of information is recognized as propaganda it can be disregarded. If enough people disregard propaganda, then the political forces seeking to obtain support will be driven back to truth in their communications with the electorates. They will not choose truth without being forced to do so, whatever their pretensions of always giving people the truth.

Part II
The Biden Administration

Chapter 4

A Mandate to Govern or Not?

It can be difficult to ascertain what the outcome of an American presidential election means. Ordinarily we determine immediately or in a few months (as in 2020) who has won the election. We know his or her political party. We know their campaign promises. We should be able to determine which political movement has won and which has lost.

But in recent years in America many have been mistaken in their conclusions. The populists appeared to have gained power with the Republicans election, but they didn't. The conservatives in the Republican party controlled the Congress and quickly deflected the President's efforts to pursue a populist agenda. The most dramatic example was how the President's proposals for tax reform became the tax reduction package of Congressional Republicans. The President had no choice but to accept the Congress's legislation and pretend to endorse it.

The progressives appeared to have missed power with Biden's election, but they didn't. Biden is a self-proclaimed moderate; he has been a liberal all his life. But he no sooner became president than he embarked on actions that were the agenda of the progressives in his party.

Populists won an election but didn't get power — the conservatives did — and the progressives lost an election — to a liberal — but did get power.

This is a reminder that appearances often deceive — the populists' appearance of getting power when they didn't, and the progressives' appearance of not getting power when they did.

The Democrats had campaigned for Joe Biden on the grounds that his opponent, the Republican candidate, was a bum. For five years they had drummed this message via the mass media and the social networks into the American public. Many Americans believed it. Biden was elected president and the Democrats presumed that the Republican president and all he stood for and had done had been rejected by the American people.

The presidential election had been close in one way and not close in another. In the 2020 presidential election Biden won by several million votes nationally. But a shift of only 43,692 votes in a few states would have swung the election to the Republicans.

A map which shows Republican and Democrat members of the House of Representative by geographic district shows that almost the entire country from New York City to the coast of California is Republican. In effect the Democrats are a party of the densely populated cities of the coasts and the Republicans of all the rest of the country (excepting a few large cities such as Chicago, Houston, and Detroit). Because the United States is a republic, this distribution of political power matters greatly.

The Democrats focused on their large victory in the popular vote and quickly moved to exploit it. It is a difficult environment in which to govern. Polls show that only 20% of Americans say they trust the federal government to do the right thing. This is the lowest of such measure in American history. In this environment, the Democrats — in full power for the first time since 2009 (that is, holding both houses of Congress and the presidency) — seek to remake American society in the progressive mode.

In his first weeks in office Biden issued a series of presidential orders granting support to the primary concerns of many of the social activist groups which constitute the core of the Democratic Party. The Democrats publicized this as "revoking the Republicans' legacy." And it was.

But had the electorate endorsed the revocation of the Republicans' legacy? Had it given Biden a mandate to pursue progressive and moderate policies championed by the Democrats? Many Americans had said during the election campaign, "We don't like the Republican president at all, but we like what he has done." Of those people many voted for the Democrats, but not for the purpose of endorsing the policies of the Democrat Party. Around 45% of the American electorate voted for the Republican president and thereby endorsed his policies. Probably 25% (especially suburban women) voted against him because they didn't like him personally (not that they knew him personally, but that they thought they knew him because of mass media — a peculiarity of modern communications), while liking what he had done. So, it may be inferred that

70% of the American electorate in the election of 2020 endorsed Republican policies.

Biden found that there was much more support for the Republican's actions than for his personality. The Democrats had waged a relentless campaign for five year of anti-Trump propaganda, but it was primarily devoted to the failings of the man himself. The result was that the electorate didn't like the Republican and voted him out of office. But did that mean that the electorate didn't like what the Republican had done?

When Biden in his first days in office concentrated on reversing the Republican's domestic policies by a flood of executive orders, he tested this question. Were his actions welcomed by the country, or only by special interest groups in the Democrat Party? Was Biden an astute enough politician to ask the question, or to determine the answer? That is unlikely.

All American politicians, including the Republicans, but especially the Democrats because of their domination in the media, live in echo chambers where they hear again and again their own views repeated. This makes them tone-deaf to signals from the people.

Being tone-deaf is a special danger to the Democrats. When a political movement has control of the media as the Democrats do in America, then they can make the smaller seem like the larger thing. This is a great advantage because it allows them to set an agenda item that they magnify into a major issue. The downside is that the media becomes an echo chamber for the Democrats and unless they are careful, they believe their own views are shared by the electorate. If they do this, they mislead themselves about the attitudes of the electorate.

The Democrats, in their excited advocacy of their various causes seem to have missed this entirely. If they received a mandate in the election of 2020, it was a mandate for a change of leadership — to Biden from the Republican — not a mandate for a change in policy.

The Republican establishment has not missed the political message. It is the reason that the Republicans believe the Republicans can recapture control of the Congress in the 2022 elections when the entire House of Representatives is up for election and when one-third of the Senate stands for election.

President Biden has misunderstood the meaning of his electoral victory. He and his close supporters, and especially importantly, the Democrat leadership in the Congress (the House and the Senate) believe the 2020 election has given them a far stronger mandate to govern than it has. This misunderstanding has caused the Democrat President to get off on the wrong foot with the American people as we shall see in the next chapter.

That Biden had overestimated his mandate was evident in the difficult negotiations which he led with Speaker Pelosi in the fall of his first year in office. The negotiations were not with his opponents — the Republicans — but with the major factions in his own party — moderates (liberals) and progressives. The progressives were blocking the passage of legislation to repair America's decayed infrastructure unless their own package of additions to the nation's social safety net was approved as well. The progressives dominated the controversy but could not compel moderates to accept their demands. Progressives seemed to outnumber moderates significantly, but this was an illusion because most moderates were afraid to express publicly their opinions. Moderates allowed two senators who were Democrat moderates to speak for them all. The reputation of progressives for both physical and political action against their opponents in the Democrat Party meant that moderates kept their opinions to themselves but did not support progressive demands.

In support of their legislative package the progressive expected to be able to call forth massive public demonstrations and contacts with Congress. They failed.

Progressives had overestimated their mandate from the 2020 elections from both their fellow Congressional Democrats and from the public generally. Biden had accepted the progressives' expansive view of their mandate and discovered to his political embarrassment that the progressives had exaggerated their strength with the electorate.

Ninety Percent Favorability with the Media

Though the media fails to provide the Democrats with feedback about the changing attitudes and expectations of the American people, it does provide great assistance to the Democrat Party in proclaiming its message to the American people. It is hard to imagine the success of the Democrat Party without its support by the national media.

For the four years of the Republican Administration the mass media (newspapers, television news programming, and social networks) of the United States stood solidly in support of the Democrat Party. Studies at universities known for their adherence to progressive politics nonetheless show more than 90% favorable ratings in media outlets for the

Democrats. At the critical time of calling the winner of the 2020 election, all major media outlets, including Fox which often supported Republican policies and candidates, supported Biden.

However, the American media are fiercely competitive among themselves, and without the Republican Administration to kick around, soon turned on the Democrats. Scandal and sensation are necessary to draw audiences, and audiences are necessary to attract advertisers, and advertisers provide revenue to media companies. In a few weeks after Biden's victory the media had begun to find scandal among Democrats (in particular, the governor of New York State became a target) and matters to criticize in some of Biden's actions. For example, he put migrant children back in the holding pens which Republicans had used for unaccompanied children and which Democrats had labeled "cages." But when the press demanded why this was done, the White House informed them that when the Biden Administration used the pens, they were no longer "cages" because the Biden Administration had different motives than had the Republican Administration.

It is likely that when Biden became president, he had significant long-term objectives in mind. But within a very short time the media was pressing his administration continually about thing after thing, and he was forced to cope with issue after issue on an immediate basis. This was the process, so familiar to people experienced in Washington, which the late Senator Daniel Patrick Moynihan characterized as the art of government: coping.

Chapter 5

Off on a Wrong Foot

First impressions matter. They remain with people a long time and are difficult to displace. The Biden Administration made a strong first impression with the American people by issuing many presidential directives — what Americans call "executive orders" — in the first days of his administration. The Administration told the American people that in doing this Biden was the most active American president since Franklin Delano Roosevelt at the start of the Great Depression in 1933.

The new president wanted the American people to see him as very active. What were the subjects of his directives? They were designed to support the concerns of activist elements of the Democratic Party, of which there are many. They were not concerned with the major preoccupations of the electorate — the raging pandemic and the struggling economy. Questioned about this, the Administration insisted that the President could not act on these matters unilaterally and that he had made proposals to the Congress to deal with each. With respect to the virus these protestations rang hollow; but they were true with regards to economic stimulus.

The result was that this president first appeared to the American people as a champion of the causes dear to the hearts of Democrat activist groups — favoring abortion, granting citizenship to undocumented immigrants, easing restrictions on further immigration, reforming police behavior, soaking the rich by increased taxation, etc. It was unclear if this was wise public relations for the following reason.

The Administration anticipated popular acclaim for the President's orders. They were surprised that many people met the orders with distrust.

From one perspective the *modus operandi* of the Democratic-run government seems to be this: It transforms political promises into policy stances and then tries to mitigate or even reverse their consequences by contrary actions. For example, in the first week of the Biden Administration the new President issued dozens of executive orders on a wide variety of promises he had made during the election. Several of his orders reversed immigration policies of the Republican Administration. These orders were to fulfill a Democrat theme promising fair treatment to people seeking entrance to the United States. Immigration had been a contentious issue between Democrats and Republicans throughout the Republican Administration. Observers quickly commented that the southern border of the United States was now opened. Immigrant caravans assembled in Guatemala with their spokespersons saying that Biden had opened the border to them. In the United States, critics pointed out that an open American border would permit drug gangs, other types of criminals, agents of foreign governments, and persons with contagious diseases besides legitimate asylum seekers to enter the country. To try to mitigate or avoid these results the Biden Administration began to negotiate with the Mexican, Guatemalan, and Honduran governments to stop or dramatically reduce the movement of caravans of immigrants toward the U.S. border.

Another example involves the issuance of presidential orders to limit climate change, another major plank in the Biden presidential campaign platform. These orders severely limited the search for fossil fuels and the transport of them within the United States. These orders threatened to limit electricity production and increase gasoline prices, among other consequences. Quickly the Biden Administration moved to increase import from abroad of oil to American power plants and gasoline refiners.

In these ways the Biden Administration sought to have its cake and eat it too. Widely publicized policy actions expressed in presidential executive orders satisfied the Democrat progressive base that its priorities were being met, while quietly pursued counter actions were taken to prevent the undesirable consequences of those actions.

In addition, the President began his administration by seeming to promise to work on major legislation with his Republican opponents in a bipartisan fashion. The President and his Congressional allies quickly abandoned that posture. Major pieces of legislation were pushed through Congress on a strictly party-line vote. It was true that the Republicans would not join the Democrats in voting for the bills. But that was because the Democrats would accept no changes except those required to get other Democrats to vote for the bills. The lack of bipartisanship could be seen as a failure of the new President to keep a promise. It could also be seen as hypocrisy. It could be seen as dishonesty. It was in fact, however, a political tactic which is described in the chapter which discusses modern propaganda techniques.

To defend the President from the charge that he had misled the American people about bipartisanship, the Administration began insisting that it was behaving in a bipartisan manner despite having no Republican support for its initiatives. Nor was it making attempts to obtain Republican support, except by behind-the-scenes efforts to persuade a few Republicans to support Administration initiatives by promising favors. Even this was not working. The tactic of saying that the Administration was acting in a bipartisan way when it was not as one of the tried-and-true elements of modern propaganda.

Biden was proclaiming unity and acting in a thoroughly partisan manner. Examples are numerous. In his first speech to the nation after becoming president, delivered on March 11, 2021, after almost two months in office, Biden discussed the pandemic. He cited the human cost to the nation (some 530,000 dead at that time) and detailed the response of his administration to it. He took credit for the rapid inoculation of much of the nation's population with vaccines against the virus. He made no mention of the achievement of the Republican Administration which preceded him in bringing vaccines to use in record time. He could have mentioned the achievement of the Republican Administration and thereby claimed bipartisan credit. In so doing he might have championed national unity. Instead, he chose to give an entirely partisan speech.

There was, however, remarkable unity in one area of the nation's politics. The unity of the Democrat Party in Congress was impressive. It made it possible to pass important legislation on a party-line vote; that is, without Republican support of even small magnitude. It also demonstrated that the Democrats believed they had the electorate behind them — that they had received in the 2020 elections a mandate to govern.

Public opinion polls in the early weeks of the Biden Administration were favorable. This was primarily a consequence of the stimulus bill with its promise of 1,400 dollar checks from the federal government for every person whose income was under a certain level. Millions of Americans were promised these checks. They wanted them. Asked about their opinions about the stimulus bill, they gave favorable answers. This was a direct purchase of favorable ratings, and it was not likely to be maintained for long as people received their checks and went on to other matters.

A significant warning of this was that all Republicans in the House and Senate — only a few less in number than the Democrats — voted against the bill. Politicians voting against direct payments to the voters? How could that happen? Apparently, the Republicans were not concerned that their votes against the bill would tell against them at the ballot box 18 months later. Gratitude and memory are not characteristics of the voting behavior of the American electorate.

Finally, the Biden Administration is being criticized as the most brutal in recent American history within the confines of the United States. Its policies at the southern border have caused the death of many migrants and the trafficking abuse of many, many more. Biden has encouraged Speaker of the House Nancy Pelosi and the Mayor of Washington, D.C. in the torture and beating of demonstrators held in the prisons of the District of Columbia. The crime of these prisoners was the demonstration that took place on January 6, 2021, at the Capitol.

In line with modern propaganda practice, Democrats had condemned the Republican Administration for brutality. But what they were referencing was the so-called brutality of failing to support the political claims of elements of the Democrat coalition. It was brutal to not support the claims of gays and transgender people, the Democrats alleged.

Major Accomplishments of the Biden Administration

A guaranteed income

The stimulus bill has a provision that provides a monthly payment per child which is essentially a guaranteed income and may be increased and extended to others without children over the years. This is new to American politics and to the American social welfare system.

A new law temporarily converts the long-standing federal child tax credit into what supporters call a "child allowance." This year, parents don't need to have paid taxes at all to collect an annual allowance of up to 3,600 dollars per child. According to the *New York Times*, "more than

93 percent of children — 69 million" will benefit from the new benefit (Matt Weidinger, https://www.aei.org/op-eds/government-allowances-are-the-new-welfare/?mkt_tok=NDc1LVBCUS05NzEAAAF82vHQPH6wd6oHVxpkbFzjgXHEZCu0e9vhDt9e72_ERnBXcTQUJGEgP6Lt-ntz54Jmh7AyBYukMsQYD-vLrcoi0DTqEsGn_G6mags5knhaEYk).

Other new government "allowances" would distribute substantial amounts of taxpayer money to tens of millions of households.

Racial preferences

The same bill has provisions that provide government loan forgiveness to African Americans and Hispanics, but to no others. This direct racial preference, and for certain minorities alone, is likely to stimulate a serious backlash from non-preferred minorities (for example, Asians) and from the white majority.

Unqualified appointees

In staffing his administration Biden did something that is now common in American government and that Republicans had done before him. He named to high positions political friends who had little or no knowledge of the topics and agencies they were to lead. This was done because political and personal loyalty were viewed by the President as more important than competence; and because they were given no objectives other than political ones. Then after these appointees had muddled up their assignments, it was asserted about them by their political friends that they were experienced at what they did and so qualified for other assignments, or for election to Congress. This process ensures that America is poorly governed.

Consider the Labor Department, or as it would be labeled abroad, the labor ministry. Its evolution in the last 100 years mirrors that of the government. During the Franklin Roosevelt administration and afterward through the administration of Gerald Ford, the Department sought to assist in the development of a trained and competent work force. It did this to help the economic performance of the nation and to help reduce un- and under-employment by providing skilled workers. It supported training and apprenticeship programs. It worked with employers and unions to retrain people as job requirements changed.

But during these years, Congress passed law after law affecting employment. The Labor Department became a large regulatory agency. Its regulatory function became more important than its labor force development function. The position of Secretary of Labor became a job for lawyers. The attorneys who now are chosen to head the Department know nothing about how to develop a trained labor force and care little. The Department is now primarily a legal agency and training in America is left without guidance to employers who train people, if at all, only for narrow tasks. As a result, people who are laid off from employment find it very difficult to get direction or retraining for new careers. Because there has been much change in the American economy in recent years, there is a large group of workers who have seen their living standards decline dramatically due to unemployment and low skill, low wage employment.

Politicians promise to assist those people. But assistance in the Biden Administration is only financial, and that not much, and the Labor Department which should be expert at training and retraining people, does very little because the Administration asks it to do little and gives it little or no support. This was equally true of the administrations that preceded Biden's for several decades.

Chapter 6

The Electoral Significance of Women

On International Women's Day (March 8, 2021) Biden signed an executive (presidential) order establishing the White House Gender Policy Council. Its duty as described in the media is to work with other policy councils to advance gender equality in domestic and foreign policy development, combat systemic bias and discrimination, including sexual harassment, and focus on increasing female participation in the labor force and decreasing wage and wealth gaps. The council will also focus on transgender rights and supporting care workers, predominantly women of color.

In a previous chapter we discussed the very important role of women in Biden's presidency, especially the tug-of-war between Vice President Harris and First Lady Jill Biden over the future of Joe Biden's presidency. In this chapter, we examine the larger and increasing important role of women in American politics. Although men still dominate elective offices, the number of women replacing men is growing rapidly and may soon become dominant just as they now outnumber men in the national electorate.

Women voters played a key role in Biden's election victory. Women are the largest voting group in America. Feminist organizations are a key element of the Democrat Party and some of its most active elements. A woman is now vice president of the United States and thought by many likely to follow Joe Biden in the presidency. For all these reasons it is appropriate to review the likely impact of women on American policy.

Because of the left's endorsement of choice about abortion at virtually any time in a pregnancy, including late in it, on the right there has emerged a counter movement which involves many women, and which opposes abortion at all stages of pregnancy.

The active participation of women in American politics has changed its flavor. If and how much women have changed the content of American politics is unclear at present.

Women vary as much as men. It is very tempting to not separate them from men and instead to just discuss people generally. But in America women insist on being considered as a different group than men. They have their own organizations — for example, the National Organization for Women (NOW), Women for Peace (Code Pink), etc. — and insist that they have been and still are victimized by a male-dominated culture.

Women played a key role in ending the Republican's presidency. Polls showed for years that suburban white women generally opposed him and they were a large enough group on their own to turn the election of 2020 against him.

The Biden Administration treats women as an important interest group in its policymaking. The Democrats insist that women are one of the demographic groups that make up their party — women are a key element of the groups that compose the Democrat Party. The spokespersons for this identity group are the feminist activists who describe themselves as very different from men while demanding both equality and equity with men.

Biden is very conscious of the political importance of women as an identity group. For this reason, he chose a woman to be his candidate for vice president. It is for this reason that Kamala Harris is at his side at almost every one of his public appearances.

Mrs. Harris was not an obvious choice to be Biden's vice president. She had been a candidate for the Democrat Party's nomination for president during the 2020 primary elections. She had garnered few votes. She had attacked Biden, who was another candidate in the primaries and ultimately successful in gaining the nomination, as a racist. Biden's choice of Mrs. Harris as his running mate for president was therefore a great surprise to most people.

Apparently, though not yet publicly reported, Biden had hoped and expected that Michelle Obama would join him on the ticket. Polls show her to be the most popular woman in America. She is well-educated, of strong personality, and experienced in the White House as First Lady. She would have been a great asset to Biden's candidacy.

Expecting Mrs. Obama to join him on the campaign trial, Biden announced that he would choose a black woman as his running mate.

For some reason, Michelle Obama decided not to run. Biden was left with a promise to fulfill. At that point Senator Harris became a possible choice, and Biden made that choice.

Women make American politics different than they would otherwise be. For one thing, they have made a subtle but major change in our attitude toward politics. In a male-dominated political environment we used to say, "I think…" Now under the influence of women voters we say, "I feel…"

"Don't tell me how you think," the women tell their men. "Tell me how you feel."

This is a contentious observation in America. There are many women who do not do this; and many men who feel rather than think. Especially when men are increasingly feminine — at least seen from the traditional male viewpoint.

At the time of the Afghan withdrawal men complained of Biden's incompetence in preparing and carrying out the withdrawal; women complained of his cruelty and lack of empathy for the suffering of the Afghan people. Biden addressed both concerns but gave surprisingly little attention to the charges of cruelty — considering that his political focus is often on women.

The change brought by women's increasing involvement and confidence in politics is real and significant. Biden is fully aware of it and attune to it. It affects substantially his own political behavior. Much of what his Administration does is to influence how women feel about their government. In fact, one of the Republicans great political weaknesses was with suburban women who did not feel good about the Republican candidate. The Biden 2020 campaign was very much aware of this weakness of the Republicans and exploited it fully.

In the context of major female participation in politics, policy pronouncements are more symbols than propositions for debate. What is important is how people feel about the qualities of heart they seem to reveal. Are the objectives stated things we feel good about? If so, that's what is of concern.

Biden understands this completely. The Republicans do not. In the 2020 campaign the Republicans seems to have assumed that because voters benefited from much that their administration had done, they would vote for its continuance. But the Democrats understood that many voters did not feel good about the Republican president and what he seemed to symbolize and would vote against him. They did. In large part this was an attitude which women voters as they matured politically into dominance over the past century infused into American politics.

During the 2012 election, polls showed that Barak Obama had a lead among women voters. Asked privately about this, the leading people in the Romney (the Republican candidate for president) campaign suggested that they were confident that women would vote the way their husbands instructed them. It appeared from the outcome of the election that if that had ever been the case, it was no longer.

Can a democracy deeply influenced by women effectively lead the world — will women exercise international power effectively? As individuals, they certainly do. But as a group, will women permit America to exercise power effectively? The answer will be a determining influence on Biden's foreign policy.

In the past, individual women have exercised power effectively. For example, in the mid- and late-nineteenth century Queen Victoria presided over the British Empire at its greatest extent. She served as Empress of India as well as Queen of England. In her role as Empress of India she presided over a colonial power which could not be termed benign. India was looted for British wealth, and many of the greatest jewels of India then found their way into the English treasury and the Queen's own collection — the crown jewels of England. Was the British Raj more brutal than native regimes would have been? Probably not. It repressed the centuries old and extraordinarily brutal conflict of Hindus and Muslims in the Indian subcontinent. All this Queen Victoria actively ruled. When at the end of World War II Indian politicians demanded independence from Britain and the then British government lost its taste for imperial power and granted independence, Winston Churchill opposed Indian independence on the ground that there would be a blood bath between Hindu and Muslim, and indeed there was. Some 5 million people died in the separation of India from Pakistan.

A woman once ruled Egypt as pharaoh; Zenobia ruled Palmyra successfully in the classical period of European/Middle Eastern history.

We know that world powers can be successfully governed by individual women. But these were not democracies in the modern sense. These women were monarchs. It is not at all clear that a nation whose political processes are dominated by women's values can be a successful world power.

One of the most interesting aspects of the Biden Presidency will be to give us an answer to that question.

Women activists helped create America's longest war. They kept the American military in Afghanistan for some 20 years, and though first Obama and then the Republican president were trying to end the American role in the conflict, women in activist groups tried to keep our presidents in the war. This occurred because women in America were very unwilling to see the rights which women in Afghanistan had gained under Western laws lost under the Taliban.

Women are impacting all aspects of American life. Harvard Business School once prided itself on being called "the West Point of Capitalism." West Point is the American university that trains Army officers. The notion was that Harvard trained tough executives to run companies in the global competition for business success. Now professors at that school write articles about how revealing in class their own vulnerability helps them connect with their students. Perhaps under the Biden Administration we will see instructors at West Point revealing personal vulnerability to military cadets.

Several years ago the teacher who had just won an award as "America's best teacher," spoke about how he was so successful in a secondary school classroom. He summarized his approach to his students this way, "Students don't care how much you know, until they know how much you care." The point was that he had to connect with each student on a personal basis before they would pay attention to the subject matter he was teaching. Personal connection was especially important because so many of his students had serious personal problems which kept them from focusing on learning. Many came from broken homes or homes in which parents argued and bickered continually; some were deprived of meals; some were bullied; etc. Vulnerability became a threshold issue before education could begin.

But these were teenagers. Harvard Business School students are adults. Most have worked for several years, many on Wall Street, before arriving at Harvard. Does addressing their vulnerabilities and having faculty members disclose their own, contribute to preparing adults for the world of work? Marshall Goldsmith, one of America's top executive coaches, and probably the most experienced of them all, has stated: "Leadership is a contact sport." Is emotional vulnerability a key contribution to preparing people for contact sports?

Many American mothers have earned the label of "helicopter moms." They hover over their children throughout their lives. They don't want their sons injured so they discourage contact sports; they don't want their sons disappointed by defeat so they discourage their sons from competitions of all sorts. This behavior from a parent produces an unusual set of behaviors in children. They become excessively self-centered and feel entitled to attention and care. They demand attention to their concerns, to their vulnerabilities, and American colleges and universities are generally now accommodating to these student expectations.

Here is how HBS accommodates its students with their overly protective moms: "Love at HBS is an annual celebration of the diverse expressions of love that exist on our campus and in the world around us. Even with the unique challenges presented by the COVID-19 pandemic, love has endured, and our students have continued to share their take on what love means to them. PRIDE is pleased to present this annual showcase of student stories from the LGBTQ+ community and our wonderful allies here at Harvard Business School" (From *HBS Communications*, February 17, 2021).

It must be said that there is a very different sort of mother who also plays an important role in American life. She wants her children to be enormously successful and pushes them from infancy to excel in all they do. She pushes her child into competitive sports which promise large financial payoffs — figure skating, skiing and tennis for girls; football and basketball for boys. She pushes them academically to get into the top secondary schools and colleges and graduate schools and pushes them toward Wall Street and riches. These women do not turn their children from competition; they don't care if sometimes they are disappointed or disillusioned; success is all that matters. This also results in some strange behavior in their children. There are not many of these kind of moms — labeled "tiger moms" in America — but their children become so successful and so often leaders that although they are few, they are extremely important in the society. The children are generally compulsive, greedy, ruthless, and narcissistic. When competence fails to win them high positions and wealth, they rely on politics whether in business or government. We now have many of them in key political offices. Some have developed superficially caring personalities that conceal the person behind. Joe Biden is one.

What is uncertain is the impact of these conditionings on young people. If the world offers them serious challenges, how will they react? We know that America, with its large population, can provide a vigorous and courageous force of professional, volunteer, and military personnel. American has about 2 million people in arms

Active personnel	1,374,125
Reserve personnel	849,450
Deployed personnel	170,000

of a potential military force of some 100 million (calculated by the rule of thumb that about one-sixth of the population of a country are of military age — these are men and in countries like the United States which accepts women fully into the military, the proportion of the population available for military service becomes not one-sixth but one-third — in America 200 million). We get some indication of the attitude of young Americans toward challenges from the difficulty that the American military has recruiting volunteers for military service. In general, young Americans are not interested in military service and do not serve. Bill Clinton fled to Canada to avoid military service; George W. Bush spent an uncertain time and role in the National Guard; Barak Obama avoided military service; so did Donald Trump and Joe Biden. This is a country which projects itself as the defender of the free world against increasing military challenges from rising nations, but most of whose young people strive to avoid military service.

The appeal of politicians to love increases as the role of women in politics becomes more significant. The governor of New York State was accused in the summer of 2021 of harassing 11 women. His efforts to delay any action against him continued for months and finally failed. In his resignation speech he appealed to "love" as his motivation in almost all that he did politically in numerous years of serving as governor. He loved the people of New York and the women he had harassed. He had been misunderstood in the demands that he had made as he had assured everyone. Love shouldn't have been so misinterpreted, he insisted.

Women play a key role in the steady transformation of the American public to a more pacifist attitude. If there are to be no serious challenges that America must meet, then this is appropriate. If a serious challenge comes to America in the form of a surprise attack, like Pearl Harbor, then this attitude is likely to be instantly set aside. But if the challenge is more cautiously presented, then the United States, like France before World War II, is likely to be unable to meet it.

Progressive propaganda recognizes the increasingly significant role of women in American life and attitudes. It offers to the nation a first female vice president who is understood to be a progressive in political attitude.

Can the United States be depended upon by its allies to offer the military protection that it used to do? Yes, at this time, but as Biden and the progressives gain control of the levers of power in America, that confidence must be increasingly qualified. This is why the Biden Administration's announcement when it took office that "America is back!" was greeted abroad with far less enthusiasm among its allies than had been expected in Washington. It was greeted by America's adversaries with a search for an opportunity to gain in the contest with America.

Meanwhile the political contest in America continues to revolve around women. Democrats fashion major policy prescriptions to attract women to the polls and obtain their votes. Biden's social spending package contains support for working mothers, for childcare and other benefits for women. One of the Democrats major allied groups has been warning Democrats that they risk losing women's votes if the Democrats do not support Biden's social spending. Republicans seem not to recognize the effort to attract women voters that the Democrats are making.

The American Secretary of State (foreign minister) is a handsome man. When he spoke to the American people about the situation in Afghanistan, virtually every point he made seemed aimed at a primarily female audience. He spoke again and again of American soldiers in Afghanistan cradling babies and toddlers. President Biden seems always accompanied by either his wife or the Vice President, and the purpose seems to be at least partly identification for the president with women voters. So strong is the appeal made by the Democrat Party and its office holders and candidates to women voters, and so effeminate the appearance and behavior of significant members of the Administration, that an interpretation of the Biden Administration is that it is one of gays on behalf of women. This is not as scurrilous as might seem since the Administration focuses its attention on domestic policy and its political strategy on women. The Democrats have embraced identity politics and women are the largest and most influential of the identity groups.

Part III
Bidenomics

Chapter 7

Biden Economics and the World

The World Economy

The Democrats are predicting the biggest economic boom since the end of World War II. It is predicted to be worldwide and to last for years. It is said to be a consequence of the enormous fiscal stimuli offered by the Republican Administration and then by the Biden Administration.

It will be wonderful if this happens. But the predictions seem to be the consequence of simple macro-economic models which have been mistaken for decades, and to which has been given a New Monetary Theory wishful thinking twist. There is much cause for concern. These matters provide a challenge to the Biden Administration. It will be ill-prepared to meet challenges if it accepts as certain the rosy future which is being predicted for the world economy.

At the highest level of concern the world economy is increasingly unbalanced. Demographically there is declining population in many areas and rapidly increasing population in others. In general, population is decreasing in economically advanced areas and increasing in economically underdeveloped areas. The great exceptions now are China, in which what was recently an economically underdeveloped area is making rapid progress and India in which underdevelopment may be giving way to rapid economic expansion. In both China and India population continues to grow slowly. Another exception is the United States in which a developed nation has significant population growth due to immigration.

Unfortunately, it appears that other regions for which there has been hope of significant progress are not making it but may be declining economically. Parts of Southeast Asia have experienced rapid economic growth for several decades and some countries have expected to join the ranks of developed nations shortly. Malaysia and Viet Nam are on the brink of being considered developed, while Laos, Cambodia, and Myanmar remain severely underdeveloped. It seems that a setback is occurring, partly due to the pandemic and partly due to less effective political leadership. Other significant regions of the globe seem to be entering a period of economic decline. This includes Africa (not only south of the Sahara) and the Americas south of the United States.

Decades of economic assistance from developed countries to Africa, Latin America, and large sections of Asia, often provided through international agencies, have turned out to have had little success.

Climate change now adds an additional threat of significant proportions. It threatens famines, pandemics, wars, and mass migrations. There are two ways to respond to the threat. One is to try to stabilize and even reverse climate change. The other is to try to offset its consequences.

Of all these challenges the Biden Administration will emphasize one — climate change. It will focus on trying to prevent it, rather than on offsetting its consequences. It will adopt much of the content of the Green New Deal program issued a few years ago by the progressive wing of the Democrat Party. A great deal of money will be directed to green initiatives.

In the developed world concern about climate change has the flavor of a mass hysteria. Politically something must be done. It cannot be shown that there has ever before been a global effort of this high ambition. Perhaps American and European efforts will be mirrored elsewhere in the world, and something can be achieved. Since there is no predecessor policy on this scale the likelihood of success cannot be predicted with any confidence.

The great danger is that in focusing its attention on combating global warming the Biden Administration will risk a nuclear winter.

The Challenge to the Developed Regions

The economic challenge to the developed regions is one of current or imminent declining population and stagnating economies. For example, Canadian and Australian GDP growth 2008–2020 was less than 0.5% per annum. The likelihood of declining population and slowing economic growth has begun in China and is likely to intensify.

The Biden Administration appears to have a strategy for answering the challenge, although it does not explain it well to the world. This is unfortunate because understanding the Biden Administration's efforts would be helpful to people at all levels.

Specifically, the Administration is trying to implement programs that will provide better and more comprehensive care for the increasing number of aged people in the American population. Secondly, it is seeking to better balance the population by inviting large numbers of immigrants to swell the numbers of prime age workers in the American labor force.

To accomplish these things the Administration proposes spending to strengthen the social safety net and permits large-scale immigration from Central America.

Taken together, these approaches are a response to the challenge of an aging population and a stagnating economy, although there are other powerful motives at play also.

Contrast the Biden Administration's purposes with the response of Europe to similar challenges, which provides an advanced safety net for an aging population but which has not developed an effective immigration policy to better balance and strengthen its population.

Beneath this high level of politics is a lower level which involves disputes over how the Administration seeks to do these things. Most public discussion including virtually all the discussion in the mass media, addresses controversy at this level. The Administration is accused of violating the nation's laws and of making serious human consideration failures in how it addresses immigration issues. The accusations have merit, but the Administration is forced into this position in part because the political stalemate in Washington prevents it from obtaining laws that would make its political strategy on immigration legal.

Now we turn to the level of economic policy which is commonly discussed in the Congress and the mass media *ad nauseum*.

Trade

Today all countries seem to be viewing trade as more of a strategic issue. This is because more is involved than transactions for goods. Theft of technology has become worrisome in the relationship between America and China. The United States is charging China with espionage via trade-related activities. Hence, America is trying to disengage its economy to some degree from China's.

The reasons for disengagement are not only economic, but they are usually justified politically on employment grounds. Most trade from Asia to America is in manufactured goods. During the Republican Administration the U.S. tried to establish a policy favoring manufacturing — trying to revive what had once been a thriving manufacturing sector in America. The Republican Administration pursued this pro-manufacturing policy in a variety of ways, including the application of tariffs on goods from foreign nations. It was at best marginally successful.

It is very unlikely that the Biden Administration will pursue the Republican policy. Were it to do so, a regionalization of supply chains might displace globalization. The U.S. would seek to outsource to Mexico, perhaps even Central America, and South America. Already the Biden Administration is offering financial support to Central American countries in order to build local job opportunities. Not only would this possibly displace Asian suppliers, especially China, but might lessen immigration flows to the United States.

Susan Land of the McKinsey Global Institute has estimated that a substantial regionalization of supply chains will divert some 15–25% of global exports. This implies that some 18 trillion dollars' worth of global trade could change destinations. For example, some 90% of personal computers purchased in the United States now come from China. Production of these computers and shipment to the United States might largely go to Mexico.

It is very unlikely that the Biden Administration will pursue the direction of trade policy of its predecessor. The Republican Administration had used trade policy to support its foreign policy. The Democrats are reversing both. For example, in his first important trade action Biden reinstated tariffs on aluminum imports to the U.S. from the Persian Gulf which the Republicans had ended late in their administration.

In place of an industrial policy favoring manufacturing, Biden has announced a Buy American policy for federal agencies. The announced purpose of this policy is to increase employment in the United States, as was the policy of the Republican Administration. The Biden policy is considerably less ambitious than was the Republican policy and is much less likely to involve dislocations of world trade.

Biden takes small steps in a certain direction and implies that they will have large results. Biden's Buy America policy is an example. It will create some demand for American manufactures, especially where there is a national security element — as in pharmaceuticals as the pandemic has revealed. Building stockpiles of goods that were discovered to be in short supply during the pandemic will also help. But these actions, however meritorious, are not sufficient to revitalize American manufacturing on a large scale.

A Reserve Currency

The United States has lived with interest rates approaching zero for about 12 years now. What had been seen as an anomaly, is now part of ordinary monetary policy, recently reasserted by the Chairman of the American Federal Reserve System (FED), America's central bank. The Republicans' somewhat higher growth of the economy had begun to allow the Bank to raise interest rates toward more normal levels. Then came the pandemic and rates fell back to zero. Unlike some European countries and Japan, the U.S. has not yet resorted to less than zero interest rates. At the outset of Biden's presidency, the Chairman of the FED promised low interest rates indefinitely.

This raises the question if there is any economic plan? The Administration sought and obtained a very large stimulus package, supposedly to combat the adverse economic impact of the pandemic. This was strange since the economic difficulty was largely due to state-level shut-down orders aimed at certain businesses, and more spending would not alleviate this. Also, the economic growth rate in the final quarter of 2020 had been about 4%, a somewhat normal rate — even a bit higher than would probably result in 2021 from the strange mix of politically driven policies with economic consequences which were beginning to characterize the Biden Administration.

The big stimulus package of the early Biden Administration was argued for in large part as a response to public opinion polls that showed some 70% of the electorate to favor the package. The key to that support was a promise of direct payments by the government to every American except those with high incomes. Not surprisingly, people favored this.

The stimulus spending made more sense as a political payoff than as an economic measure. At the time of the first major stimulus package Congress had passed the bill with little support from the Republican in the White House. But when came time to send out the checks, Trump put his name on the checks and claimed credit for the whole effort.

The flood of national government spending under both administrations could be seen as a contest to see which party could deliver more financial benefits to its supporters. The Republicans used both tax decreases and spending increases. The Democrats used only spending increases.

The total of all this spending threatens to undermine a major source of the United States' position in the world — the role of the American dollar as the reserve currency of the world. Until now the dollar has remained stable because the EU and Japan have expanded their debt at the same pace as America. This may not continue much longer as American public debt begins to increase at a dramatic new rate. Biden Administration spending has not been offset directly by tax increases, so large amounts of debt were floated by the federal government to support the spending. The Republican Administration had enacted some tax increases (in the form of no further tax deductions for some common sorts of people's spending) which were targeted at states that are Democrat strongholds. It was widely expected that these tax increases would be immediately reversed by the Biden Administration. They were not. The taxes were kept in place in order to lessen the national debt increase created by the increased spending. In this way, the Biden Administration demonstrated a preference for spending above even tax reductions for its strongest supporters.

In America there is now an assertion that being "a reserve currency" is the root of evil. The thinking seems to be that if the dollar isn't a reserve currency, then the U.S. won't have the financial tools to over-inflate its economy. In addition, since the U.S. is not responsible enough to regulate its own financial system, it doesn't deserve to be trusted with reserve currency status. These are the arguments, but they are to a degree contradictory. The 2008 Global Financial Crisis is exhibit A and a likely coming second financial crisis will be exhibit B.

People are worrying about big federal spending and deficits and are thinking that if the dollar were not a reserve currency, the U.S. could not be on this spending and borrowing binge. In light of this and the likely coming consequences, it is not as safe as it used to be for the world to trust the U.S. with the world's reserve currency.

The American and increasingly the global strategy is to implicitly tax passive savers by providing negative real interest returns in the present, and in the future by inflationary devaluation of debt for the purpose of current government spending and encouraging speculative windfall gains on land, stocks, and bitcoins. The long-term effect will be the impairment of the nation's real productive potential for essentials.

Chapter 8

Biden Economics and the United States

America's Economy under Biden

We now reach that level of policy making which gets almost all the public attention — the level at which who gets what is decided.

There was a time when this was not so blatant as it is today in America. For almost 30 years after the end of World War II it was possible to appeal to Americans' love of country when trying to get them to act. By the mid-70s this had almost entirely disappeared except with World War II veterans. In its place was a commitment to self-interest and nothing more.

The Biden Administration describes its economic program as having the objectives of distributing money to the poor, using resistance to climate change as a reason to update our energy and transportation infrastructure, and investing in research and development to match Chinese efforts in electronic and space technologies. Large-scale spending will be devoted to each. With respect to distributing money to the poor, it is unclear whether funds will go to the poor or to advocacy groups on behalf of the poor which are active in the Democrat Party.

The Biden Administration achieved a 6–7% real GDP growth in 2021. Wall Street is proselytizing the story that 2021–2022 will mirror America's post WWII boom. This has propelled corporate shares higher.

There will be a great deal of spending by government, accompanied by much personal consumption expenditure. Spending can be channeled into three different categories. The first is production of goods and services in the United States — what we measure as Gross Domestic Product (GDP). This is job creating. The Biden Administration projects attained the increase in GDP this year over last to be about 8% — a very rapid rate of growth. This created millions of jobs.

But spending can also go into imports. We have had imports this year at such a high level that our major ports through which imports enter the U.S. have been clogged with shipping and long delays of unloading have been experienced.

Finally, spending can go into inflation. More money chasing a limited availability of goods and services will cause prices to rise. Spending cannot increase output beyond the full employment limit, and growth cannot be sustained without new capital formation and technological progress, both strongly discouraged by Biden's tax policies.

We face a contest between production, importing, and inflation for the high level of spending that will occur. Production that makes adequate provision for new capital formation and innovation is best for America, but there are certain impediments to a rapid increase in production. There are shortages of some key inputs — a major shortage of computer chips is delaying automobile and other production. There are disruptions in supply chains which developed during the pandemic and delay production. Industry groups that are involved in shipping and other transportation activities are warning that global supply chains are in danger of collapse because of shortages of labor caused by pandemic-related restrictions on transport workers that have now been in place off and on for years. Should this happen, the Biden economy will be dealt a significant blow. It is not clear that the Biden economic team is able to address this danger successfully. Greater economic disruptions due to supply chain disruptions are virtually certain.

Finally, the behavior of customers changed during the pandemic in ways that are uncertain. For example, the hotel industry used to host large conventions at which thousands of people filled hotels. Are people going to be comfortable returning to in-person gatherings? If not, hotels will have excess capacity and production of services will be lower than anticipated by the Administration.

Big tech companies are under increasing criticism. In part it is that they are accused of predatory behavior of the type prohibited by anti-trust legislation. In part it is the censorship they do of content posted on their sites. The Biden Administration will be under pressure to break them up.

Probably the Administration will refuse to do this. The Administration will be alleged to be protecting the companies for political reasons. But there are economies of scale in big technology and the U.S. needs large firms to be able to conduct research and invest at the level necessary to compete with the Chinese. So big tech cannot be broken up. The Administration might propose a graduated tax on the companies which would not interfere greatly with their ability to compete with the Chinese.

What Biden calls investment is primarily progressive social programs. This is consistent with modern propaganda techniques.

Since Biden displays no concept of what are traditionally called investments which can lead to real economic growth, discussion of his economic policy as if it is growth oriented is pointless. The trouble is that there is no link in Biden's "deficit and spend" strategy supporting technological progress, and there are strong government-created incentives for opting out of the labor force. Hence, spending won't generate a growth dividend, even though it is comforting to Democrats to image that somehow it will.

Real economic growth 2015–2020 was 2.7%. It was a negative 4% in 2020 under the impact of the pandemic. The economy in 2021, the first year of Biden's presidency, is likely to grew at a faster rate as it recovered from the pandemic, but then there is little likelihood of a higher growth economy than in 2015–2020.

The American economic system has not been working well for the masses. The Biden Administration with its allies in Congress has responded by spending in order to create jobs and proposes to improve the jobs by raising the minimum wage. The Administration also proposes to subsidize people directly to provide funds for living. Biden is trying both. Both have risks.

The system is in an acute state of macro-economic disequilibrium due to excess deficit spending. It is dysfunctional at the micro level due to anti-competitive regulatory ineptitude and inefficient anti-meritocratic and anti-growth government transfers. Yet Biden calls this circumstance the threshold of dazzling prosperity.

Biden's Reach

The Chair of the Federal Trade Commission has laid out before a Senate Committee a program that reaches across almost the entire economy of the United States. It proposes to impose outcomes on the economy that the Administration believes to be just. It rejects what the Administration views as rigged marketplaces. The program promises a fair and thriving economy for consumers, workers, and honest businesses. The FTC proposes to make businesses smaller and shape "the distribution of power and opportunities across our economy" (Mark Jamison, "The FTC moves toward a command economy," AEIdeas, September 28, 2021).

This ambitious program was described to Congress on April 21, 2021, by Lina Khan, Chair of the FTC. It expresses an aspiration of the progressive wing of the Democrat Party for reshaping the American economy. Biden has not yet spoken to it explicitly, but Chair Khan is his appointee, and she speaks for the most energetic wing of his political party. Biden has been following progressive policy proposals on other significant issues. He likely has this program in mind as opportunities arise for the FTC to implement elements of it.

The wide scope of this plan is reminiscent of Soviet central planning. It may be thought of a program of co-option since a frontal assault on the economy's many parts is deemed politically too conspicuous. It seeks to subvert the economy in order to achieve the stated goals. It is a Communist Party approach to ends of a similar nature.

Alternatively, Khan's memo is so ambitious that it is hard to image the FTC having the personnel to carry it out. From Biden's perspective it has the dual purpose of comforting progressives with a nod toward their aspirations. It also creates a regulatory environment in which firms can be singled out and persecuted for political objectives. Normally in America the tax authorities are employed for this purpose by the political party in power. The FTC here offers itself as another tool for this purpose.

It may be objected that Ms. Khan does not speak for the President but only for herself. That she is the chair of an agency which is semi- or fully-autonomous. That the FTC is part of the agency branch of government which joins the Congress, the Presidency and the Courts to have become in recent decades a fourth branch of government. We discuss in a later chapter the possibility that the emergence of a fourth branch of government of that nature has occurred. It would follow that Ms. Khan might be stating a progressive vision of the American economy independently of the President's views. Even if this is so, President Biden has during his time in office been championing progressive aspirations continually.

An Age of No Limits

It seems that America has entered an age of no limits. Government spending has reached levels previously inconceivable except in wartime. Debt is at historic highs for government, businesses, and individuals. The government uses its own debt creation power to encourage individuals to add debt by promising to forgive debt owed to the government itself. Student loans are being forgiven for some and loans made to businesses during the pandemic are being forgiven to many. There seems to be a general feeding frenzy. People who warn that these things will have to be paid for are ignored, because no one thinks of the adverse long-term consequences, preferring to temporize.

The broad outlines of the economic approach of the Biden Administration are taking shape. It has many moving parts, and several seem inconsistent with each other. Because of that it is probably too much to refer to it as a plan.

The big stimulus bill funds a whole set of liberal, not so much progressive, favorite causes. It is redistribution on a large scale, with the tax increases that will make it truly redistributive on the way.

Fiscal Policy

The United States House of Representatives has now authorized a total of almost 6 trillion dollars in spending on the pretext of counteracting the negative impact of the pandemic. While not all has been spent by any means, expenditures on this level, and the expectation that all will eventually be spent, is driving American GDP growth at a rapid rate — the first quarters of the Biden Administration saw inflation-adjusted growth at some 6% at an annual rate. The Biden Administration will claim credit for bringing about this rapid expansion of the economy. The development of vaccines and their distribution to inoculate the population and allow the economy to flourish are substantially due to the efforts of the Republicans. This is being ignored by the Biden Administration. Further, the Administration endorses slower economic growth in order to facilitate efforts to protect the environment and counteract climate change, despite claiming credit for a more rapid economic expansion than usual in America in recent decades.

Allegedly for the purpose of continuing a rapid rate of economic growth the Biden Administration is proposing large spending bills. A roughly 1 trillion dollar program to repair and expand the nation's infrastructure is likely. Such a large expenditure is required for several reasons. First, the United States in recent decades failed to maintain its infrastructure. This is because bills to build roads, bridges, ports, and airports failed to provide funds for their maintenance. Undone maintenance piles up until the bill is so large as to be almost too big to tackle. The Biden Administration, seeking reasons for further stimulus spending, is determined to tackle the backlog. Second, the American system involves extensive permitting and unrestrained cost increases as some people try to limit construction (via permit restrictions and delays) and others to profit from it (via cost increases). The Republican Administration was seeking to constrain and even reverse these barriers to infrastructure efforts, but the Biden Administration, with its political roots in the nation's cities, does not seem committed to continuing the effort. Third, the bill provides for spending on (described by the Biden Administration as investments) elements of the Green New Deal to combat climate change.

A key question is whether rapid economic growth can be made to last until the Congressional election of 2022, or more importantly into the presidential election of 2024. Probably the answer is no, at least not without continuing high levels of fiscal stimulus. Already the United States has piled up a debt level above the size of its annual GDP. Can it continue to add stimulus by debt financing, which is the issue for fiscal stimulus?

Republicans say no. But the answer is probably yes. The consequences are liable at some time in the not-so-distant future to be calamitous, so that Congress may balk at continued additions to the deficit. But Democrat Party discipline in Congressional voting may give us another large stimulus bill in 2022 intended to impact the 2022 Congressional elections.

In March 2021, Larry Summers, once Treasury Secretary for President Clinton, denounced the Biden fiscal policy as the most irresponsible in recent decades.

Despite being irresponsible, it may not work. After 2021 America is not likely to grow faster than 2–3% per year. Secular stagnation is still in command.

A Shrinking Labor Force

The U.S. has a steadily shrinking proportion of people working. The decline has been dramatic in recent years. Both parties attribute this to the impact of the pandemic. This is appropriate, to a degree. But the downward trend began in 2008, a decade before the pandemic.

However, the secularly stagnant, declining labor force participation rate from 2007 to 2021 is the more important fact. America is creating a society where a shrinking working class supports more and more non-working people.

Rather than be concerned about this many people in both political parties are accepting it as necessary. They are justifying shrinking labor force participation by the argument that automation is reducing the need for employees and that artificial intelligence (AI) will soon add dramatically to that. This would seem a rationalization rather than a cause. There would seem to be no limit to employment in service occupations — for example, teachers unions in some of our large cities are now asking that they be provided with daycare for their children. People could be employed in providing this service, whom neither robots nor artificial intelligence are likely to replace.

The Democrats are comfortable with an economy made up of large firms (which support the Democrat Party in various ways) and many lower-wage or non-working people. At the end of the second decade of the twenty-first century there was a spat of predictions that jobs would be scarce in the future due to automation and that the government should therefore provide a minimum income to all citizens. When the private economy seemed slow at bringing the prediction to reality, the Democrats set out to achieve it. Part of the purpose was to extinguish small business, despite endless prattle about encouraging entrepreneurship. Even under government anti-virus loan programs, small business was charged high rates of interest and given less favorable terms than bigger business gets from banks ordinarily. Proposals to increase the minimum wage struck at the financial viability of small business. Lockdown orders associated with the pandemic hit small business very hard. Since small business is historically a foundation of the Republican Party all this made very good political sense to the Democrats.

Biden supports this vision of a Democratic future — one of big businesses and many non-workers supported by government largess. Critics label the Democrat vision a cradle to the grave hyper-welfare state.

Problems with Bidenomics

Certain problems with Bidenomics are evident from national jobs reports. There is much slower job growth in the U.S. economy than the Administration had predicted. The Administration had spent money to increase employment; it had spent much of that money on subsidies to workers that caused people to be uninterested in taking jobs. The two elements of Biden's economic policy were at odds with each other and so job creation was modest. The Administration might have been expected to anticipate this — but it did not.

The waves of pandemic that washed against the shores of the nation's populace surely impacted the economy and its measurements in important ways. But they were not evaluated by top officials of either the Trump or the Biden Administrations. American economic assessment is rendered mistaken much of the time by the meaningless institutionalization of past practices on auto-drive across administrations and through the decades regardless of the changed circumstances.

It is not only the pandemic that has changed the economy. The steady evolution of tax law has made a major change in the economy. In the past most Americans paid federal income tax. Today, most do not pay federal income tax. Low earners have been exempted from income tax by law. Many very high earners are exempted from federal income tax by the form in which they take and spend income (that is by so-called loopholes in the tax law). Specifically, in 2020, some 61% of American households filed tax returns but paid no income tax. If non-filers are included, then 74% paid no income tax. The federal income tax is the major source of federal tax revenue, and it is paid by the middle class and some upper earners. If Biden's insistence that his Administration's proposed income tax increases will not impact the middle class were to be true, then there would be very little increased revenue from the tax rate increases. His insistence probably is not true.

In their political posture the Democrats hold that taxes are a necessary evil and that the rich should pay the lion's share. But when the Biden Administration considers trying to pay for its very large expenditure programs with tax revenues, it faces the need to raise taxes dramatically and to do it in the income categories in which people pay taxes. Such an effort faces staunch Republican opposition and will be very unpopular even if accomplished. The alternative is to continue massive borrowing at the federal level to finance spending program thereby raising both federal budget deficits and the total national debt. Traditionally the fear is that if debt rises too rapidly it will either undermine the national credit or stimulate inflation, or both. To offset concern about these dangers there has been offered a supposed new form of monetary theory in which the size of the federal deficit has no adverse consequences. Possibly this is true for a short term. It is very unlikely to be true for a longer term (for example, a period of a few years). Already inflation is rising rapidly in the United States the Biden Administration's spending packages becomes law.

In a speech on capitalism given on July 9, 2021, President Biden said, "Let me be very clear, capitalism without competition isn't capitalism, it's exploitation." The President's speech addressed a concern in America about the growth of large corporations to apparently dominate the economy. Surprisingly, market concentration has declined from the consumer perspective (not by industry definitions). "Viewed from consumer's vantage point 44.4% of all industries were highly concentrated in 1994 compared to 36.6% in 2019" (Laurent, Belsie, *NBER Digest*, July, 2021, p. 4).

The Administration is concerned that competition in America is being weakened by a dramatic fall in the rate of new business formation. The White House noted on July 9, 2021, that new business formation has declined almost 50% since the 1970s "as large businesses make it harder for Americans with good ideas to break into markets."

It is ironic for the President to attempt to assist the formation of small business. This is because progressives have been actively attempting to ruin small business since it is normally conservative and Republican. Progressives make a political alliance with big business. Again, the President is caught between progressives and liberals of his own party — a topic to which we will return later.

Chapter 9

Biden's Political Economics

Blowing Financial Bubbles

The New York Times reported on April 2, 2021, that a house in the Washington, D.C. suburbs was put on the market. It was in bad shape — a "tear-down." The broker received 80 offers and sold the house for almost double the asking price. This occurred in a very short time.

This housing frenzy was created by the Biden Administration's easy spending policies which attracted to Washington D.C. speculators and job-hunters hoping to live off the Administration's largesse. The Fed's low interest policy funded the run-up in housing prices by making loans for buying houses cheap. This is compounded by the absence of safe investment alternatives. Stocks in the current bubble market are probably overpriced, and people receive negative returns on bonds and bank savings after adjusting for inflation. Speculation is thought by many today to be a form of "prudence."

Washington is not the only place that the housing market now has a quality of frenzy. In Palm Beach, Florida, for example, a house which sold in 1989 for 2.25 million dollars sold in 2021 for 45.6 million dollars. There are numerous such examples.

Real-estate price inflation is a common occurrence in financial bubbles. Other assets and items also enter the frenzy territory. Prices rise exponentially for bitcoin, a digital asset with a basic value of zero, and rise and fall for share prices for companies that are in long-term decline. "Asset bubbles have a clear cause: the massive expansion of money and credit" (John Greenwood and Steve H. Hanke, *Wall Street Journal*, February 21, 2021, 4:58 pm).

Biden is turning a blind eye. His Administration says that it is focused solely on mending the labor market. With the fervor of messiahs, Federal Reserve Chairman Jerome Powell and Treasury Secretary Janet Yellen insist that the only way to save the labor market and reach full employment is to continue to pour fiscal and monetary fuel on the fire. But their prescriptions and prophecies, modeled on the playbook of the 2008 financial crisis, can be questioned today.

After that crisis, the Fed began quantitative easing, which massively expanded its balance sheet. At the same time, commercial banks were busy shrinking their loan books and writing off losses from mortgage debt and securities, which meant the Fed's injections did little more than offset the contraction of commercial bank balance sheets. As a result, money growth from 2010 to 2019, as measured by the Fed's broadest money measure, M2, averaged only 5.8% a year.

While money on the Fed's books grew rapidly, money in the hands of the public grew slowly. Spending and inflation were restrained, and the post-crisis recovery was anemic with inflation persistently below the Fed's target. In contrast, China's money-supply growth exploded in 2009 and 2010, averaging 23% a year. China not only achieved a strong recovery as a result but also a jump in inflation, which moved from −1.8% in July 2009 to 6.5% by July 2011. Money matters.

Fast-forward to February 2020. Since then, the quantity of money in the U.S. economy, measured by M2, has increased by an astonishing 4 trillion dollars. "That's a one-year increase of 26% — the largest annual percentage increase since 1943" (John Greenwood and Steve H. Hanke, *Wall Street Journal*, February 21, 2021, 4:58 pm ET).

American financial markets are experiencing a colossal bubble fueled by radical credit expansion tactics, "New Monetary Theory" and Washington's penchant for increasing public expenditures without raising taxes. New Monetary Theory is the assertion that the FED can expand the money supply without limit and without negative consequences so that the economy can receive whatever degree of stimulation is needed to meet economic objectives.

Pushing expenditures to unprecedented levels, as progressives are pressing President Biden to do, is not hard in a democracy like America's in which most politicians bid for votes by promising more and more spending.

Secretary of the Treasury Janet Yellen is Biden's key person in dealing with the economy. She is a Berkeley economist with tight ties to the Democrat Party, a series of high government positions, and close financial ties to Wall Street.

In the first days of the Biden Administration, she promised that if the 1.9 trillion dollar stimulus package was enacted by Congress, then in 2021 full employment would be restored without significant inflation.

She insisted that while the American economy was in a dramatic transformation caused by recovery from the pandemic, response to climate change and a return to outsourcing and while directives of the President were crippling industries and eliminating many jobs, macro policy spending alone would cause the economy to recover and move forward dramatically.

When the Administration's plans for further spending required tax increases, Yellen proposed that because of the negative effect of a higher corporate tax rate on American firms, and the likelihood that our firms would move profits abroad where they would not be taxed by the U.S., other countries should establish a minimum corporate tax rate worldwide so that the U.S. should not be disadvantaged by its own actions. There has been no rush abroad to assist the U.S. in this way.

Restraining Inflation

The Biden Administration is pushing so much fiscal and monetary stimulation of the economy that inflation expectations are growing. In order to restrain inflation, the Administration will either cut back its stimulus dramatically, undermining its economic growth targets, or will have to find another way to control inflation — perhaps even wage and price controls. It will likely do three things.

First, it will allow American firms to continue to anchor their supply chains in Asia and Mexico in order to keep costs low. Biden may try to start outsourcing to Central America to create jobs there in order to slow the flow of immigrants north. This reverses the Republican Administration's efforts to restore American manufacturing. It is likely that before long the Biden Administration will declare that for a successful economy, the United States needs more trade, not less. Then the Administration will seek multinational trade agreements to open more of the world to U.S. companies, while remaining silent about the further opening of the U.S. economy to foreign suppliers.

Second, if faced with a sudden leap in inflation, the Administration will likely turn to formal wage and price controls. It will set a limit for price increases of all kinds and establish an administrative board to enforce the regulations. This will introduce major dislocations into the economy and will collapse of its own failures in about 18 months.

Third, the Biden Administration will consent to a rise in interest rates but will soon discover that this crowds out domestic spending (because interest payments are a large component of the Federal Budget), torpedoes the housing market (mortgage payments will then exceed potential buyers' ability to pay), and risks precipitating a replay of the 2007 financial crisis.

It is possible to make such a firm prediction about wage and price controls because this is what happened several decades ago when a Republican Administration faced a similar situation.

It is possible to run effective price control programs. The United States did that in World War I, World War II, and the Korean War. But those models have not been followed since. The methods have been forgotten, and the people who developed and ran those programs are deceased.

A Summary of What Bidenomics Is and Will Be

Biden will push up minimum wages while bringing immigrants in to provide a cheap labor supply.

He will continue the extinguishing of small business (including entrepreneurial start-ups) via minimum wage increases, virus-responsive lockdowns, and lack of anti-trust enforcement.

He will continue pouring money into the economy (expansive fiscal policy), at this point through "stimulus bills."

He will support the FED keeping interest rates very low (expansive monetary policy).

He will support a strong dollar (an over-valued foreign exchange rate).

All this will threaten inflation so that continuing to rely on cheap foreign sources of imported goods is necessary.

He will resort to an ineffective program of direct price control to counter even more inflation.

All this will threaten to drive unemployment up, so he'll propose subsistence level transfer payments and he'll talk about education and training and all kinds of things to make people more capable of doing work that isn't available in sufficient amounts. Meanwhile in order to get work many people will work off the books at lower rates than the new minimum wages. The shadow economy will grow.

Tax increases will be substantial and will not be limited to high income earners and corporations only.

The result will be a slow growth economy accompanied by rising unemployment rates — but the unemployment rates can be kept down by providing transfers to people for not working. They will be out of the labor force and so not counted as unemployed.

All these elements reinforce each other and are likely to be inevitable consequences of each other.

Raiding the Federal Treasury

It is instructive to view the Biden stimulus bill of 2021 as another of a series of trillion-dollar raids on the federal treasury. The first was about 1 trillion in 2008, and by 2021 the price had risen to 2 trillion. This perspective on federal spending is an unusual one, and not popular. But it is instructive. This perspective ignores the issue of the need or lack of it for these massive spending bills, a topic which is highly complex, and here discussion focuses instead on the simple politics of these measures.

The first massive spending bill was a Republican bill pushed against Democratic opposition in the mist of the financial crisis of 2007–2008 under Republican President George W. Bush. It bailed out big banks and was perceived in Washington as a bailout to Republican constituents.

It was followed by another trillion-dollar spending bill pushed by the incoming administration of Barak Obama. It was hailed as a necessary stimulus for the economy in the mist of the so-called "Great Recession" which followed the financial crisis. It provided federal financial support to a plethora of Democrat institutions and voters. It was seen in Washington as the Democrats getting their own trillion-dollar package to mirror the one the Republicans had just achieved.

Then came the pandemic. This time some 4 trillion dollars in spending was authorized from the federal budget, but it was done in a series of bipartisan legislation. It appeared that both parties had learned to like the big spending game and had agreed to do it on an even grander scale.

The Republicans left office and the partisan game might have ended. But the Democrats wanted to renew it. Biden proposed a roughly 2 trillion dollar spending package labeled a stimulus to counter the economic impact of the pandemic. Republicans proposed that such a package be negotiated on a bipartisan basis as had the 4 trillion dollars in spending in the previous year (2020). The Democrats refused and passed the bill on a party-line vote. No Republican voted for it. The Democrats had renewed partisan raids on the Treasury and upped the ante from 1 to 2 trillion dollars.

The Republicans defended the first trillion-dollar raid as necessary to keep the nation's banking system from collapsing. The Democrats defended the second trillion-dollar raid as necessary to lift the economy out of a recession. Both parties defended the 4 trillion dollar raid during 2020 as necessary to lift the economy out of the pandemic economic collapse. The Democrats are now defending their 2 trillion dollar raid as necessary to lift the economy out of a continuing pandemic-caused recession. Beginning in the winter of 2021 the Democrats proposed a 3.5 trillion dollar package of programs which would have extended the game much further. Economists linked to each party defend these spending packages as necessary to strengthen the national economy. President Biden is especially adamant in defending the Democrat's proposed spending even against determined resistance in his own party. He even goes so far as to insist that the largest spending package will be without cost to the American taxpayer. Economics is said to be the cause, but politics is the purpose of the spending, and the clear beneficiaries are the constituents of each party.

Seen in this political perspective, each party has been raiding the Treasury for vast sums to benefit its supporters and has been loading the American public with very large increases in the national debt. Again, partisanship is exploiting the opportunities presented by being in control of the American government, not serving the interests of the America people.

Part IV
Biden's Domestic Policies

Chapter 10

Biden's Complex Game: Immigration

Immigration is one of the most fought-over political issues in America. Because of this, the Biden Administration must deal with it carefully. Immigration has been politicized to such a degree that most Americans have a conviction about it and are not interested in facts unless those facts support their preconceived notions.

In a previous chapter is a discussion of the role of immigration, legal and illegal, in Biden's broad economic policy for the United States. In this chapter, we address how the Administration handles the current confused and inequitable immigration system, if it can be called a system, of the United States.

The immigration issue has both short and long-term political aspects. Today, large-scale immigration is a desired policy for the Democrats for two reasons. High levels of immigration provide employers with a cheap labor supply. And immigrants tend to vote, overwhelmingly, for Democrat candidates. Immigrants who are not citizens are not legally entitled to vote in most jurisdictions in the U.S., but American election laws and their enforcement are notably loose. Immigrants seem a sure source of Democrat votes, even if it takes a while for many of them to become legally entitled to vote.

Biden's immigration plan is intended to do three things. The first is to bring a steady flow of immigrants into the country. This is a major bone of contention with the Republicans, who generally want to discourage immigration in order to limit to a smaller number the flow of immigrants. Perhaps surprisingly, the Republicans are less responsive to business demands for additional labor than are the Democrats.

Second, Biden's plan has as a key objective to legalize as many immigrants as possible, so that they become reliable Democrat voters. Where that is not possible, they may be assisted in voting Democratic anyway.

Third, Biden's plan is to make the immigration process more orderly. In place, for example, of the current flow of illegal immigrants across the U.S.'s border from Mexico, with the largest group originating in Central America, Biden wishes to establish American immigration processing centers in Central American countries.

Biden envisages immigration as a good. He proposes a path consuming 8 years by which immigrants illegally in the United States (there are estimated to be at least 11 million and possibly as many as 30 million) may obtain legal status as American citizens. He proposes to legalize immediately smaller groups (still a million or so) who are not legally in the United States but have been here several years as children.

For the long term America is seen by progressives not as an ordinary nation which is concerned to protect the jobs and health of its citizens by controlling immigration closely, but rather as a very unusual country which is in fact a global nation. This term, coined by a former American diplomat, Strobe Talbott, suggests that the United States see itself as opening its borders to people of all nations, and reflecting in its growing population the demographics of the world. It is a unique conception. Only the Romans at the time of their empire, had such a conception — that they were meant to govern all the peoples of the world. But Rome governed by having an elite, Roman citizens, who were a governing minority within the empire. "Why to be a Roman," went an old slogan, "was to be better than a king." The empire was universal in conception.

America as a global nation is a similar conception, except that there is, officially at least, no official governing group — instead, immigrants become citizens after time — Biden is proposing an immigration law to formalize that process — on the same basis as all other citizens.

An alternative perspective, more common in the world outside the U.S. than is the perspective of a global nation — sees a country (the U.S.) built by the labor of generations of people who have been here until it is a beacon for others, who come illegally into the country and by joining liberal and progressive politicians take over the country and under the rhetoric of democracy and equity use government — including taxation and redistributive spending — to divert the wealth created by other people to their own benefit. It is a process that is partly illegal (the immigration part) and partly legal (the government redistribution part). To people of this point of view the immigration process seems morally reprehensible, and so is vigorously fought.

The American immigration situation is different from that in the other main center of immigration — Europe. Immigrants pouring into America are primarily from Central America. They are of the same religion and culture as Americans generally. Many speak English, and Spanish has become a common second language in the United States. They meld into the general culture.

Another major source of immigration to America is Asia — Chinese, Indians, Vietnamese, and others. While of very different religion, culture and language these immigrants are generally anxious to fit into the general culture and make significant efforts to do so.

In America only in the short run, for a single generation, do subcultures emerge. The possible exception to this, which is now being determined, involves a large migration to the United States from Somalia which was fostered by the Obama Administration and may now be resumed by the Biden Administration. Somali immigrants are Muslim, and many do not speak English. They gather in communities outside some of the northern cities. Some have entered politics and a couple have made their way to the House of Representatives as Democrats.

The Somali pattern in the U.S. is more like the pattern of immigration in Europe. In Europe immigrants generally come from the mid-east and Africa. Most are Muslims and do not speak the language of the country in which they arrive or settle. Most enter enclaves of previous immigrants who do not meld into the local populations.

In the United States in pursuit of their goals, the Democrats are willing to ignore a dark side of illegal immigration — crime. Republicans point to victims who are American citizens. Democrats ignore the outcries of the victims. They simply don't care about the victims. In part, this is because when the victims are white males or the families thereof, they resent them deeply already. Biden accepts this.

The turmoil and danger that roils border communities in Texas and Arizona is welcome to the progressives. The inhabitants of those areas are mainly ranchers and small businesspeople. They are Republicans. If they are threatened and harmed, that is a positive for the progressives in the Biden Administration. In this way, there is a form of civil war under way in America today. It extends to other parts of the country as well, taking different forms than along the border. Biden, in endorsing progressive non-administering of immigration law along the southern border embraces violence against people who are citizens of the United States but not his political party's supporters.

Europe has substantial immigration, much of it illegal as in the U.S. Immigration is a similar political problem in America and Europe in that many immigrants are socially and culturally diverse from the existing populations and problems grow out of differences. In addition to social and cultural differences there often grows competition for jobs between immigrants and previous residents. This is mitigated in the U.S. and in Europe by immigrants who are willing to take low-paying and difficult tasks not desired by the previous population. Immigration to the European Union is not of a type which can be easily and effectively integrated into the European society. This is exactly the opposite in the U.S. where mass immigration from Latin America is dispersed throughout the nation and is integrated into the nation's work force quickly and effectively.

The United States now receives about 3 million immigrants a year — about 1% of its total population. (https://www.dhs.gov/immigration-statistics/yearbook/2019/table1). Of these about 1 million arrive legally and about 2 million arrive illegally. This estimate for illegal arrivals is the figure generally accepted privately in the American business community. It is not supported by official statistics nor by public estimates from business sources. Official and officially public estimates are closer to half a million illegal arrivals per year.

These numbers are very large in international comparisons. Some countries receive very few immigrants. Instead, if they need additional workers, normally for low-skill jobs, they issue work permits and they effectively prevent illegal immigration. Most countries are in this situation. America is not.

In America the argument against a large volume of immigration is that many immigrants, not all, are able to take jobs away from American citizens. They cause unemployment among American citizens and keep wage levels down for many Americans.

The approach of the Republican Administration was the opposite from that of Biden's. The Republicans attempted to reduce immigration significantly in the name of reducing unemployment for American citizens. The Republicans' wall worked — where it had been built. It funneled those seeking entry into a central location where they could be registered, counted and controlled rather than have a porous border of two thousand miles where they could slip across.

Biden did not run on a platform of increasing immigration, but rather on one of reducing the alleged inhumanity of the Republicans' approach.

The Biden Administration has very strong support from the American business community for its immigration policy. In general, American business seeks about 2 million additional low-skilled workers each year (6,000 a day across the southern border), and cares very little about whether they are legal entrants or not. American business will rarely say this publicly because of an expected political backlash.

The politics of the approach of the Biden Administration are potentially explosive. Polls show almost 80% of respondents opposing the Biden Administration's immigration actions and inactions. Immigration is a political loser for the Administration, meaning that opposition to increased immigration is substantial and comes from both the political right and left — that is, from within the Democrat Party itself as well as from non-Democrats.

Opposition to Biden's Policy

Opposition to the Administration's immigration policy rests on five pillars.

First, that large-scale immigration by working-age people is depriving Americans of work opportunities and increases non-employment of Americans. This is so, but it is not clear that there is a large body of citizens that American businesses want to hire, or who want to work for them. A cabinet member in the Obama Administration observed, "We are trying to keep out of the country people who want to work in order to make jobs for people who don't want to work!" This, he implied, was self-defeating.

Second, with illegal immigration across our southern border comes not only workers but also criminals and foreign agents of all sorts and from all over the world. Illegal immigration is asserted to be a national security threat.

Third, illegal immigration has fostered the development of large criminal organizations who not only profit from the trade in illegal immigrants but are the source of massive criminal activities in the U.S. itself. Drug addiction and human trafficking are currently the major criminal activities which the cartels engage in within the United States.

Fourth, the process of illegal immigration involves massive human rights violations of the immigrants themselves. It is an awful trade in people.

Fifth, a primary purpose of the Administration permitting a large volume of illegal immigration is believed to garner votes for the Democrat Party. The expectation is that the immigrants will be thankful to the Democrats for letting them enter the country — many in 2021 arrived at the U.S. border from Central America wearing t-shirts that had spread across the chest the slogan, "President Biden let us in." The immigrants are expected to be grateful to Biden and to vote, legally or illegally, for Democrats in American elections.

Of these five objections, only the first and fifth deal with the issue of the volume of immigration. The others are about how it is done. But the first objection is so powerful politically that it prevents the Administration from legalizing immigration at the desired level, and so by legalizing the immigration process, resolving the other four objections.

This is the political basis of the human tragedy that occurred at the southern border of the United States in 2021.

The Administration responds to these objections by trying to conceal what it is doing from the country and from much of its own party. To do this it relies on many elements of modern propaganda techniques which are described in detail in an earlier chapter of this book.

Biden's Response

Biden has emphasized that the border patrol under his direction has been sending all illegal immigrants except children and their parents back to Mexico, which is in conformance with American law. He does not mention that this applies only to the illegals who are apprehended by the American border patrol. Most are not.

Today some immigrants turn themselves in to the American border patrol. Some are returned to Mexico, some to their home countries, and some are processed and released into the United States. Some have dates set for hearings before specialized courts about their application to become American citizens. Some do not. Those who have court dates sometimes appear. Most do not. Some who do not appear are apprehended by federal police (ICE) and are deported. Many American cities have declared themselves sanctuaries for immigrants seeking to avoid arrest for being in the country illegally. This means that local authorities do not help federal police apprehend undocumented immigrants and will even hide them from the feds.

In the past, illegals would cross the border and flee on foot into the brush on the American side. They would make their way into the interior where smugglers (now called traffickers) or friends would meet them and take them further into the U.S. But recently, the illegals are picked up almost immediately after crossing the border by "coyotes" — traffickers — who are driving old SUVs, vans, and trucks which they have purchased in the U.S. The coyotes drive the immigrants north. The vehicles are ordinarily full to overflowing with people.

If they are spotted by U.S. agents, the coyotes drive the vehicles off the road. The illegals jump out and race off into the brush where they are very difficult to apprehend. One of the reasons that there are sometimes tragic accidents is that the vehicles may turn over as they are driven off the road and the immigrants are injured or killed. Most however get away into the brush — what Congress people from the north like to call the "countryside," as if it were well-watered, which it is not, and covered with grass and trees, which it is not. This is more evidence of politicians speaking to the expected ignorance of their constituents who in most of the country know little or nothing of what the southern border of their own country is like.

Most people who illegally cross the border do not get apprehended or sent back to Mexico or their countries of origin but make their way successfully into the U.S. Biden knows this. He favors it but does not mention it publicly.

The primary immigration problem with which Biden must contend is that of Hispanics and the southern border of the U.S. But it is not the only immigration problem. For example, during the summer of 2021 a question arose about roughly 100,000 refugees from Afghanistan occasioned by the American military withdrawal from that country. Apparently, the Administration was concerned that there would be substantial opposition to resettling those people in the United States. Most Afghans were taken by plane to other countries than the U.S. while American authorities sought permanent homes for them. Several thousand were admitted to the United States, but virtually no publicity was given by the Administration to this fact or to its magnitude. In some respects, the reception granted to Afghans was not different from that granted to Hispanics. The less said by the Administration about them, the better, despite the Administration welcoming them.

Progressives favor open borders. Biden is adopting their position in practice while publicly being silent about it or even claiming to do the opposite. Progressives welcome immigrants including those who come illegally. Yet their domestic policies threaten the freedoms and opportunities for individual advancement which make the U.S. attractive to immigrants. Over time if the progressives remake American society as they are attempting to do, immigration will fall of its own volition. But this will take several decades.

Chapter 11

Demographics is Destiny

The Foundation of the Immigration Problem

The foundation of the immigration issue is that there is rapid population growth in many underdeveloped countries that are both poor and poorly governed. And in the developed, rich countries there is slow population growth because the women don't want children and can avoid it with modern medicine. The result is that people in the poor countries want to get to the rich countries and there is room for them.

A Gallup poll in 2018 indicated that 27% of some 600 million people who live in Latin America and the Caribbean would leave their countries if they could do so. This is some 162 million people. Not all these people wish to go to the United States, of course. Some will be satisfied to flee to other Latin American countries and some to Europe. But the majority will head for the U.S. if that is possible. The pressure on our southern border will be intense for years!

Large-scale immigration from Latin America to the U.S. is a consequence of the failure of American-sponsored economic development in Latin America over the last several decades. Americans have known that there was a race between economic development and population growth in the region, but America promised more in terms of economic development than was delivered.

Large-scale immigration from Latin America to the U.S. is also a consequence of the failure of democracy in the region over the decades since the 1970s. Prior to that Latin America had seen many dictatorships. Then they faded and democracies took over in most of the countries of the region. Democracy promised much in personal freedom, social advances, and economic progress. It delivered little in most countries. The result is that people are trying to flee poverty, gang violence, injustice, and political corruption.

It can be no surprise that in the U.S. there is a tug-of-war over how much immigration to allow through the southern border with Mexico. Most of the immigrants come from Central America. American law doesn't permit much legal immigration from that source. So there has been a great deal of illegal immigration. For a variety of political reasons, the Democrats endorse the illegal immigration. They endorse it uncritically. Sick people and criminals are welcomed with the healthy and honest. The Republicans tried to shut the illegal immigration off. Republicans say the immigration should follow legal procedures, knowing that legal procedures would permit very little immigration from Central America. Yet the American business community welcomes large-scale immigration to obtain people who will work effectively for them, noting that Americans who are not employed often don't want work and if they do accept employment are not as productive as recent immigrants. In Congress a battle goes on endlessly about a thorough revision of the immigration laws to resolve the problem of illegal immigration over our southern border. No resolution is ever reached.

Illegal immigration has evolved into a business for criminal cartels that is now on an enormous scale. Almost all people coming across the southern border are trafficked by the cartels.

The United States over recent decades allowed illegal drugs to become a large international crime operation. Cartels from Mexico and Latin America built a booming business shipping drugs into the United States for sale. America fought the drug traffic but ineffectually and the business grew and grew. Then the cartels moved into the business of trafficking people to the United States. Again the U.S. resisted, but ineffectually and the cartels grew ever larger and more aggressive.

Why has the United States been so uncertain about enforcing its own laws? There are three reasons.

First, there is strong support for the drug trade among American drug consumers — after all, the reason there is a drug trade is that many Americans choose to consume illegal drugs — and as for illegal immigration — employers want the additional labor. There is not support for vigorous enforcement of the laws.

Second, there is activist opposition in the United States for any law enforcement activity that might involve innocent people being hurt. Full enforcement of the laws against the drug trade or illegal immigration would certainly involve innocent people being injured, even killed. This is against our values, opponents cry.

Third, the cartels spend a great amount of money easing opposition to their activities, and this is now done with such careful disguise that it is not known to the American people but only to experts about the cartels.

Hence, the cartels continue to flood the American border with illegal immigrants from many countries and the United States is ineffective in stopping them.

Most immigrants come from central America, but people from South America and Asia also come. Because the border is porous, agents of foreign governments also enter the United States in this way. Most immigrants entering the U.S. illegally are young adult males. But there is a sizable minority of families and children traveling without adults. These are a special problem of exploitation. Here trafficking by the cartels is exploitive in the extreme. If immigrants make it into the United States, as most do, then the cartels pursue them to exact further payments, or to punish them if the payments are not forthcoming. The cartels therefore have units in the U.S. for both human trafficking and drug distribution.

There are many restrictions and checks to get into the U.S. by plane or over the Canadian border. There are effectively few on the southern border. There are restrictions and checks by American law, but they are not effectively enforced.

Why is this? Progressive politics desire this outcome and Biden follows those politics. Progressives prefer large-scale immigration to provide votes for them and to help create a proletariat in America which will support them. In this aspect of his immigration policy Biden is satisfying the progressives, who praise him greatly.

I (Mills) have a friend who runs a large company based in the U.S. He has employees in Europe who are very important to the company. Sometimes he needs to bring them to the U.S. He complains bitterly of the difficulty and delays of getting them visas to come to the U.S. Sometimes by the time a visa is approved, the work need is over. Now, under Biden, his best course of action is to buy his employee an airline ticket to Mexico and in Mexico hire a car and bodyguards to bring him to the southern border of the U.S. where he can cross and catch a flight to the headquarters of my friend's company in the northeast. The bodyguards are to protect his employee in Mexico, not in the U.S.

Biden's Administration again placed immigrant children in special facilities as the Republican Administration had done. When Republicans did this, the facilities were labeled "cages" by the Democrats. The same and similar facilities are not so labeled now. The Biden Administration asserts that it has no other alternative given the situation of the children. But though the Biden Administration's assertion is correct, progressive spokespersons condemned Biden for his action. "It is not alright," a progressive spokesperson exclaimed. "It was never right, and it will never be right!' In the matter of immigration, the Biden Administration quickly fell into controversy with Democrat progressives.

Biden's first actions in office reversed key elements of Republicans' policies at the southern border of the U.S. This was accompanied by mass media reports of Biden's welcoming attitude toward immigrants. Immigrant activist groups in the United States informed their contacts in Central America that the American border was again open. Finally, people with families abroad told their family members abroad that the border was again open.

Immediately the number of legal and illegal immigrants on America's southern border began to rise. Immigrants wore t-shirts praising Biden. In particular, the number of unaccompanied children crossing the border illegally rose dramatically. Thousands of children were intercepted by American border patrol officers and interred. This was a building tragedy. Children without family support, without means of existence, were placed in their thousands in holding pens.

The political fallout was instantaneous. Critics spoke of a "crisis" at the border. The Biden Administration vigorously denied a crisis but only a month after he had entered the White House Biden dispatched senior advisors to the border to observe the situation. There were two alternatives available to the Administration in dealing with the situation. One was to return — practically if not publicly — to the Republicans-era means to stem the tide of migrants. In fact, the Administration did so to a substantial degree. In the fall of 2021 large numbers of Haitians fled their earthquake and hurricane-ravaged country to cross into the United States over its southern border. The Administration flew these illegal immigrants back to Haiti. The Administration made no mention of this because its progressive wing opposed the policy. Taking advantage of the Administration's silence, its opponents broadcast news of the Haitians crossing into the

United States but said nothing of the Administration returning them to their homeland. The impression was intentionally left that the Haitians remained in the United States.

The American political parties continued to jockey with the lives of millions of immigrants, while failing to attempt to resolve a problem recognized by almost every American.

Chapter 12

President Biden Confronts the Pandemic

America was among the hardest hit of the nations by the pandemic. It had more cases and more deaths than most, even adjusted for population. Its economy was greatly disrupted. Its political process guaranteed that the pandemic would become a center of bitterly partisan conflict. Yet America did much to pull itself out of the clutches of the virus. Biden had little to do with this, but he has claimed credit for it.

The background is that for 25 years the Center for Disease Control (CDC), the American public health agency, had quietly studied the possibility of a pandemic and how to deal with it. Some 700 people, mostly professionals, worked on the matter. A full response plan was prepared. Obama, late in his presidency, created an interagency committee at the White House level to manage a U.S. response. Predictions of a pandemic were made, including by Bill Gates (personally) and the Gates Foundation.

Trump became president and a year and a half into his presidency disbanded the committee. When the first reports of the Wuhan virus came out of China and the American public health committee offered its analysis of how the U.S. should respond, the Trump Administration rejected it wholesale. As the epidemic developed in the U.S. the Republican Administration had to take notice.

The Republican Administration adopted a policy which in the end was likely the major contributor to its election defeat in November 2020. Ironically, it took the one action by American administration that had an important impact in lessening the pandemic. The Republicans at the outset of the infection launched a program to build vaccines against the virus and funded it liberally. Within a very short time by historic measures several vaccines were available.

The Republican president had acted within the context of a strategy to counter the vaccine. Like any president's strategy his had both a substantive and a political aspect. Substantively the Republican decided to end the pandemic by the creation and distribution of vaccines. Politically he decided to encourage the American people to face the disease with confidence that it would be overcome.

The Republican's strategy worked, but it took too long. The Democrats criticized it for ineffectiveness for a year before the vaccines became widely available. There was no more effective element of Biden's campaign than his attacks on the Republicans for the spread of the virus throughout America and the suffering and death it caused. By election date in the fall of 2020 Americans who were not ill were complaining of having to defend themselves against the danger. Most were isolated in their homes. They spoke of being "too – tired of spouse." They spoke of being "too – tired of everyone." People's lives at work and home had been disrupted and they were in an angry mood. At the time of the election much of the nation had lost loved ones; they were in financial distress; they were tired of being stuck at home. An upset and angry electorate entered the voting booths. It is not too much to say that the virus caused the Republicans' defeat in the election of 2020.

The Republicans seemed not to recognize the adverse political consequences of the pandemic. Biden understood it and capitalized on it. When Biden took office in January 2021, he announced that dealing with the pandemic was his top priority.

The Biden Administration had used the virus as one of its two major political weapon against the Republicans (the other was continuous vilification of the character and personality of the President — this was the case whether or not the criticisms of the Republicans were merited). The incoming Biden Administration was fully aware that the pandemic was raging in the U.S. and that it must deal with it. From the date of the election to the inauguration were almost four months. One would have thought that the incoming administration would have prepared a full-scale program to address the virus. The Republican Administration made this more difficult by refusing for many weeks to share information on the federal government's current anti-virus programs. But there had been discussion of various strategies for dealing with the virus since its inception. The Republican Administration had adopted one course of action; the Democrats had condemned it for its failure.

Yet when the Biden Administration took office, a new strategy implemented by new programs was nowhere to be seen. In a flurry of presidential executive orders — said by Democrat supporters to be the most extensive start to a new administration since that of Franklin Roosevelt at the height of the Great Depression in 1933 — the pandemic played no role.

Instead, the massive confusion of the vaccine rollout simply worsened.

Biden's White House did attempt to alter the politics of the virus by targeting black and Latino communities for vaccination sites. In doing so the White House utilized its own measures of suitability of counties in the various states and rejected those offered by the American public health agency, the Centers for Disease Control (CDC). So much for science when it encountered politics in the brand-new Biden Administration.

A Chaotic Vaccine Rollout: A Parade of Fools

The vaccine roll-out in the United States both failed to counter the virus quickly, and it also infuriated many people. People spent day after day trying to get reservations for vaccinations. People waited hours to get vaccine shots and tests for the virus. When vaccinated or tested, they were usually unable to pull their vaccination certifications, or their test results out of software packages. In general, vaccinations or tests were well administered once people got to the sites. But provision of results was not. Almost every one of the many different organizations which provided shots or tests had software programs built to provide people with certifications and results. Generally, they failed to work properly and failed to provide the necessary information.

The first weeks of Biden's Administration were characterized by continuing confusion in the rollout of vaccinations that had been occurring in the last days of the Republican Administration.

Since this had been the situation which was developing when a Republican was president, the public expected better of the Biden Administration. It was not better. Articles in local newspapers read in the Biden period, "We're stuck with the 'worst possible' vaccine rollout" (Thomas L. Knapp, *The Palm Beach Post*, February 24, 2021, p. 20a).

The evidence was that Biden's people were no better than the Republicans'. The problem was a national one, not merely partisan. What is partisan is the criticism each administration made of the other.

In the vaccine rollout two very serious mistakes were made from the outset by the Republican Administration and then both were continued by the Biden Administration.

The first was that in a situation of a serious shortage of vaccine, the two administrations sought to increase demand for the vaccine. What should have been done was to seek to reduce demand in the beginning. Instead, chaos was created by millions seeking inoculation who could not be supplied with vaccine.

What caused the federal government under both administrations to try to increase demand for vaccines of which they had only very limited supply? They were concerned that many Americans might not be willing to be vaccinated. There was cause for this concern. But at the outset of inoculation, when vaccine was in short supply, it was a god-send that many people weren't sure they wanted it. This attitude reduced demand at a time when reduced demand would help provide for a calm rollout.

There was instead a steady drumbeat of appeals from Washington for all Americans to get vaccinated. So great was the demand that very soon priorities had to be established for who could get the vaccine. It was not until several months into Biden's administration that the initial demand for vaccination was filled.

The second big error was to fully decentralize distribution of the vaccines. Distribution was assigned to each state with almost no guidance from the federal government. The result was 50 different systems for distribution of the vaccines. This led to serious difficulties for both the Republican and Biden administrations.

The Republican Administration initiated both errors. The Biden Administration continued both.

There was no real excuse for this. Distribution of the vaccination was a problem in rationing. The United States had extensive experience in rationing during both world wars and the Korean War. Tires, gasoline, and other products were rationed, not vaccines, but the process was identical. The United States should have known what to do with the vaccine. But neither administration consulted the past. Neither approached the few people living who had experience in how to ration.

For example, the government at one point had to ration vaccine against COVID-19. There was likely to be big competition for vaccination because it restores mobility to people. But simultaneously with the first distribution of vaccine, the government to bipartisan applause started a public relations campaign to convince millions that they needed the vaccine. Polls showed that about 40% of the American people are suspicious of the vaccine and wouldn't take it. This was considered a huge problem that had to be addressed immediately. At the outset of a rationing campaign the government was trying to increase demand. This was certain to make rationing more difficult and introduce chaos. It did.

Having many people not wanting the vaccine initially was a blessing — it would take pressure off the distribution. Some 330 million people need vaccine, and since generally two doses each, 660 million doses. To have some 130 million people withdrawing from the contest for vaccine was a gift from heaven. Months from the start of vaccination, when the first 220 million had been served, then there was time to try to persuade people who hadn't taken the vaccine to do it. By then, if the rollout had gone well, most of those people would have decided it was safe and would be seeking it.

But instead of this imminently sensible approach, the government acting on media publicity of a supposed crisis of unwillingness to be vaccinated, did the opposite. The result was a disaster in distribution of the vaccine as the shortage was magnified by the public relations campaign. There may have been some additional cases and deaths in consequence of the confusion and turmoil accompanying the roll-out of the vaccine.

But despite the roll-out chaos large numbers of people began to be vaccinated. At the end of his first month in office, Biden announced that enough vaccine would be available to inoculate the entire U.S. adult population by the end of May (an advance of the target date by two months).

The result was failure. Significant resistance to vaccination emerged. In an international survey the U.S. had a larger proportion of its population resisting vaccination against coronavirus than any other country but Russia.

Why has this happened? The Democrats saw the turmoil caused by the pandemic as the Republicans' greatest vulnerability in the 2020 elections. They sought to add to the problem. The top Democrats before the 2020 election called on people to not get the vaccines because Trump was involved in creating them. (Later, when they were begging resistors to get vaccinated, Democrats changed course and insisted that Trump had not been involved in the creation of the vaccines.) In 2020, the Democrats insisted, because Trump was involved, the vaccines were likely dangerous and ineffective. People heard them and grew cautious. When they had won the election and gained power, Democrats began to champion the vaccines. In response, some Republicans began to call for people to avoid vaccinations and exploited the fears of people who were already anti-vax. This they did to gain political advantage against the Democrats. It has been working. Vaccination resistance in the United States is largely, perhaps primarily, a result of our partisan politics.

With Biden now President, almost half the American population remained unvaccinated, and vaccinations slowed dramatically. Appeals by President Biden for people to get vaccinated were largely ignored. The Administration began efforts to expel anti-vaccination propaganda from media and social media channels.

In simple summary, the Democrats had warned Americans that vaccines developed by the Trump Administration would be unsafe. Many Americans had accepted the warning. When the Administration took office, it needed to administer the Trump-developed vaccines as quickly as possible, so it had to reverse its warnings about the safety of the vaccines. Opposition to vaccination had now two origins — one which had developed over many years involving convictions people had developed about the danger of vaccinations, and another created by the Democrats themselves in the 2020 presidential campaign. The Biden Administration was unable to counter on a large scale either of the sources of resistance to vaccination. The result was another spike of virus infections in the summer and fall of the Biden Administration's first year.

The United States under Biden was the only country in the world to have lost the lives of 1 of every 500 people to the pandemic and to still be losing almost 2,000 lives a day.

Having continued a mistaken policy of the Republican Administration the Biden Administration retreated into a tried-and-true political response. It blamed the Republican Administration for the fiasco in distribution.

Chapter 13

Mishandling the Pandemic

A State-By-State Approach

The U.S. is a large nation geographically and it can be argued that a national approach is too broad to be effective. Yet the only alternative considered by either administration seems to have been a state-by-state approach. There are 50 states. The only two alternatives considered appear to have been either 1 national policy or 50. The federal government has no central directive capacities other than mandates and edicts to deal with public emergencies. But the United States falls naturally into several regions each of which has somewhat similar population distribution characteristics (for example, urban or not) and internal travel patterns. The best way to have addressed the pandemic would likely have been on a regional basis. Neither the Republicans nor the Biden administrations made any attempt to do this. This contributed to the mismanagement of the virus.

American states have their own governments which are generally subordinate to the federal government. Governments at the state level are dominated by either Democrat or Republican legislatures and governors. In the intense partisan political atmosphere of the United States the Republican- and Democrat-dominated states took different directions in dealing with the pandemic. In general, Democrat states imposed strict general lockdowns on their populations and vaccination mandates. Republican states did not. Political controversy surrounded the different approaches taken by Democrat- and Republican-controlled states.

The Texas Challenge

By March 2021, the third month of the Biden Administration, the American effort to counter the pandemic was in disarray. Vaccines were increasingly available and despite what the media called "chaos" in their distribution; millions of people were getting vaccinated. Preventive measures remained necessary. The federal government was urging, but not insisting, that the states continue to require people to wear masks and keep a distance from one another. Yet suddenly Texas (the second largest state in population) dropped all preventive regulations and reopened all businesses, churches, etc., as if the pandemic didn't exist. Since there is free movement of people among the states, if the pandemic resumed its spread in Texas, it would soon pass into the rest of the country. A lead federal contagious disease scientist commented that he found this action by the government of Texas to be "inexplicable."

Why was this done in Texas? No reason based in medicine or public health was offered by the state's leaders. It was done on a political basis only. First as political distraction. Texas had just been through a disastrous week of freezing weather and winter storms in which the state's electric power system had failed and so had its water supply. Opening-up despite the virus was good news to the population. Second, it was defiance by the Republican-led state directed at the leadership being offered by the Democrat-led federal government. Again, partisan politics triumphed over sensible public policy in America.

Challenged about the decision made by the Republican leaders of Texas, a prominent Senator from Texas responded, "No one in Texas is prevented from wearing a mask." So, apparently, if individuals in Texas wanted to, they could wear masks. The implication was that a person could protect themselves from the virus by wearing a mask if they wished.

Of course, a person wears a mask primarily to protect others, not themselves. If others don't wear masks, then that threatens you. That is the essence of what it means for a disease to be contagious. Thus, the Texas Senator's response was disingenuous, and indicative of the political games being played in America with the response to the pandemic.

Why did the federal government do nothing to reverse Texas' course? The pandemic was a national crisis, not a state-level one. States with very different approaches to controlling the pandemic had very similar outcomes in terms of numbers of cases and deaths per capita. This occurred because people traveling carried the disease with them from state to state.

At the outset of the pandemic the then Republican president had left the management of the pandemic to the states while he focused on encouraging the development in record time of vaccines to combat the virus. He had succeeded dramatically in bringing vaccines to the public.

But the states had garbled the management of prevention of the virus' spread. A state with an effective plan to control the virus found its number of cases and deaths being raised by contagion coming from other states. A state with an ineffective plan to control the virus simply exported the virus to other states. Travel was the Achilles heel of every state's contagion-control plan.

An undercurrent of resistance to vaccination was also rumbling through the nation encouraged by both some Republicans and some Democrats. Republicans tended to question the reality of the disease — so people didn't really need a mask or a vaccination. Democrats questioned the safety of the vaccines in particular reminding African Americans that decades ago some of their parents and grandparents had been secretly used to test new vaccines.

When employers sought to require employees to be vaccinated as a way to abolish the virus from workplaces, lawsuits were filed in some states to prohibit employers from requiring vaccinations.

Federalization

Biden didn't federalize the response to the pandemic. When some states opened businesses, Biden appealed to them to reverse that decision. He begged them to reverse it; he pled with them. They ignored him. His leadership in this area that he had identified as his highest priority in his first months in office was completely ineffective.

With open travel state boundaries mean little. For example, by early April almost one and one-half million Americans were traveling on a single day on the nation's airlines. Millions more were traveling by automobile.

Such a large volume of travel among the states meant that a national approach was needed. The Republicans had rejected a national approach. President Biden also rejected a national approach. Biden could have used his new presidency to impose a national policy. Why didn't he?

The political resistance was too great. Democratic-run states like California and New York were deep in lockdowns. Republican-run states like Texas and Florida had largely abandoned efforts to constrain the virus and their businesses and other institutions were open and operating. Virus constraint was a political snake-pit for President Biden. Better to let the roll-out of the vaccine mitigate the virulence of the pandemic over the last months of the winter and the spring of Biden's first year in office.

Again, extreme political partisanship — the different approaches at the state level of Republicans and Democrats — had prevented America from executing an effective public policy.

Politics Drive the Pandemic Agenda

It was quickly apparent that neither policy analysis nor science would drive Biden's agenda. Politics would drive his agenda.

In accordance with the strictures of modern propaganda, when things went badly, the Biden Administration accused the Republicans of exactly what they (the Democrats) were doing. This was sufficient to cause most of the American mass media to ignore the evidence of politics in Biden's Administration dominating other influences.

Democrat-run states continued business shutdowns to combat the virus. Biden supported this and urged the method on other states. What was never made public was that the COVID shutdowns devastated small business, eliminating a great deal of it and placing most of what remained on a tenuous basis. The Democrat governors who imposed shutdowns and President Biden when he called for them, wanted this to be the result. Historically, small business has been the heart of the Republican Party. To destroy it is a Democrat priority, though never publicly acknowledged. An enormous step in this direction was made in the shutdowns. In the matter of small business, the Democrats sought shutdowns and disruption for the benefit of the Democrat Party.

The Special Challenge of International Travel

Travel moves the variants of the virus around the world, and into the U.S very quickly. But how is that to be dealt with? Can it be dealt with? Do the airports and border passages need much more effective tests for the virus? Is it travel that should be shut down, perhaps instead of stores and schools? The Republican Administration attempted to shut off most international travel into the United States for fear of the spread of the disease.

The Democrats criticized this bitterly as unnecessary, discriminatory and racist in origin.

The Biden Administration made no significant effort to resolve the problem. Possibly the level of border controls required to make them impermeable is not plausible in the U.S. given the decentralized policies at state-level and the resistance of many people even to wearing masks and keeping social distances.

During the Biden Administration the United States remained unprotected from the import of the virus from abroad — both by flights and by entry over the nation's southern border.

A Missed Opportunity: A Strategy to Combat the Virus

A coherent nation-wide strategy was available to combat COVID-19. It was suggested to the Republican Administration in the early days of the contagion and ignored. The Biden Administration ignored it as well.

I (Mills) sent a proposal to the President in February 2020 — as others did also. It suggested a national program. The elderly and those with medical conditions who were most at risk would have been quarantined. The older population and those with medical complications should have been isolated in the beginning and given priority in vaccinations when vaccines became available. Meanwhile, less endangered age groups and those without medical complications, should have been required to wear masks and socially distance from one another. Large gatherings like rock concerts and football games should have been banned. There should have been no lockdowns. The strategy should have been nation-wide, applying all over the country in the same form and to the same degree. There would have been a determined push to develop vaccines. This is the one recommendation the Republican White House adopted. Vaccinations would have been provided as soon as possible. There would have been strict limitations on travel from abroad, and on immigration. There would have been no shutdowns of schools or businesses.

The Republican Administration rejected this approach, preferring to assign anti-COVID policy to the 50 states. Had the recommended strategy been implemented by either administration, and certainly if by both, then the number of cases, the number of deaths and the economic disruption caused in the United States by the pandemic would have been greatly reduced. This is to say that the damage of all sorts done in the United States by the pandemic was largely self-inflicted, as a result of ineffective federal government leadership by both political parties.

Yet, in the aftermath of more than a year of confusion, examples of success of a different approach could be found. In some states, for example, colleges could avoid mandates to shutting down. A small college (2,400 students) in the middle of a large city — West Palm Beach — never shut down. It had a few cases of the virus, quickly isolated in a dorm and quickly cured. If we had had a national program like this, much suffering of many kinds could have been avoided. The Republicans erred badly in not doing this. Biden is erring badly in not having done it even this late in the progress of the pandemic.

Part V
Biden and the Post-American World

Chapter 14

Biden and the World: A World Order Disintegrating

Biden's Confidence in Himself

As former Chairman of the Senate Foreign Relations Committee and an active participant (as vice president) in the Obama Administration's foreign policy, Joe Biden has experience with the issues of American foreign relations and knows the major international players. The final decisions on both goals and tactics of American foreign policy are being made by the President himself. Nonetheless, he is very cautious about making any statement that could be misconstrued or cause a foreign policy crisis. At his first press conference whenever he was asked a question about foreign relations, he turned to a briefing book and read from talking points prepared by his staff. No other president in recent decades has done that.

The Biden Administration is reacting to the Republicans' "America First" slogan — and its implementation — on a high-level basis. This is good. The United States needs to think through an overall strategy on a long-term basis.

But what the Biden Administration has come up with as a foreign policy strategy is very questionable. It seems to be more posture and wish than a real strategy. It reflects the drift of Democrat political thinking.

American foreign policy, says the Biden Administration, is for the working class. Biden's National Security Advisor Jake Sullivan said, "Everything we do in our foreign policy and national security will be measured by a basic metric: Is it going to make life better, safer and easier for working families?"

Thus, the central organizing principle of Biden's foreign policy is not about foreign relations at all. It is about domestic politics. And the Biden Administration knows this. The Administration must strengthen the domestic foundations of American power, it tells us. With a strong America — one that adheres to Democrat policies — the U.S. can withstand the challenge from China which Biden sees as the central contest of our time. The dangers to the foundations of American power are those which the Republicans embody: unilateralism and populism.

Again, Biden's policies are not only rooted in domestic political concerns, they are nothing but that. It appears that the Biden Administration does not think it can cope with rational problem solving. Instead, it prefers to manage a propaganda narrative. Critics see the Biden focus on domestic politics in everything it does, including foreign relations, as a form of social pathology.

The concept of Biden's Foreign Policy for the Working Class highlights an apparent ploy of posing as the sword and shield of a working class that Democrat progressives despise.

The Biden Administration presents itself as the champion of all elements of American society. It represents itself as focused on each element. It champions all demographic groups except white males. It champions the working class and the poor. We have seen how the Biden Administration presents itself as focused on the good of the working class. But it also says it is focused on the poor.

It is very difficult to infer from this foreign policy slogan the Biden Administration's approach to foreign relations. But there are other clues. Biden is committed to diplomacy above all other tools of foreign policy.

The Background to Biden's Diplomacy

In 1990–1991 the Soviet Union collapsed, and the United States stood on the brink of the dominion of the world. China was still an underdeveloped nation. Russia was a shrunken remnant of its old superpower self. President George H. W. Bush had been well-trained by experience for the role of leader of the United States in its new importance. Democracy was potentially ascendant world-wide; financial capitalism in the American model was triumphant and its tenacles were spreading rapidly, even into Russia.

But America soon squandered its opportunity. President Bush mismanaged the American domestic economy and lost his re election campaign to the governor of Arkansas, a charming politician with virtually no international experience or even knowledge of history — a man totally ignorant of the role he should play as leader of the world. He was followed by a son of former President Bush — a man as equally unprepared for a significant international role as was his predecessor. George W. Bush allowed the terrorist attack on New York City on September 11, 2001, to temp him into invasions of Iraq and Afghanistan and thereby to waste American power in lesser, tragic, conflicts.

Meanwhile, Russia recovered, and China modernized dramatically. By 30 years after its being propelled into global dominance, the United States had squandered its opportunity to shape the world. In the third decade (2021) of the third millennium it faces dramatic challenges in many parts of the world, and at home is wallowing in bitter partisan political division.

Into this difficult situation stepped America's new president, Joe Biden.

This is the background of our story.

There is confusion in America about decades that have gone awry. The Republicans approached the challenge with principles that Biden has rejected. The Democrats, having failed to lead the world effectively, are in the process of changing their objectives. While liberal (or centrist, as Biden prefers to call himself) Democrats still give allegiance to freedom, progressives stress social justice instead. Justice is to be achieved by social engineering of progressive design. Their concept calls for demographic minority domination of public discussion. They stand for a leftist political morality and the end of traditional personal morality. They seek social woke, not personal liberty, contributions or excellence.

Diplomacy as the Key to Foreign Relations

Biden is committed to diplomacy. As such, he may underestimate or even ignore the threat of war. If a rival country is committed to peace and diplomacy, that may be reassuring. But if that country is aggressive, Biden's commitment to peaceful diplomacy may make the United States seem vulnerable to war.

The moderate Democrats, of whom Biden is one, strongly favor diplomacy as a method in international relations. They value allies and are willing for the United States to carry a disproportionate share of the cost of military and other obligations. America's European allies are a diplomatic strength and a military weakness. Biden appears unaware of this. His Administration ignores the issue. Biden is attempting to return to the Obama-era focus on American diplomacy. This is the meaning of Biden's slogan, "America is back."

When questioned about America's response to numerous problems in the world, including Iran's development of nuclear weapons, North Korea's building long-range missiles, and America's objections to the building of a natural gas pipeline from Russia to Germany, Biden's Secretary of State Blinken responded essentially to each, "We'll get people together to talk about it."

To his critics Biden's focus on diplomacy means simply a policy of appeasement of America's enemies. For example, Biden has announced that the Republican-era imposition of sanctions on Iran failed to stop the Iranian regime from pushing ahead with its effort to create nuclear weapons. Biden proposes therefore to return to negotiations with Iran over a nuclear arms limitation agreement. His spokespersons refer to an objective of lengthening and strengthening the Iran Nuclear Deal.

Biden stresses his commitment to America's democratic allies. He says nothing of America's non-democratic allies. He seems to equate alliances with the promotion of democracy. He speaks of them as if they were one in the same. He appears to have dual objectives for alliances: security and democracy. When Biden speaks of alliances, he notes the increasing challenge of authoritarian states to democracy Biden then links alliances with America's efforts to turn back the challenge to democracy.

Alliances are important in the multi-faceted rivalries of today. But it might appear that the American alliances with Europe are much less important than those in Asia. This is because the greater challenge to the United States comes from China, not Russia or other countries near to Europe. The Biden Administration says this repeatedly. America's major alliance facing China in the Far East is not NATO but the Quad — Japan, Australia, India, and the United States. The Quad has economic as well as military strength and directly confronts China.

Yet Biden seems to live in a past world in which Europe was the most important of American alliances — that is, NATO. It is our NATO allies with whom President Obama worked out the Iran Nuclear Deal, and it is to them that Biden is turning to try to revive that deal. It is to Europe rather than to our Middle Eastern allies to whom he turns to deal with Iran. It is to Europe rather than to our Asian allies that he turns to deal with Iran even though Iran finds its strongest allies in the Far East — in

North Korea and China. It appears that Biden's foreign policy thinking is rooted in his experiences during the Cold War and in the more recent experience of the Iran Nuclear Deal. This bodes ill for the United States — it represents a misallocation of American focus and strategic interest.

In comments about the Middle East Biden seems to express a desire to greatly lessen the American alliance with the Saudi Arabian monarchy. This desire seems to emanate largely from the non-democratic character of the Saudi regime. It also has roots in the discrimination (from the American viewpoint) of the Saudi regime against women — a serious human rights failing in the Democrats' view.

Also, with respect to the Saudis Biden's distaste for an alliance reflects his almost exclusive focus on diplomacy in international relations. Saudi is primarily an American military ally directed against a military and terrorist threat from Iran. Biden has already embarked on a diplomatic initiative directed at the Iranians, to which the Saudis would contribute little. Hence, Biden's willingness to let the Saudi alliance slip.

Interestingly, Biden's disposition against the Saudis does not seem to arise out of support for Israel against a major Arab power. Biden appears to share the distaste for Israel that is rooted in progressive support for the Palestinians and the conviction that Israel persecutes Palestinians. This progressive conviction is strongly entrenched on many American university campuses.

It does not appear that Biden rejects Jews or Israel. Jews play a very important role in the Democrat Party and Biden has worked successfully with them for many decades. But with respect to Israel his position today is another of the many in which he has accepted a progressive point of view.

Biden's close linkage between alliances and democracy is probably a strategic error, as is any strategic direction which dilutes one objective with another. Duality of objectives means that the concentration on a single purpose which is at the core of successful strategy is abandoned. In Biden's case, it may be that the purpose of enhancing democracy will cause him to eschew allies which are important to America's security. This is probably already happening with the Saudis.

Biden is locked into developments which have occurred in the past 4 years. He has been handed a set of allies in Asia, for example, which is much more firm than previous alliances. Each of the countries in the Quad is strong enough in its own way to stand against China, but each benefits greatly from having America as an ally. The other countries of east Asia are more cautious in their dealings with China and feel they must be.

Biden undoubtedly is uncomfortable with this situation, but it is the inevitable result of China's growing strength and assertiveness. He cannot change it.

As best can be determined from the Biden Administration's statements, Biden's four foreign policy objectives are:

(1) Restore good relations with U.S. allies
(2) Establish a better approach to China and Russia
(3) Obtain another nuclear agreement with Iran
(4) Pursue vaccine diplomacy to promote international dealing with the pandemic

Biden adds other objectives which he defines as more important. For example, he says that dealing with climate change is his top priority. Biden refers to climate change as "a global existential crisis," showing the penchant for exaggeration that his progressive supporters continually demonstrate.

Biden thrusts American domestic politics into America's international relations either intentionally or unwittingly. It is probably the latter, since he is so deeply immersed in American domestic politics that they dominate his world view. For example, his foreign policy slogan is "America is back." Of course, America never departed from the world scene, though it changed some of its policies under the Republican Administration. The need for America to return to the world stage was a Biden campaign posture in the 2020 American elections, which Biden now projects onto the world stage, apparently believing that the world sees the world situation from an American perspective. Biden seems to believe his own rhetoric in circumstances of this nature — what is called in Silicon Valley, drinking one's own Kool Aid.

Biden also refers to promoting democracy as at the top of his foreign policy objectives. Yet under Biden the United States has now missed opportunities to advance democracy by weakening its enemies. Biden failed to eliminate the Taliban (when they emerged from hiding at the start of the U.S. withdrawal in August, 2021), and to free Venezuela and Cuba from police-state dictatorships. Each required the use of hard power, which Biden was unwilling or unable to do, and so the American support for democracy in the world appears limited to diplomacy (talk). In fact, it rather appears that Biden's support is more easily gained by leftist dictatorships than by democracies, a result of his support for the progressive wing of his party which in the case of Venezuela and Cuba actively supports dictatorships.

Biden's attitude is even more schizoid than it so far appears. The Democrats seek hard power military options to support color revolutions.

When fighting broke out in mid-May between Israel and Hamas, the Biden Administration blamed the previous Republican Administration for the failure of the Abraham Accords to prevent the conflict. Partisanship made it impossible for the Biden Administration to build on the positive start the Republicans had made, rather than junk it and try to go back to the Obama Administration policy of years previously. It also made it impossible for the Biden Administration to accept the likelihood that Hamas had initiated the violence at this time in conjunction with American progressives to pressure Biden into support for the Palestinians rather than the Israelis. This sort of American domestic political jockeying which occurs in the international field is likely to be a continuing feature of the Biden Administration.

A key element of Biden's presidency is the people he chooses to assist him in his Administration. In foreign policy the Secretary of State is the most important appointment. Antony Blinken, Biden's Secretary of State, is a long-time associate of Biden's. Blinken has worked for progressive publications (specifically, *the New Republic*). Blinken was a member of the National Security Council (NSC) staff from 1994 to 2001 that pushed "shock therapy" for Russia. Putin still holds a grudge against Washington for Russia's 1990's hyper-depression.

Blinken was an architect of Obama's Syria policy. On December 16, 2014, he was deeply involved in fomenting the color revolution in Ukraine 2013–2014 in his capacity of Deputy Secretary of State, designate. He was influential in formulating the Obama Administration's response to the annexation of Crimea by the Russian Federation in the aftermath of the 2014 Ukrainian revolution.

Another key Biden associate in foreign policy is John Kerry who appears to have sort of a diplomat at large assignment. There has been much controversy recently about John Kerry's discussions with the Iranians and whether he revealed matters about Israel's activities that he shouldn't have revealed, as the Iranians have indicated. But to a large degree this is off the mark, as are all such discussions. The thing that matters is whether the policy he is pursuing is successful or not — that is, are the Iranians going to give up their nuclear weapons program as a result of the Biden Administration's diplomacy. If so, whatever Kerry is saying is justified. If not, it is not justified. It is not possible to judge the success or failure of a policy by examining tactics or pieces of the effort to implement it. The media's report-by-report approach to important policy matters usually takes this form. This is something that journalists and media commentators do all the time, and it is essentially without value. What matters is the success or failure of policy, not how it is conducted.

Biden's America: The Arrogance Returns

When Biden said to great publicity that "America is back," he not only declared that Trump's "America first" policy was ended, but, to much less public notice, he implied a certain arrogance in American behavior. America was back not only to assisting its allies and asserting involvement in the major international concerns but also to an assertion of dominance that became noticeable a few months later in how Biden dealt with the imbroglio in Afghanistan. There the U.S. and its NATO allies were involved in a long conflict that had settled to an almost stable situation with the radical Islamists, the Taliban. Very few casualties were being taken by the Western allies; most of the fighting and dying was being done by anti-Taliban Afghans. Yet, without consulting his allies Biden initiated a unilateral American military withdrawal that plunged Afghanistan into chaos and marooned thousands of the troops and civilians of American allies in an Afghanistan suddenly controlled by the Taliban. Biden's America was back, and it acted unilaterally and with an arrogance remembered and unwelcome.

That the arrogance is inbred in Biden and not simply a creature of the Afghan situation was demonstrated immediately afterward. The French had a contract to supply conventional submarines to Australia. It was a large contract and central to the economic health of the French armaments industry. The United States undercut the French contract by offering to supply Australia with nuclear-powered (not nuclear armed) submarines. The Australians canceled the French contract. In numerous contacts between French and American diplomats in numerous settings prior to the announcement of the American contract, the Americans had given no hint of their developing contract with Australia. Upon its announcement the

French were furious and withdrew their ambassador from Washington, something which had not happened in the modern era.

Biden had brought America back to the international arena with all its previous involvement and generosity but also with its accustomed arrogance.

At the G7 meeting in Britain on June 27, 2021, it became clear that Biden's foreign policy is essentially nostalgia. He acts like the G7 democracies still dominate the world. But as the Chinese immediately said, those days are now gone. China need not heed the demands of the G7 and Russia need not fear NATO. Biden may accept that these statements are true. If so, then his pronouncements at the G7 are merely posturing for his domestic political audiences.

The only way to restore G7 dominance would be to invest heavily in hard power, and this Biden has no intention of doing.

Chapter 15

End a War by Losing It: Afghanistan

At the time of the American Civil War in the middle of the nineteenth century a song was current which had as some of its verses "Tenting tonight, tenting tonight, tenting on the old campground/Many are the hearts that are weary tonight, hoping for the dawn of peace." Abraham Lincoln was then President of the United States. He could have provided peace by simply withdrawing federal troops from the rebellious southern states. He did not do so. He prosecuted the war at the cost of several hundred thousand northern dead until African Americans who were held slaves were freed and the union was reunified. Lincoln did this although the Supreme Court of the United States had just a few years earlier declared that African Americans were not and never should be citizens of the United States. In his turn, Joe Biden heard the prayers for peace and supplied it by withdrawing troops from Afghanistan and leaving the women of that nation in slavery. He did the opposite of what Lincoln had done. It is no surprise, therefore, that a large part of the American public is upset. It is also no surprise that the Afghan fiasco has generated soul-searching in America about America's role in the world. Biden initiated all of this on his own.

Numerous commentators are referring to Afghanistan as the most recent element of a "post-American" world. Apparently, this means that much of the world now is effectively outside of the Pax Americana. What the United States had established through the years of the Cold War and consolidated at the collapse of the Soviet Union — a world responsive to the behavior desired by the United States — a rules-based international order — was no longer. No longer was it sufficient to note that the world was now multi-polar — that the United States had rival superpowers. It had gone beyond that to something rather like the Cold War — a world in which America leads one group of nations and the authoritarian powers dominate another. There had been one world under American domination, now there were two worlds — an American and a post-American world. Afghanistan is to be a major example of this.

Biden's conduct of the American withdrawal from Afghanistan was criticized from the beginning. Large-scale errors had apparently been made. For example, the American-supported Afghan government was expected by American officials to remain in office for several months after the withdrawal of American forces. That government fell after the first stages of the American withdrawal so that the last stages of the American withdrawal had to be made under the observation and even supervision of radical Islamic elements — the Taliban. The Americans abandoned Bagram Airforce Base about 25 miles north of Kabul — one of the strongest military bases in the world. In its place the Americans relied on a small, one-runway airport within Kabul — difficult to defend and difficult to provide access to without interruption by the Taliban. Also, a date was set for the withdrawal to be completed which did not allow for the completion of the withdrawal mission.

American forces had entered Afghanistan soon after the jihadist attack on New York's World Trade Center and the Pentagon on September 11, 2001. Afghanistan had changed dramatically from the entrance of American troops in 2001 until their exit in 2021. It appeared that the Biden White House had not appreciated the extent or significance of the change. Afghanistan had gone from being a generally rural country without an effective central government to one which had elements of urban sprawl, sophisticated living, and central government outreach. In an important aspect of the transition the capital city, Kabul, had grown from a population of half a million in 2001 to a population of four and a half million in 2021 and was the center of a growing national government outreach. Afghanistan was becoming a modern nation when the Biden Administration decided to hand it back to a rural militia.

It was apparent that both a strategic error in withdrawal and tactical errors in the conduct of the mission were made. But American civilian and military leaders refused to acknowledge either. Before the mission ended some mid-ranking officers were resigning from the military in order to protest the willful blindness of their high command. Willful blindness to errors is one of the most serious limitations an organization's leadership can have. It foreshadows even more fiascos in the future and on what could be a much larger scale. It speaks especially badly for Biden. His demands for support were the central cause which generated willful blindness as to the failures in the planning and execution of the withdrawal from Afghanistan. About this Biden insisted that there would be plenty of time to critique the experience of the mission after it had been completed. Perhaps there will be post-mortems in the war colleges — with no consequences for the Afghan mission or for any subsequent mission until in the distant future a new generation of political and military leaders have arrived in positions of power.

There is a perspective of some Americans, including those who now govern it, that America is best thought of very much outside the framework of international power. These people are averse to any conception of America that might seem to imply imperial or colonial trappings. In this perspective America cannot be thought to fight long or colonial wars, or to bear the costs abroad of international involvements except in the form of international organizations (UN agencies in particular). In this view America may be seen as a model nation: as a global nation in its population's demography (as diverse as possible) or its democratic government (where democracy refers to nothing else than the policies of the progressive left). Nor can the United States ever consider the secondary or indirect impact globally of a foreign intervention. The likelihood of the great American air base at Bagram in Afghanistan having a deterrent effect on China, Russia, and Iran because of its central location cannot be considered. Appearance is everything and the key is to avoid any appearance of imperial or colonial acts. In general, this American attitude is firmly opposed to any continuing unilateral or almost unilateral commitments abroad. America in this expression is not a super-power. It is first among equals in international organizations and one of a group among allies. It is not suited to the position of a dominant power, and it cannot be one.

The American withdrawals from Iraq and Afghanistan conform to this perspective of American power. There must be no empire-like elements in the American portfolio of global involvements. Instead, in this perspective America acts on the international stage only in international groups.

Unfortunately, for major conflicts with substantial powers like China or Russia, whether a nation state or a loose alliance like radical Islam, alliances are not the best way to conduct a war. In fact, they are often counter-productive. Successful wars must be fought by individual or dominant powers.

American soldiers had been in Afghanistan and supporting a friendly government for 20 years. The Republican Administration had been trying to withdraw American forces from Afghanistan, asserting that the war had lasted too long and been too expensive for the results obtained. The Republican White House set a public deadline for the withdrawal of American troops from Afghanistan for May 1, 2021.

Biden did not want to withdraw on a date Republicans had set. It would look like he was following their lead. In mid-April Biden made it clear he would not withdraw American troops by May 1.

Soon thereafter, he announced that he would withdraw American troops by September 11, 2021. That would be exactly 20 years since the attack on the World Trade Center in New York City in which some 2,500 American civilians had died. The American invasion of Afghanistan had been to deny Al Qaeda a base from which to stage further attacks on the United States.

By April 2021, American intelligence agencies were reporting that only 200 or so Al Qaeda operatives remained in Afghanistan. Most of those who remained after decades of attrition at the hands of U.S. troops were in Iran. It seemed safe to withdraw American forces from Afghanistan. Drones, long-range bombers, and spies were expected to be relied on by the United States to keep Islamic militants from terrorism directed at the United States in the aftermath of American withdrawal.

It was not so simple as it might seem for an American president, formally in charge of the war-making power of the government, to end the Afghanistan war by withdrawing all American military forces from that country. This Biden would learn as had Obama and Trump before him.

The American Constitution vests all power to declare war in the Congress. Congress declares war and the president wages it, subject to oversight by Congress. There was opposition to withdrawal in Congress.

Domestic interest groups and advocacy groups which supported the modernization of Afghanistan opposed withdrawal. Advocacy groups like Code Pink defended the new freedoms of the women of Kabul. They resisted any effort to remove American protection from them. This was a critical concern for Democrat politicians. Because of the position of women's advocacy groups in the United States, President Obama couldn't get out of Afghanistan. The Republican didn't finish pulling our troops out before he lost office, and the opposition to withdrawal was building so fast that the Republican might not have been able to do it. Biden found it difficult to withdraw also.

Finally, the military-industrial complex lobbied to continue the conflict because it was profitable to them.

Despite all this opposition Biden was able to withdraw all American forces from Afghanistan. His ability to do so indicated the strength of the American democracy and of its presidency. Whether or not it was a strategic mistake was another matter.

There was almost no public discussion of the geo-political consequences of withdrawal from Afghanistan. Americans tend to compartmentalize decisions. The decision to withdraw from Afghanistan was based on the situation in Afghanistan. But no country is isolated from the rest of the world. The Taliban would quickly develop a close relationship with the Islamic fundamentalists in Iran. Iran is now a Chinese ally. China would seek a relationship with the new government of Afghanistan. The Taliban would be desperate for financial aid and for technical assistance. China would offer both — for a price. Afghanistan would serve as a bridge connecting China closely to Iran and the middle east. This was impossible while the Americans had a strong presence in Afghanistan. It is all too easy now that the Americans have gone.

American withdrawal from Afghanistan will turn control of Central Asia over to China and its allies in Iran and Pakistan. This region used to be in the sphere of influence of Russia. Now it will be China's and if that stimulates a more vigorous rivalry between Russia and China, that will be good for the U.S. But more likely, China will dominate the region now that America has left Afghanistan and that will strengthen our rivals and weaken ourselves.

Probably China will find a way to gain control of Bagram airbase, one of the strongest on earth. China might come to control Bagram either directly or indirectly. Directly, China might seize the base with its own military force. That would probably initiate conflict between China and the Taliban. China might consider it a tolerable price to pay for such a prize. Alternatively, China might obtain control of the base indirectly. It might obtain a contract with the Taliban to operate the base for the Afghanis. China has the technical competence to run the base, which the Taliban does not. In such a fashion China obtained years ago operational control of the Panama Canal from the government of Panama.

In the aftermath of the fiasco in Afghanistan it can be concluded that the U.S. has learned nothing in 75+ years of conflict in regional wars — Viet Nam, Iraq, Afghanistan. Our opponents have learned more than we have. Our opponents have learned how to defeat us. We have the continuing capability to win battles, but we have a continuing incapacity to use them properly as a route of political success. Americans can be outwaited and outwitted — the Taliban did both.

The final U.S. evacuation of Afghanistan, leaving behind many people who had worked closely with the Americans to modernize their country, was an unmitigated disaster — for the Afghan people and for the U.S. geopolitically. It was a consequence of the Trump Administration and the Biden Administration. It was a consequence of the bitter domestic political rivalry between the two parties. At the time of the final collapse, the U.S. was said by objective analysts to have been "blind and deaf" to the realities of the situation in Afghanistan. The capabilities and ambitions of the Taliban leadership had been totally underestimated by the Americans. In pursuit of a domestic political advantage the American political parties were each telling people that only negotiations would have promise with the Taliban — at a time when the Taliban were maneuvering successfully not for a negotiated settlement but for a total victory. The fiasco of the final stage of the Americans in Afghanistan was an American failure and it indicated in the arena of geopolitics and military conflict the incompetence to which the American government had decayed.

At the time that the Taliban was overrunning Afghanistan, the White House pronounced that the Taliban had to be careful about alienating the international community. The Taliban cared nothing for the international community, of course. But the White House pronouncement indicated that the White House was still in the perspective of a world in which America led an alliance of nations that dominated the world and could impose its will on errant governments. Biden was still living in that world which had disappeared a decade or so previously.

To withdraw from Afghanistan Biden had to overcome energetic opposition. To justify his decisions Biden answered his critics in several speeches given in late August 2021. He was very determined in his answers. He apparently believed them. Sometime, somehow, for Biden the American invasion of Afghanistan had morphed into an American response to a request for military support from the Afghans. In his mind he made a courageous decision not to continue to spend American lives fulfilling the request of the Afghans for support in their civil war, forgetting that it was the Americans who gave birth to the large-scale civil war in Afghanistan. The Afghan intervention was not a civil war into which America was asked to intervene. To say that it was, was an effort to revise history to blame Afghans for the intervention and failure of Americans.

Biden believed the account he gave of the Afghan War in his press conference on August 16, 2021. From a different perspective he demonstrated that a war can always be ended by losing it; and political face can be saved by blaming your allies for the loss.

The method of withdrawal from Afghanistan was a fiasco and a tragedy. It indicated incompetence in leadership and execution. To many Americans it was inexcusable and unforgivable.

In addition, the American withdrawal demonstrated that in some situations America remains an untrustworthy and dishonest ally. China quickly began to tell Taiwan that America is an unreliable ally who will not fight for them. This may ring true to the Taiwanese.

The withdrawal also shows that America lacks the breadth of vision that allows it to be a global superpower. Biden could not assess America's role in Afghanistan in the context of the global contest for power among the great powers. Biden decided that Afghanistan should be made to join the post-American world.

Biden's judgment of the strategic aspect was dependent on the U.S.'s intentions. If the U.S. is intending to withdraw from its large footprint in the world — to concede control of much of the globe to China, Russia, and Iran — then this is a key part of that. If the U.S. intends to continue to assert dominance, then the withdrawal is a strategic error of the first magnitude — it is Biden's Blunder.

Biden remains president of the U.S. and in charge despite his Afghan mess. But he discredited himself as leader of the free world and is no more. If Biden did not expect these consequences, he should have.

He didn't consult with NATO allies which had troops in Afghanistan about U.S. withdrawal. The U.K. had thousand or so citizens there which it did its best to evacuate before the deadline set by the American president.

There was a viable alternative to endless war in Afghanistan. By the time of Biden's withdrawal there were only 2,500 American military personnel in Afghanistan and the Taliban were contained by Afghan government ground forces supported by American air power. The system was established and working and was not that costly for the United States. We might have stayed forever. We might have maintained air support for the Afghan ground forces, and that would have stymied the Taliban.

Now the Taliban has taken over the entire country. We need a base in Central Asia to limit Russian and Chinese influence. We have abandoned that as well. In the context of Biden's world-wide foreign policy, the U.S.

still claims to impose a Western world order on the world while steadily reducing its effective footprint.

All Biden's speeches about his reasons for withdrawal from Afghanistan do not provide a convincing rationale to many listeners. There would seem to be more to his thinking, and it would seem to be kept secret. There appears to be a pro-jihadist element of the Democrat Party. It has expressed itself in the Iran Nuclear Deal and again in the Afghanistan withdrawal. It probably does not endorse militant Islam or the tactics of terrorism. But it is convinced that jihadists can be successfully appeased; that they can be negotiated with; that they will keep agreements; and that they are not a mortal threat to the United States if appeased. It sees them as having serious historical and current victimizations, and it agrees with them on certain key issues of international politics, including anti-colonialism and that Israeli treatment of the Palestinians is reprehensible. Out of this attitude toward jihadism come the actions of the Biden Administration in Afghanistan and the defiance with which criticism of the actions and their results has been met by the President.

That there should be a pro-jihadist element high in the Democrat Party need not be a surprise. Before World War II there was a pro-Nazi element of the Conservative Party in England which sponsored appeasement as the best policy for dealing with Hitler. Even Winston Churchill, before he later changed views, praised Hitler as a political leader. The appeasers formed a conception of Hitler in their minds as a responsible German patriot and believed that his objectives were no more than reasonable German purposes. These they were determined to appease. A similar process appears to be underway in the minds of top leaders of the Democrat Party. They believe the Taliban are not so bad; that they can be worked with; that there is no need for conflict with them. This last is the meaning of President Biden's repeated assertions that the United States has no national interests in Afghanistan.

Chapter 16
Sovereign Democracy: Russia

Russia is a natural ally of America against China. Russia has natural resources and living space which China needs for its large population. Russia shares a border of thousands of miles with China and clashes have been common in the not too distant past. Already millions of Chinese reside in Russia east of the Urals, though this is denied by both governments. The potential for tension between the two countries exists, but their common opposition to American influence impels them to cooperation.

Despite their natural differences, China and Russia have worked out a *modus vivendi* that allows them to work together against the West. The last unresolved territorial issue between the two countries was settled by the 2004 Complementary Agreement between the People's Republic of China and the Russian Federation on the eastern section of the China–Russia Boundary. Pursuant to that agreement, Russia transferred to China a part of Abagaitu Islet, the entire Yinlong (Tarabarov) Island, about half of Bolshoy Ussuriysky Island, and some adjacent river islets. The transfer was ratified by both the Chinese National People's Congress and the Russian State Duma in 2005, thus ending the decades-long border dispute. The official transfer ceremony was held on-site October 14, 2008.

Today the alliance of Russia and China moves the danger of open conflict between China and the West to the borders of Europe. If Russia were on our side, then the danger of conflict would be moved 7,000 miles from the borders of our NATO allies, and we would have a much easier time confronting China world-wide than we do now. We were in fact very strong allies of the Soviet Union during World War II despite its having a much more despicable leader then (Stalin) than now (Putin). So American distaste for Putin and his regime should be no barrier to an alliance against China, just as Stalin and his regime were no barrier to an alliance against Nazi Germany.

For domestic political purposes the Democrats have chosen to make an enemy of Russia when it could have been a frenemy. Mrs. Clinton exploited the legacy of anti-Soviet sentiment from the Cold War period to rationalize her electoral defeat in 2016. She blamed the Russians for supporting Trump against her and on that basis the Democrats tried to remove him from office. Despite the failure of that effort the Democrats have never ceased to vilify the Russians. Some conservatives allow themselves to be swayed by residual anti-Russian communist sentiment into an agreement with the Democrats.

The complaint is that the Russians are "trying to undermine our democracy." But what does that mean? The Democrats created the phrase to say that Russia was trying to get Trump elected. It appears that it doesn't have any meaning other than a partisan complaint. Putin is many of the bad things Democrats claim, but the Russians have not seriously impacted our political processes however much they might like to and even play at it.

We should seek to have the Russians be our allies against the Chinese, but this will not happen on our terms only. They are far more valuable to the Chinese as allies (they have big weapons) than to us, so our gain would be denying their support to the Chinese.

Russian Attitudes Toward the West

Russians are dominated by their history, as perhaps all of us are. Americans have great difficulty comprehending the Russian mindset because we have no history comparable to theirs, and most Americans are largely ignorant of Russian history. Russia has been invaded from the West many times. Almost every major Western nation has invaded Russia at some time or other. Russia has, of course, invaded the West numerous times and controlled eastern Europe for long periods. The result of all this conflict is a deeply held suspicion of the West and its motives. The United States sees itself as the leader of the West. Below is a summary of the Russian view of the west penned by a senior advisor to President Putin in 2021:

"For the thousand years that Russian civilization has existed, the attitude of the conventional West towards us has not fundamentally changed.

And the crusaders, and the Poles, and the Swedes with the French, and the Germans with the Americans went on campaigns to Russia ... on various occasions, but always to destroy us — because they considered it a historical absurdity that the seventh (now) part of the land, and together with according to some estimates, almost half of the planet's resources belong to some incomprehensible Russians ... Over the centuries, Russia has been a special civilization of the imperial type, which has created an order within and around itself that resists chaos, is ready and capable — at different times in different ways — to defend this order. Thanks to a strong state and our army, Russia even today has the opportunity to act at its own discretion, and order in it depends on its own will" (Andrey Ilnitsky, "Russia's Choice: Forks, Threats, Opportunities and Solutions," *Eurasia Expert*, April 30, 2021. Ilnitsky is deputy chief of the Executive Committee of the United Russia Party).

The Russians are objective observers of trends in warfare. They see the Americans as continual aggressors against Russia using all forms of warfare. They credit us with far more effectiveness than we often do ourselves. Below is Ilnitsky's commentary:

"Our opponents also have a very intense discourse on the nature of the war. There are 'cognitive wars' to defeat consciousness, 'cyber wars' aimed at destroying the critical infrastructure of the enemy, there are 'network — centric wars' related to the information-technological type of military operations, various kinds of 'information-algorithmic wars' with the use of artificial intelligence, 'proxy wars' on the territory of third countries and regions, and similar hybrid influences and conflicts that are being prepared/waged below the 'waterline' of a direct military clash of powers — in the so—called gray zone. Finally, the concept of societal warfare was recently introduced. In reports from RAND Corporation, this type of war, aimed at destroying the social infrastructure of the enemy, is being developed in particular detail ... the goal of war is tomorrow is the destruction of self-consciousness, a change in the civilizational basis of the enemy's society ... Mental warfare is a war aimed at changing the worldview. Moreover, if manpower and infrastructure can be restored, then the evolution of the worldview cannot be reversed — this is the main threat of mental war! ... The task of any war is the same — the object of influence must eventually be deprived of sovereignty and go under external control. If for this earlier — in a classic war — it was necessary to seize territory and destroy the enemy's manpower, now this is not necessary. You can destroy the state and destroy the country by changing the consciousness of society. Let me remind you that once in recent history we have already seen such a war and, alas, lost. When the great Soviet Union with the most powerful army in the world ceased to exist literally in weeks, because society — and this is the essence — itself chose a different path. ... we, having lost the mental war, lost a great country — the USSR.

"Not everyone has learned these lessons. In Ukraine, for example, as a result of systematic work on rebooting the worldview, through "zeroing and rewriting history," young people were almost without exception turned into Russophobes of the neo-Nazi persuasion. And we continue to wonder why these people who speak the same language with us suddenly become our enemies ... Mental wars are an aggressive complex impact that is directed not only on the information field, but also on education, upbringing, and work with society. In my opinion, for our de-ideologized society today, this is the most dangerous type of war.

"...according to the Americans, there are noble Wasp (WASP) in the world — with Anglo — Saxon roots — and everyone else, and Americans know better what they want. Why go far if U.S. Secretary of State Anthony Blinken recently announced that the world, you see, 'needs America to lead.' Paranoia, of course, but there is nothing to be surprised at: exclusivity has simply eaten into the American mentality. They really think so. And here there is no need to harbor illusions: no matter who is in the White House, the policy towards us will remain unchanged. Its essence is best defined by the phrase of the same Leonid Shebarshin: '*The West needs only one thing from us — that we are not there.*' Do we have the initiative in this mental and ideological confrontation with the enemy?'
" (Andrey Ilnitsky, "Russia's Choice: Forks, Threats, Opportunities and Solutions," *Eurasia Expert*, April 30, 2021).

The Biden Administration seems to have no sympathy for Russian views, nor does it seek understanding of them as a bridge to accommodation. The American Administration views Russia as seeking a return to the Middle Ages in which the world is Balkanized. It also believes that in such a world Russia is too weak economically and demographically to compete. Russia is thought to be especially at the mercy of China whose size gives it an enormous advantage of scale in all things economic and military. Russia is therefore the perfect example of a failed state in the knowledge society clinging to power through energy exports that will go away as the world transitions to renewables. The expected collapse of Russia will make the world a better place.

The Russian interpretation of the American attitude is correct, and this source of conflict will remain active. It is unfortunate because it is unnecessary.

Consequences of the Russia–China Alliance

The consequence of Russian suspicion, Chinese aggrandizement, and American confusion is that we now face a loose alliance — growing tighter by the day — among China, Russia, Iran, North Korea, Cuba, and Venezuela against us. It is a world-wide alliance with military strength perhaps as great as ours and growing steadily and rapidly.

This is a disaster in the causes of which Biden has been a wholehearted participant. Biden has a reputation for focusing on diplomacy, and his Party the same. Yet with respect to Russia, Biden uses remarkably crude language. The previous president, Biden says, "is Putin's puppy." Putin, Biden grumbles, "is a killer." Putin will pay, Biden says, for having intervened in the election of 2020 in favor of the Republicans, though the American intelligence agencies say any Russian effort had no effect on the election at all.

Continuing the Democrat crusade against Russia, Biden is likely to press hard against Russia, at least publicly. The Democrats are angry that Russia interferes in American elections; that it asserts itself on the world stage diplomatically and militarily against American interests; that it challenges American propaganda with its own; that it cozies up to American allies in Europe, particularly Germany; and that it threatens American allies in Eastern Europe. These things are, of course, what an enemy does, and Democrats see Russia as an enemy. They have done their best to make it so. Biden is being urged to put pressure on Russia where it is thought to be vulnerable — specifically on Russia's President Putin by trying to undermine his government. "This is a place where America should advocate democracy more and more strongly," Biden is being told.

Biden will do that. He will also propose sanctions and threats directed at Putin, while seeking allies to line up behind America in pressuring Russia. This will be a classic demonstration of Biden foreign policy — insults, threats, sanctions, and American leadership of a group of allies, all stopping short of any actions sufficient to constrain Russia from whatever it seeks to do. Russia has insulated itself against American pressure by its increasingly close linkage to China.

America has failed to work out a positive relationship with Russia in the aftermath of the collapse of the Soviet Union. President Bill Clinton's promotion of destruction "shock therapy" for the Russian economy's "transition strategy" made this much more difficult. The Democrats have chosen to treat Russia as an enemy as part of their domestic political battle with the Republicans.

Biden will seek to lead an alliance — perhaps NATO — into positions that restrain Russian ambitions. Biden was part of the vilification of Russia and Putin that the Democrats orchestrated during the Republican Administration. Biden will seek to justify the Democrat's actions taken then by the direction of his policy toward Russia now.

Biden's America has an ambivalent attitude toward Russia. It thinks Russia is weak and insignificant. It sees Russia as a past power with a small, fragile natural resource-based economy, a small and declining population, and an increasingly dictatorial government. It is not worthy of American attention.

But America, particularly the Democrats, also describe Russia as a malignant and capable adversary which keeps meddling in American domestic affairs very effectively.

Biden will continue this confused and contradictory opinion. It makes American policy toward Russia internally confused but always adversarial. Russia is an American enemy — to Biden.

Many American politicians complain today that Putin is trying to make Russia again like it was under the Czar. This seems to mean that it is an autocracy linked strongly to the Orthodox Church and opportunistically aggressive internationally. This is likely true. But Americans might ask themselves how the U.S. would be governed if instead of Canada and Mexico as neighbors, it had Germany and China? If instead of having virtually no damage done to our homeland and few civilians killed in World War II, America had had as Russia did, most of its heavily populated regions devastated and some 15 million civilians killed?

A legitimate American answer might be that all that is in the past. That Russia need not be prepared today for anything like that because America will preserve peace in the world.

Unfortunately, America does not seem to be able to provide this peace. American power is declining largely because of internal differences and debilitating political partisanship. Russia cannot depend on the United States to protect it. It must be prepared to defend itself. Hence, Putin's attitudes and Russia's behavior. Since America finds his attitudes and Russia's behavior threatening, and threatens Russia in return, the situation is that Russia has become an enemy of the U.S. and has joined in a coalition with America's other enemies.

The hostility of the Biden Administration toward Russia may move from rhetoric to action. In 2021, rumors are circulating that the Biden Administration is involved in a plot to assassinate the President of Belarus, a Russian ally. Efforts by the U.S. to assist in the removal of the president of Belarus stretch back to the Obama Administration. They have all failed. We have seen no hard proof of a Blinken trademark "color revolution," but it is possible that there is some validity to the rumors. It is possible that the Biden Administration is so hostile to Russia and its friends. This goes far beyond the Democrats' objective of damaging Republicans politically.

Despite the temptation to search for and find rational motives for such actions, it increasingly appears that Washington is driven in matters relating to Russia by imaginary demons (a Kremlin global menace), political fanaticism, venality, power-seeking (color revolutions) and vendettas (following Hilary Clinton's electoral defeat). Fashioning rational explanations for the Democrat approach to Russia seems a bit like putting lipstick on pigs.

Perhaps Biden as president will see the danger that is threatened by Russia's alliance with China and will seek to distract Russia from it. In the early days of his Administration Biden extended a small olive branch toward Russia. He failed for a few days to denounce Putin as Democrats had denounced him repeatedly for the 4 years of the Republican Administration. Biden also failed briefly to criticize Russia for intervention in American elections as his Party had done ceaselessly for 4 years; and he failed to warn Russia to make no further interventions in American elections. Instead, he offered talks toward an accommodation with Russia. In doing this Biden revealed awareness about the potential threat posed by Russia's increasingly close relations with China and Iran — both American rivals and opponents of the American sponsored world order. But Biden abandoned his olive branch quickly.

Part VI

The Rise of Global Military Insecurity

Chapter 17

Is the U.S. Ready for Armed Conflict?

Threats to the United States and its allies grow more serious daily. What the Soviets used to call the "correlation of power" is measured recently in a book by the authors of this book: Steven S. Rosefielde and Daniel Quinn Mills, *Beleaguered Superpower: Biden's America Adrift* (Singapore: World Scientific Publishers, 2021). The correlation of power is trending much to the disadvantage of the United States and its allies.

It is difficult to compare spending on military force made by the major powers, even though comparisons of this nature, based on official figures, are cited continually in debates over military strength. In general, it is asserted that the United States spends almost twice what any other nation does, and indeed China spends officially about half what the U.S. does. Yet China hides defense spending so that their official figures are almost certainly serious under-estimates, and the United States hides social spending in its defense budget so that our official figures for military spending are over-estimates. In addition, for American eyes the CIA compounds the confusion about Chinese defense spending with underestimated dollar value derivatives. It appears that Chinese spending on military strength is about to exceed that of the United States, and under Biden will almost certainly do so.

It is unclear what is the readiness state of the American military. On the one hand there are elite units which are probably the best in the world. There is equipment that is top-notch. There is advanced technology. Military personnel are a volunteer force which is highly professional. It is possible to believe that the American military is the best in the world by some significant degree and so it provides a very hard shell to the American world presence.

There is an alternative perspective. Much of the advanced equipment is said to be poorly maintained and often inoperative. Officers of the elite units tell people that they do not trust higher ranking officers who are said to be bureaucratic and inexperienced in warfare. Higher ranking officers are concerned about the attitudes of the soldiers and unsure that they will fight. The cost of weaponry is so great that the high levels of America expenditure on weapons is undercut. The aircraft carrier Gerald R. Ford cost some 13.5 billion dollars. The George F. W. Bush cost some 6.5 billion dollars. But this isn't all. For example, a Jeep that began World War II at a cost of 14,000 dollars now much altered (improved) but carries a price tag of some 525,000 dollars. This is more than half a million dollars for a Jeep that still carries only four people. America is having trouble selling equipment like this to its allies, and it would seem to be evident why — there are much less expensive ways to accomplish almost the same thing.

Biden and the Military

Despite Biden's predilection for diplomacy, he will increase the U.S.'s military presence in many areas of the globe, in pursuit of limited objectives. It is hard to see how these actions add up to a strategic policy. For example, Biden has increased to a few thousand the U.S. and NATO troops in northern Iraq and Syria, thereby restoring our commitment to the Kurds and forestalling Russian influence in the region. The actions caused Putin to complain that the U.S. was trying to contain Russia. This is correct in the region in which Syria, Russia, Turkey, Israel, and Iran all jostle for influence and control. The Republicans had been in the process of disentangling the United States from the Middle Eastern tangle, but Biden halted the U.S. withdrawal immediately. When the Republicans made U.S. troop reductions, there were bitter complaints that the U.S. was abandoning its allies, the Kurds. Biden has responded to these complaints by restoring American power, though only on a limited basis, to the region and to the support of the Kurds.

It is likely that Biden will further entangle the U.S. in the developing turmoil around Venezuela — another cockpit of geopolitical ambitions into which the Republicans avoided getting the U.S. significantly involved. Probably Biden's actions are largely concessions to special interests in the U.S. which have interests in the areas and are not intended by Biden to be part of larger American strategic plans. When Biden claims to the world that the U.S. is back, he means not only that it has returned to international organizations and to diplomatic engagements but also to small military presences in hot spots around the globe. Biden intends the U.S. to again be a full player, it may be said, in the geopolitical wrestling which is continually taking place around the globe.

Yet the withdrawal of American forces from Afghanistan suggests that this is not so. Strategically, Afghanistan is centrally located in Asia and America had a major air base there. Biden abandoned it. In effect, the U.S. has pulled back significantly from global engagement in that important area.

Perhaps more importantly, Biden's comments during the American pull-out from Afghanistan suggest that Biden is very uncomfortable with the use of force. In mid-August 2021, Biden told the G7 members that the reason he would not extend the pull out deadline for Afghanistan beyond August 31, 2021, was to avoid danger to American military personnel. Apparently, President Biden thinks that the most important obligation of the American president to the American military is to see that none of them get hurt. Echoing the confusion that Biden's comment caused in the United States, a reporter the next day asked Speaker of the House Nancy Pelosi, a supporter of Biden's position, a question to the effect that if the American military in Afghanistan were not for the purpose of protecting American citizens and allies who were in danger from radical Islamists, then what was the American military for? Mrs. Pelosi had no coherent answer, as none of Biden's supporters did. In fact, Biden's apparent conviction that the military is not to be put in harm's way was echoed by the Chairman of the House Armed Services Committee (Smith, Democrat) on Fox News of August 30, 2021, the day the U.S. ended its withdrawal from Afghanistan. Representative Smith implied that the mission of the American military was to avoid casualties by withdrawal. It is remarkable to think of a military whose purpose is to avoid combat with an enemy in order that no one get hurt. It is understandable that critics are suggesting that had Mr. Smith and Democrats like him overseen our government during World War II, we would have lost the war.

Biden is again involving the U.S. in pursuit of his overreaching purposes — America's own security and the promotion of democracy. America was once the single global superpower, the hegemon, and it continues to try to play that role with its involvements in all parts of globe, despite the rising challenge of the other claimants to superpower status. It is not likely that Biden will accept formally a multi-polar world. But it is likely that he will not be able to resist multi-polarism practically because he and the Democrats generally are unwilling to pay the price that maintaining global dominance requires. Instead, vast sums will be expended on involvements that have no strategic purpose.

America is drifting without clear direction through the titanic changes in geo-politics wrought by the emergence of China as a global superpower.

The Military Situation

For America the hard-power contest is not just a spending race with China and Russia. It's a technological race as well. Americans presume that we are leading, but we may not be. Biden is being confronted with some difficult problems of catch-up, perhaps like John F. Kennedy's problem when the Soviets launched Sputnik.

President Biden's first defense budget will be marginally lower than the Republicans' proposed budget. It will reduce real American military spending by roughly 2% and will be further diluted by increased social programs mislabeled as defense activities. It is not the 10% reduction sought by progressives in the Democrat Party. But there was little time for the new Biden Administration to work that out. Given the opportunity of a largely peaceful world, a large decrease in military spending will likely be proposed for 2022.

Social Engineering in the American Military

American military spending is not just on personnel and hardware. Much is on social engineering that doesn't provide a clear contribution to military strength.

The American military has become a jobs source for Democrat identity groups. The impact on military effectiveness is yet to be determined.

In some perspectives, there is nothing wrong with this. But if social engineering is a focus to the exclusion of things more directly related to combat readiness, and absorbs money, other resources and attention instead, then it could be a problem. When counting expenditures on the American military, it should be realized that social engineering costs are being included and compared with the hard-combat expenditures of our rivals. It should also be noted that supporters of these programs insist they improve the readiness of our military, and within the narrow context of a military which is required to do many things to accommodate special groups, they possibly do. If there are to be pregnant women in airplane cockpits, then it makes sense to have maternity suits for them.

"We're making good progress designing body armor that fits women properly, tailoring combat uniforms for women, creating maternity flight suits, updating requirements for their hairstyles. And some of it's going to take an intensity of purpose and mission to really change the culture and habits that cause women to leave the military," Biden said on International Women's Day, March 9, 2021.

Biden's Pentagon leadership on March 31, 2021, reversed course from the policies of the Republican Administration and offered transgender people in the American military wider access to medical care including assistance with gender transformation.

No one seriously suggests that this policy will strengthen the U.S. military. Instead, this policy change is to make the American military more equitable for transgender citizens of the United States who meet military standards for enlistment, which presumably have been altered to accommodate them. This may be equitable, but it is clearly social engineering with domestic politics in mind rather than an effort to strengthen the preparedness of the American military.

On January 25, 2021, on his fourth day in office, President Biden signed an executive order reversing the ban on transgender troops that was imposed by the Republican Administration. Mr. Biden's order also called an immediate halt to involuntary discharges of transgender troops who were already serving. "Simply put, it's the right thing to do, and is in our national interest," the White House said in a statement.

A White House spokesperson described Mr. Biden's order as an overdue recognition that no one who can meet the standards should be barred from military service.

In 2016, the Obama Administration allowed people who had transitioned to a new gender to join the military. This was represented by the Biden Administration as continuing a decades-long trend toward inclusion that stretched from the desegregation of the armed forces in 1948 to the repeal of the ban on openly gay troops in 2011.

It is reported that some people who have struggled with gender identity see the armed forces as a haven from discrimination against them in the civilian world.

The Republicans had prohibited transgender people from the military. The Republican president argued that they might have high-cost medical needs and be non-deployable. Democrats insist they can be deployed.

Most young people in America have no interest in military service. When told that the nation needs their service, they express the modern American attitude: someone calls out "The ship is sinking. This is terrible." The response is, "Oh, I wish you didn't feel that way about it." The result is that it is very difficult for the military to get volunteers. There are said to be about 200,000 transgender Americans of military age. In an era when the military finds it difficult to fill relatively small recruiting goals, transgender people may fill the ranks. Biden is fully comfortable with this transition.

Biden is committed to progress in these matters and attention to social engineering in the American military will increase during his Administration.

Biden is More Bellicose than is Expected

It is surprising that the Biden Administration is sometimes unexpectedly bellicose. But it shouldn't be, because the bellicosity has its roots in the past of high members of Biden's Administration. They do not seem to limit their aggressiveness by calculations about American strength. They seem instead to recall the past years when America was the world's sole superpower, and they act from that conviction.

On March 24, 2021, the President of Ukraine announced that it is the official policy of Ukraine to take back Crimea from Russia. This statement is a virtual declaration of war by Ukraine against Russia. This does not imply a judgment that the conquest by Russia of Crimea from the Ukraine was justified. But the conquest is a *fait accompli*.

Ukraine's president was encouraged to this action by Biden, who stated in the American view Crimea belongs to Ukraine. Further, the American Secretary of State promised full American support for the territorial integrity of Ukraine. The American Secretary of Defense then added that the United States promised unwavering U.S. support for Ukraine's sovereignty (see http://ronpaulinstitute.org/archives/featured-articles/2021/april/05/why-is-the-biden-administration-pushing-ukraine-to-attack-russia/).

For Ukraine to retrieve Crimea from Russia implies a major war and one that Ukraine is unlikely to be able to win without full military involvement by the United States. It is very unlikely that such a high level of support from the U.S. would be forthcoming. This then is a surprisingly provocative bluff by Ukraine with American backing.

Probably this is a false bellicosity. The Ukraine is unlikely to attack Russia — its survival instinct is better than that. Knowing this, the Biden Administration can push Ukraine toward an attack in order to warn the Kremlin off actions in various places that the U.S. wishes to avoid.

Finally, the American withdrawal from Afghanistan also raises a question about the Biden Administration's willingness to use military force to back any ally. Biden Administration bellicosity may be no more than empty bellicosity.

Still, the United States has always been unpredictable. It appears pacific sometimes, and militant the next. Serious errors can be made by presuming that Americans will or will not fight at any given moment.

Chapter 18

The Loss of a Major War

The more forward-thinking strategists in the United States are preparing for the loss of a major war. The concern is how great the devastation accompanying that loss will be.

A loss is almost certain because of the poor state of readiness of American forces. During the Biden Administration the focus of high-level command attention has been on a variety of political, not military, objectives. The composition of the nation's armed forces has been altered to meet politically determined demographic purposes which mirror efforts being made in civilian society. There is nothing wrong with demographic integration of our armed forces, except, as now, when it becomes an objective itself and supplants military effectiveness as the primary purpose of our military leadership. An officer corps which was already full of careerists seeking their next promotions has learned to seek advancement from political correctness rather than in military effectiveness. In addition, the Biden Administration will be limiting military capability by reducing both the nominal and real expenditures of the American military. The Biden Administration will fail to rectify gross overspending on certain items by the Pentagon. All this will add up to declining military strength.

It is likely that when America is finally challenged by a major power on the modern field of battle — conventional warfare supplemented by cyber and space battle — the U.S. is almost certain to lose. Either apparent weakness of its armed forces or overreach by the United States will tempt an enemy to war and a lack of readiness will cause the U.S. to lose. What will follow defeat is an enormous shift in American attitudes and a rebuilding of the nation's armed forces. How much damage will have been done to the nation; how many lives will have been lost; how long the rebuilding of the society and its military strength will take, are questions that cannot yet be answered.

American Decline

Biden is approaching American foreign policy in the manner described in previous chapters. He must also address in some form the more serious problem of the decline in American power and influence in the world. The essence of this decline is the emergence of major challenges to the United States from China, Russia, and their allies.

The U.S. decline is because of years of bad leadership. America's big opportunity followed the collapse of the U.S.S.R. in 1990–1991. We have had since as presidents Bill Clinton, George W. Bush, Barak Obama, and Donald Trump — and a steady decline in American power in the world.

In a 45-minute speech at Harvard reported in the *Harvard Gazette* for April 9, 2021, Bill Clinton reflected on his foreign policy performance as President of the United States. He accepted the judgment that his greatest foreign policy success was his interaction with Russia in the aftermath of the collapse of the Soviet Union. He explained how he had pushed the Russians to get out of eastern Europe, then brought Russia's former satellites into NATO. He had also pushed Russia to become democratic. During his effort, the Russian security forces in the personification of Vladimir Putin seized power in Russia. Clinton, who barely knew Putin, commented, "I always enjoyed my private conversations with Putin because I could be brutally frank with him ... But it was clear his model for Russian greatness was basically the czars." Clinton disapproved of that and spent his administration trying to deny Russia the greatness it sought.

While Clinton was President, Russia suffered a hyper-depression with more than 3 million deaths above those that would normally have been expected. Clinton's "shock therapy" policies were co-responsible with those of Yeltsin for this disaster. Putin and the Russian power services (the military and the security services) consider Clinton's policies a deliberate effort to decimate Russia and to weaken Russia. A strong case can be made that it was Clinton who lost Russia to the West.

It seems that Clinton then and now has no concept of geopolitics on a global level and of America's interests on that level. There was no long-term gain to the U.S. in Clinton's effort to weaken Russia. America would be far better off today with Russia stronger in Europe and able to confront China in Asia, than it is with Russia as an enemy of the United States and an ally of China — which is a consequence of Clinton's efforts.

Clinton was president at the most important period in American history since World War II. He was there in the immediate aftermath of the collapse of the U.S.S.R. He was there when America was the sole superpower and was in position to remake the world in its own image of what would be just. What did he say at Harvard about his concept of what he was doing as president in that unique time of opportunity?

"I thought it was my job to try to build a world that America would be happy to be a leader in, but could no longer dominate," Clinton said. He has succeeded. We are now in a world in which America can be a leader, but no longer dominates. As a result, we are confronted by the growing strength of authoritarian powers who endanger us. Clinton in his talk at Harvard acknowledged victories and challenges in his international dealings, but no failures. He failed with Russia (he weakened Russia but made it an enemy) and succeeded in putting America and its allies in danger today.

George W. Bush led the United States into two initially successful wars in the mid-east, but he had no idea what to do with his successes. It is reminiscent of the remonstrance which Hannibal of Carthage received from his brother after Hannibal's great victory over the Romans at Cannae. Hannibal had failed to hurry to Rome before it could have been put in defensive mode and so missed his chance to end the war victoriously. "You know how to win a victory," Hannibal was told, "but you don't know how to use it!" Similarly, Bush knew how to win wars, but had no idea how to exploit them successfully. The result is that 20 years later America had won neither.

Obama presided over the emergence of China onto the world stage as a superpower. He did nothing to restrain it or to constrain it.

The Republicans stirred the geopolitical pot but failed to bring anything to a successful conclusion. They left America still in geopolitical decline and facing increasingly dangerous challenges.

And so it is that America has entered a long period of decline largely because of the ineptitude of her presidents.

American presidential candidates can talk convincingly to party groups and town halls. They can hold babies and smile. They can try to demonstrate that they are just ordinary people. These are key characteristics of successful politicians in a country which wants to think that its president is someone just like its citizens. But these abilities have nothing to do with leading the country.

Dictators and their successors don't have to do this stuff. They can be chosen or emerge for other, better, more relevant reasons.

It is argued on behalf of America's current system of choosing presidents that when the candidates mingle with the electorate and kiss babies, they gain greater public confidence than otherwise, and that this is important to the health of a democracy. This is likely true and may improve domestic attitudes. But there is little contribution to how America tackles world affairs. There is a balance to be attained and imbalances to be avoided. Now there is imbalance on the side of too much public confidence and too little effective national leadership.

The Failure of the U.S. to Defend Its Neighborhood

For example, the U.S. has failed to defend its neighborhood. For two centuries the United States kept the Americas safe from foreign intervention. The United States helped expel French troops from Mexico in the 1860s. The U.S. drove Spain out of Cuba at the end of the nineteenth century. To some degree American protection came not only with American intervention and exploitation but it also preserved the independence of all other nations in the Americas.

But American protection of the Americas has steadily eroded since the 1960s. The Kennedy Administration decided to let the Russians have a base and close ally in Cuba, insisting only that the Russians not place strategic weapons in Cuba which could be used against the U.S. (this was what the Cuban Missile Crisis was about). But from that base the Cubans and their Russian allies have moved to add Venezuela to their alliance. China has also been allowed to develop a strong position in Venezuela, several Caribbean islands, and Panama. Russia and China continue to extend their influence in our neighborhood.

Writing about Russian military tactics in World War II German General F. W. von Mellenthin emphasized, "Bridgeheads in the hands of the Russians are a grave danger indeed. It is quite wrong not to worry about bridgeheads and postpone their elimination. Russian bridgeheads, however small and harmless they may appear, are bound to grow into formidable danger-points in a very brief time and soon become insuperable strong-points" (F. W. von Mellenthin, *Panzer Battles*, Norman: University of Oklahoma Press, 1955, p. 185).

Americans for decades have ignored this sage advice. We have not worried about Russian bridgeheads in the Caribbean and we have postponed their elimination. What began as a Russian bridgehead in Cuba soon became too strong for us to be willing to try to eliminate it. Now it has pushed its way into Venezuela and controls that country. Russia has invited its ally, China, to participate in the bridgeheads as well.

The Republican Administration was aware of the Venezuelan danger to America. Russian long-range bombers are based there that can attack the continental United States. The Venezuelan government is propped up by Cuban troops. The Republicans fulminated against the Russian/Cuban/Chinese control of Venezuela and attempted to over-throw it politically. The Republicans failed and took no further steps.

In early March 2021, the Biden Administration granted temporary protected status to Venezuelan refugees. This was its response to a serious threat in the Caribbean. The Republican Administration had done less.

It is very unlikely that Biden will do more. The bridgeheads remain. They are certain to become stages for further infiltration of the Americas — politically and militarily.

Military Alliances Against the U.S. — Our Enemies Gather Their Power

There is already a continual elbowing of each other by the United States and its rivals. Their strength and number and alliance are growing. What will be the result? Will it be a second Cold War against Russia and China and their allies? Or a hot one?

The end of March 2021, saw the announcement of a pact between China and Iran, an example of U.S. adversaries uniting to advance their strategic ambitions.

"The two sides signed what they described as a twenty-five year 'strategic partnership' that amounts to a significant deepening of ties. China will invest several 100 million dollars in a variety of Iranian projects, including nuclear power, ports, and oil and gas development. In return China will get a steady supply of Iranian oil. The two will also deepen their defense cooperation as China will transfer some military technology" (*Wall Street Journal*, March 30, 2021).

This is important. The United States has been trying to limit Iranian power, particularly nuclear weapons, for decades. Under Biden, it is reviving that effort. It is talking to Iran about limitations. But China is now able to provide Iran with nuclear weapons and with means to avoid U.S. sanctions. The outcome of Iran's nuclear ambitions is now in the hands of the Chinese and Biden is unable or unwilling to recognize that.

This is what the U.S. should have been trying to avoid for two decades. It has failed. Now China is linked to Iran and to Russia and the strength and reach of U.S. rivals is compounding.

The U.S. now faces an almost complete military alliance between China and Russia; close military cooperation between Russia and Iran; allies in Cuba and Venezuela; and hostility from North Korea, which is what we used to term a "satellite" of China. This is a very formidable military challenge, and one that the United States and its allies are not clearly strong enough to counter.

The U.S. has the world's strongest military, but it is not necessarily strong enough to defeat the combination of nations that has been raised against it. The U.S. is commonly said to spend much more on defense than other combinations of nations — but these statistics are being misread. The U.S. gets far less for its expenditures than its rivals, in part because so much American money is spent on social engineering of its military. Moreover, in comparing military spending among nations the CIA uses purchasing power parities that drastically understate Chinese and Russian defense activities.

Biden will see all this from his perch in the White House. Whether he can or will do anything about it is uncertain. His domestic allies do not or will not see the danger because they are focused on other priorities and are accustomed to denying facts they do not find to their liking.

Further, and making things more difficult, is a blooming alliance between Iran and North Korea, directed at the United States and subordinate and friendly to the Russians and the Chinese.

On March 25, 2021, North Korea tested two short-range ballistic missiles. The missiles threaten South Korea and Japan. The tests violate UN Security Council resolutions. It is not likely that the Biden Administration will do anything effective to enforce the UN resolutions or reduce the threat to our allies.

Chapter 19

The Decline of American and the Rise of Chinese Globalization

China is a rising power. It has geopolitical aspirations that conflict with American involvements. Only a few years ago America viewed Chinese aspirations as a challenge limited to the Far East. In a remarkably short time China has become a rival to the U.S. all over the globe. China is active in Africa; it is involved in the Caribbean. It has recently signed a 25-year alliance with Iran that involves it in the Middle East. European nations are considering how best to arrange their trade relations with China. In the most dramatic of its challenges to America, one which is largely ignored in America as too extreme — as mere hyperbole — to be considered, on May 2, 2019, China's media called for a "people's war" on the U.S. (https://www.cnn.com/2019/05/14/asia/china-us-beijing-propaganda-intl/index.html).

In consequence of all this, most Americans now view China as an increasingly dangerous rival. Many refer to China as our worst enemy. For them the issue is simply whether the United States can put China into a permanent disadvantage *vis-à-vis* the United States, or whether the American position in the world will shrink in the face of Chinese expansionism.

There is much disagreement in the United States over China's future. The dominant point of view, pressed by the media, holds that China will soon surpass the United States as an economic power and in so doing will put America into a lesser position in the world.

There is a well-informed group of commentators that voice a different view. They assert that China will collapse soon. According to Gordon Chang speaking on Fox News on March 4, 2021, China is facing a demographic collapse. Chang says China will have a smaller population by 2200 than the U.S. In face of this calamity China cannot catch the U.S. economically, Chang insists, and its global reach will soon begin to recede. That Chinese demographic trends might change dramatically is not considered in this expectation.

U.S. Attitudes Toward a Rising China

The popular attitude in the U.S. toward China until recently welcomed the peaceful rise of China. This favorable attitude was accompanied by the conviction that as China modernized economically it would democratize. That has not happened in China. Instead, the opposite has occurred. The Communist Party of China has strengthened its tyranny and extended it to Hong Kong. Watching this, the popular American attitude has changed to one of suspicion and fear.

The American attitude is at that place now, with a majority of opinion seeing China as a competitor. A leading edge of thought is urging that China must be thought of as an enemy.

Biden, reflecting in part his advanced age, reflects the original view of China as an emerging economy whose modernization is on balance good for the whole world.

In foreign policy his Administration continues to see China as part of a world which is under American suzerainty and whose role in the world is to play a part in the Western World Order.

The United States is now transitioning through these attitudes toward China. Americans who adhere to older attitudes favoring supporting a modernizing China are increasingly denounced as favoring an enemy. This gives the American debate about China an increasingly excited edge.

For example, an article whose author was stated to be a high-ranking U.S. official identified as "Anonymous" reads in part as follows: "The single most important challenge facing the United States in the twenty-first century is the rise of an increasingly authoritarian China under President and General Secretary Xi Jinping … Because of the scale of China's economy and its military, the speed of its technological advancement and its radically different worldview from that of the United States,

China's rise now profoundly impacts every major U.S. national interest" (Opinion: "To Counter China's Rise, the U.S. Should Focus on Xi" — *POLITICO*, January 28, 2021).

Sources of Possible Conflict

According to public opinion polls Americans now see China as America's most serious threat. But it is unclear what Americans mean by this. China increasingly displaces American firms in the world marketplace, causing unemployment and loss of higher-paying jobs in the U.S. In so doing, China is an economic rival to the United States. China also threatens some existing American international relations — especially in East and Southeast Asia. But a person might ask, "so what?"

China is a growing power economically and so it will challenge America's economic and political role in parts of the world. This is to be expected. In the past several decades Japan and Germany have both done the same. But in recent decades neither Japan nor Germany — for good reasons rooted in World War II — challenged American geo-political dominance world-wide. But China is doing that. It is doing so diplomatically and militarily.

The military challenge seems most concerning to Americans. So much so that a new Cold War seems to be developing. China is building and testing weapons to confront American conventional military power, American power in space, and American cyber power. Americans are complaining about this vigorously.

In the past military conflict has often arisen out of commercial rivalry between nations. For example, Britain may be said to have waged a series of wars in Europe from the sixteenth through the twentieth centuries to suppress a sequence of rising trade rivals (first Spain, then the Netherlands, then France, then Germany). Geopolitical conflict followed commercial rivalry among nations.

Perhaps surprisingly, despite the publicity they get, trade tensions do not seem to be central in the increasing tensions between the United States and China. Trade played a critical role in past international conflict, as we have seen above, but this does not seem to be the case in today. Biden is seeking to enter the Transpacific Partnership. He is trying to reestablish economic ties with China and thereby position the U.S. on a better footing with our allies. All this probably means a resumption of outsourcing by

America determined primarily by the cost and quality concerns of American corporations.

Hence, the Biden Administration's economic concerns are not likely to intensify geo-political rivalry. Instead, geo-political rivalry seems to be causing some commercial tension. It appears to some observers as if the United States is threatening a rising geo-political rivalry. An influential bipartisan group seems to insist that American geopolitical dominance be continued as it existed at the time of the collapse of the Soviet Union in 1990. That is, whatever the label given it for political appearances, the U.S. should retain its role as hegemon even in east Asia.

The danger of military conflict is evident. Graham Allison of Harvard University has found an analogue for today's situation in the rivalry between Athens and Sparta two and one-half millennia ago. That rivalry resulted in a lengthy war that destroyed Athens' empire. Athens, the quasi-democracy of the period, tried to stop the increasing strength and influence of Sparta, a totalitarian country, and in a lengthy war, failed. Allison warns the U.S. to avoid the trap of trying to limit the growth of a challenger by force which is what Athens is supposed to have done. The trap is being mired in war instead building national economic strength.

More than a geo-political rivalry is involved, because the United States represents the democratic aspirations and realities of many nations. If the United States misplays its hand, then democracy is threatened in many other countries.

Liberals in the United States are inclined to pay attention to China's internal affairs, complaining when they see what they consider to be human rights violations. They accuse China of genocide against the Muslim population of its far western provinces. They accuse China of a different form of human rights violations in its take-over of Hong Kong. These criticisms anger the Chinese Communist Party.

Biden refers to China's treatment of Hong Kong and the Uighurs as "cultural differences," and so abandons the U.S. human rights positions which are at the core of liberal attitudes.

American Policy Toward China in Biden's Era

President Biden now confronts the issue of what American policy should be with respect to China. He spent several decades in the American Senate during the period in which America supported in many ways the modernization of China and anticipated that as China modernized it would become democratic politically. His family even participated financially in Chinese modernization — perhaps he did also. Fear of direct conflict between the two countries is new to him.

Today the U.S. is being encouraged by many of its most articulate foreign policy experts to assume a much more hostile posture with respect to China. We are being urged to substantially strengthen our conventional military posture in East Asia, directly confronting China. We are being urged to increase dramatically our space and cyber military forces to confront Chinese efforts in those areas.

Which way will Biden go? At the broadest level he has defined his role with regards to China as "proving democracy works." He foresees a peaceful competition in form of governance and economics.

Focusing on this, he will try to cool off the building hostility between the two nations. But he will also make moves that suggest some strengthening of American force in East Asia.

The United States must decide how to respond to increasing Chinese assertiveness. The U.S. could accept China as an equal power in the world, accepting a multi-polar world. We could give up our hegemony and our attempt to retain our hegemony. This might make sense as accepting with good grace something that history is going to make inevitable.

Alternatively, we could decide to contest what the Chinese like to call the "peaceful rise of China." We could seek to strengthen our alliances in the Far East against China and add new partners to them. We could move our business supply chains out of China to other developing nations (India and Viet Nam in particular). We could compete with China in Africa and Latin America in providing economic support. We could build our military in the western Pacific to deny China any further advance of its political control.

Joe Biden is now in charge of the U.S. decisions on these matters. In the past he has favored Chinese development, as most Americans have. Longer than most Americans he has continued to support Chinese economic gains. "They are not our enemies," he said during the 2020 presidential election campaign. As we saw in an earlier chapter concerning Biden's economic policies, he is likely to be forced to continue American outsourcing of its business supply chains to China.

All these matters incline Biden to accommodation as the rise of China on the world stage continues. He will pursue diplomacy and eschew conflict when possible. Within a few weeks of becoming president, he sent his new Secretary of State with a delegation to meet with Chinese counterparts. At that meeting the Chinese lectured the Americans on human rights abuses in America and the American foreign minister apologized for American shortcomings.

But, whatever Biden's inclinations, Congress — including key figures in both political parties — is unlikely to allow him to abandon our grasp on hegemony. There are various reasons for this. The liberals and progressives deplore human rights violations in China. The conservatives have economic reasons.

Populists don't care much about human rights abroad and wish to end outsourcing in order to bring manufacturing back to the United States. Their champion, the Republican president, was prepared to give up hegemony in order to strengthen the American economy.

Biden inherits a confused and complex situation in which most Americans have views about what our policy should be toward China. This has developed in recent years and very quickly. The American media stress danger from China and now every American is aware of that. A decade ago, the American president had considerable freedom of movement with respect to China. No longer.

Biden's decision-making is always driven by domestic politics. What to do about China is now a hotbed of contesting views. Finding a coherent course through the political minefield will be difficult for Biden. American policy will be inconsistent and there will be from the American side two sources of risk of overt conflict. First, the American side may be so confused that the Chinese mistake it for a fatal weakness and grow overly aggressive. Second, the Americans might step over a line in resisting Chinese rise and China might feel required to resist strongly.

What then should be American policy toward China? It has progressed in the last several decades from thorough support for Chinese modernization to a rising animosity toward China's increasing strength.

The American resistance to China's impact on employment in America, about which there is so much talk in America, is not a serious cause of the increasing opposition to China in America. The opposite is the case. It is America's resistance to growing Chinese global power that causes American opposition to its increasing interdependence with China. It is displacement in global power than first and foremost concerns America — and economic complaints follow that concern.

Trade With China under Biden

Globalization is a two-pronged process. The first prong is economic. America has successfully enticed much of the world into accepting its commercial market principles and transnational economic institutions. Global productivity has increased on balance as authoritarian economic planning and autarky receded, and market forces expanded with American big business benefiting disproportionally. America in the process has strengthened its spheres of political influence. This is the second prong.

China under Xi Jinping has responded with a double counterstrategy of capturing control of existing transnational institutions (e.g., WTO) and creating its own alternative transnational networks (the Shanghai Cooperation agreement and the Belt and Road Initiative). It seeks to expand its economic and political gains from transnational market integration at America's expense.

China is the world leader in the production of rare earth materials which are needed in the production of advanced technology products. They are in many places but are rare, in that a large amount of earth must be moved to collect even a small amount. Ecologically it is a very messy process, and China is willing to do it. The Biden Administration with its concern over the quality of the American environment is likely to leave the production of rare earth materials to China. Again, in the Biden Administration national security needs will give way to domestic postures.

U.S. Harassment of China

Biden will be pressured strongly in two ways regarding China's winter Olympics which are scheduled for the winter of 2022. One element of the Administration will urge him to stage a semi-boycott. He'll be urged to allow American athletics to attend, but not American tourists or corporate sponsors. The purpose of this is to show the Chinese our concern at their invasions of the human rights of their citizens so that the Chinese government will behave better. What it is likely to do instead is anger the Chinese government without achieving anything on the human rights front.

Realizing this and wishing for Chinese support in climate control, another element of the Administration will urge Biden to allow full American participation in the Chinese winter games. This, Biden will be told, will gain Chinese good-will and help in the climate negotiations.

Part VII
Biden and China

Chapter 20

An Ideological Contest with China

There is emerging an ideological aspect to the American Chinese rivalry. This is surprising since the end of the Cold War brought common acceptance of the notion that the great ideological contest between communism and democratic capitalism had ended. This was the so-called end of history. The rivalry that emerged between the U.S. and China in recent years has been thought to be free of ideological overtones.

But that is no longer the case. The ideological dispute now emerging is more about national governance than economic systems, although there are profound systemic differences including China's prohibition on private freehold property ownership.

The primary dispute is between Chinese-sponsored authoritarianism and American-sponsored democracy. The Chinese are increasingly pointing to what are said to be the serious limitations of democracy and contrasting to them the great successes of Chinese Communist Party leadership in China. American government is said to be confused, chaotic, and unable to get important things done. In contrast, Chinese government is said to be responsible for the tremendous economic advance of the country and its current rise to great power status. China now champions its authoritarian system as a better choice for other nations than American-style democracy. (Incidentally, Putin's Russia does the same.) This ideological contest is certain to intensify in the coming years. Biden is strongly supporting the American model (by which he means the Democratic Party's progressive rule) for governments all over the world.

In a later chapter we note the dumbing down that is occurring in America's schools at the instigation of progressives. The challenge is to meritocracy and high performance in all areas of life. A consequence is that the authoritarian states will soon stand for creativity, innovation, brilliance, and performance in all fields. It is possible that beyond its rhetoric, America will stand for cradle to grave anti-meritocratic social indulgence.

Biden's America will wish to see the authoritarian challenge in terms only of human rights, but the authoritarians will present their challenge in other terms as well — including public order, social harmony, economic progress, social problem-solving, and educational achievement. The challenge is already being presented in those terms by both China and Russia.

American thought-leaders are beginning to perceive the ideological challenge from the authoritarian powers, in particular China. They are becoming self-critical about it.

In a monologue on HBO's *Real Time* host Bill Maher called Americans a "silly people" for allowing themselves to be mired in culture war struggles, such as the politically correct canceling of children's books, while our superpower competitor China is laser-focused on political, economic, and military dominance.

"You're not going to win the battle for the twenty-first century if you are a silly people. And Americans are a silly people," Maher asserted. He then referenced the latest "cancel culture" controversy — the woke mob's targeting of children's author Dr. Seuss over purported racism in his books. "Do you know who doesn't care that there's a stereotype of a Chinese man in a Dr. Seuss book? China. All 1.4 billion of them couldn't give a crouching tiger flying fuck because they're not a silly people. If anything, they are as serious as a prison fight."

Maher pointed out that China has "built 500 entire cities from scratch, moved the majority of their huge population from poverty to the middle class, and mostly cornered the market in 5G and pharmaceuticals" in two generations. Meanwhile in America, "half the country is having a never-ending woke competition deciding whether Mr. Potato Head has a dick and the other half believes we have to stop the lizard people because they're eating babies. We are a silly people," he continued.

"Do you think China's doing that, letting political correctness get in the way of nurturing their best and brightest?" Maher added. "Do you think Chinese colleges are offering courses in 'The Philosophy of Star Trek,' 'The Sociology of Seinfeld,' and 'Surviving the Coming Zombie Apocalypse'? Those are real and so is China. And they are eating our lunch. And believe me, in an hour, they'll be hungry again" (America at the End of Empire Is civilizational decline reversible? Mark Tapson https://www.frontpagemag.com/fpm/2021/03/america-at-the-end-of-empire-mark-tapson/).

Perhaps America is more impacted by the authoritarian challenge than it admits to itself. The Republicans' Secretary of State (foreign minister) had suggested that America's primary goal is to end the rule of the Chinese Communist Party in China. Biden sponsors democracy worldwide. But America increasingly adopts authoritarian measures. Censorship is now widespread in American social media and in the schools and colleges. Propaganda management by the techniques of the Nazi and the Soviet regimes is now common in America. Efforts to silence political opponents are becoming common in America. Indoctrination in the place of education is becoming common. Morality is being defined in terms not of personal behavior but of political correctness.

Examples abound. Since Harvard is thought to be one of the world's top universities, it is helpful to take an example from there. On May 1, 2021, the *Harvard Gazette* endorsed the teaching of an instructor by writing that she "keeps diversity, equity, inclusion, and belonging at the core of her curriculum." The core of her curriculum is all political, not educational. She's an indoctrinator, not an educator, and it's what Harvard now espouses.

These are major shifts in American political behavior, and they all have their origin in authoritarianism. It can almost be said that the dictatorships are winning the battle of ideas in America itself.

Is the Chinese Criticism of U.S. Merited?

According to Chinese spokespersons the U.S. is an unreliable country with no credibility. What makes this statement credible itself is the domestic politics of the U.S. in which Republican and Democrat administrations following one another closely (as often as every four years) denounce their predecessors and proclaim that they are altering policies dramatically, even when they do not do so.

Chinese criticism of the U.S. has merit. Political chaos in the U.S. seems to drive the decline of the U.S. role in the world as the Chinese allege. From a different perspective the decline of the U.S. role internationally drives political chaos in the U.S. The first implies that what is happening internationally is driven from the U.S.; the second implies that what is happening internationally is driven by countries outside the U.S. Is China driving the U.S. decline? Or is the U.S. decline opening the way for Chinese advance?

It is tempting to say both — that there is a feedback loop from one to the other so that events are driven by both causes. But this may be too simple, and it suggests that not much can be done to reverse the dynamic. However, if it is political chaos in the U.S. — the Republican reverse Obama/Biden's policies, and then Biden reverses the Republicans' policies — that is driving America's international decline, then America can reverse that decline by stabilizing its politics — even though that cannot be achieved amicably and may require a dramatic victory by one side or the other.

Chinese Propaganda Inside the U.S.

There are also issues with respect to the role of China within the United States. The U.S. is suddenly trying to meet the Chinese on propaganda grounds in the U.S. itself. The Chinese have established institutions on many American college campuses that are supposedly to promote understanding and cultural exchanges for China with Americans. They are called Confucius Institutes.

The action of the U.S. in this matter is reminiscent of American resistance to the activities of Hitler's German American Bund before World War II and its elimination when the war began.

The U.S. Senate in the first week of March, 2021, approved, by unanimous consent legislation introduced by Senator John Kennedy, Republican of Louisiana, that would increase oversight of Confucius Institutes. Kennedy said the China-funded cultural centers "are under the control of the Chinese Communist Party in all but name."

One of Biden's executive orders in the early days of his administration reversed a Republican order regulating the relations of American universities to the Confucius Institutes. The Republicans had required the universities to report the amounts of money and size of these organizations on their campuses. The Institutes are thought to be centers of espionage and propaganda. Biden eliminated these requirements.

These actions of Biden have been greeted by the Chinese as accommodations for the purpose of improving American-Chinese relations. These American policies will make U.S.-Chinese relations seem calmer and more peaceful, but possibility at the risk of increasing the likelihood of a brutal confrontation later. They make the U.S. seem weak and vulnerable, and so encourage Chinese adventurism while also giving China a further advantage in its contest with the U.S.

Chapter 21

China and COVID-19

Wherever it originated, COVID-19 seems to have come out of China and triggered a global pandemic. Questions about the virus' origins and China's responsibility for the chaos that ensued have emerged strongly in the U.S. and elsewhere in the world.

Why did the U.S. not pursue the origin of the virus more vigorously? Neither the Republicans nor the Biden Administration have done so.

A Tacit Conspiracy of Silence

There were minor barriers to determining the origin of the virus which have received much publicity. For example, neither the World Health Organization nor the U.S. have been able to get free access to the Chinese research center in Wuhan which is likely involved in the origin of the virus.

The bigger barrier is that if China created the virus and unleashed it on the world, then the consequences of that fact are too awful to contemplate. That would be an act of biological warfare, which must be responded to with a commensurate act of war and with overwhelming force. Neither the U.S. nor any other government wishes to be compelled to act in this way.

So American leadership avoids the issue. The Republicans were willing to keep alive the suspicion by referring to the virus as the China virus. Biden ordered, as one of his first steps, federal employees and agencies not to refer to the virus as the China virus or the Wuhan virus.

How has the Chinese regime interpreted Biden's action — with thanks for helping contain a potentially disastrous situation? Perhaps, but the danger, of course, is that China has interpreted Biden's action as one of weakness.

Suppose the release of the virus was accidental, then Biden's action was constructive.

Suppose the release of the virus was intentional, then Biden's action was very questionable. The Russians or the Iranians or the North Koreans may be soon to follow China in biological attacks.

Biden and the Republicans have both silently pursued the same policy with respect to China and COVID-19. This is disguised by cosmetics, since for campaign purposes, both political parties wished to highlight differences. The Republicans insisted on referring to the virus as the "China virus" or the "Wuhan virus." Biden insisted that it not be referred to by either term. The pundits opined that the Republicans were trying to blame China for the virus, while Biden was trying to relieve China of any responsibility.

American politicians spoke of the responsibility that China has for the spread of the virus around the world. The Republican Administration was prepared to lay the responsibility heavily on Chinese shoulders, the Biden Administration less so. American politicians called on the world to let China know that it could never do something like this again. It was unclear what the Americans thought the world would or could do about it if China did the same thing again.

The world is different than a decade ago. Now biological weapons, space-based weapons, and cyber weapons are available, and nations are developing them and experimenting with them. Some of those experiments may go wrong and the consequences might be very serious.

Secrecy about Biological Weapons

A final historical parallel is instructive. In 1944, Allied warships were gathered in the Italian port of Bari in support of the Allied invasion of Italy. Italy was being defended by German troops. Unexpectedly a German air attack was made on Bari. An American supply ship in the harbor was hit by a bomb and exploded. The ship was carrying mustard gas, the highly deadly poison gas used in the First World War and outlawed thereafter.

Many American and British service men died from the gas at Bari. Doctors put mustard gas on their death certificates as the cause of death.

From the first, the Allied command covered up the incident. Prime Minister Winston Churchill of Great Britain was informed of the event. He ordered that all the death certificates be altered so that the gas was not identified as having been on the site and involved in the fatalities. Churchill ordered that no admission that the gas had been present in Bari be released to the media. It was about 70 years later when the story finally leaked out.

Biological warfare is real. It is experimented with around the world. It could have been involved in the COVID-19 pandemic, but the United States presidents prefer not to know, at least publicly.

An Important Precedent

There is a case like that of COVID-19 involving the American presidency which has set an important precedent. This is not widely known in America and its truth is controversial.

In 1963, President John F. Kennedy was assassinated in Dallas, Texas. He was in a motorcade and was shot three times. He died in a local hospital or on the way to the hospital. Vice President Lyndon Johnson immediately assumed the presidency. An investigation began into who had committed the murder.

President Johnson asked the Chief Justice of the Supreme Court, Earl Warren, to head a commission to study the event and assign responsibility. Warren did so and after an exhaustive investigation issued a voluminous report finding that a single assassin, Lee Harvey Oswald, acting alone, had killed the president. He had shot the president from a building, the Texas School Book Depository, which stood alongside the president's parade route. He had shot him three times from behind his vehicle as it made its way down the street.

What was not revealed publicly was that President Johnson had told Chief Justice Warren at the time of the creation of the Commission that if Warren's commission found that Oswald had not been acting alone, about 100 million people could die.

Suitably warned, the Chief Justice saw that the Warren Commission reached a conclusion that Oswald had acted alone. In the meantime, back in Dallas, Lee Harvey Oswald had been murdered a few days after the assassination while in police custody. He was never able to testify as to what had happened, or even if he had been involved in the shooting. He had denied involvement from the moment of his apprehension.

At the time there were numerous conjectures that Kennedy had been the victim of a conspiracy. Suspects were the Mafia, right-wing extremists, Fidel Castro, and the Soviets — all of whom had credible complaints against President Kennedy.

The Warren Commission Report put to bed for most of the American people these speculations. It also served as a prime example of what was said to be a penchant among some Americans for conspiracy theories, which penchant had no foundation in fact.

But what had President Johnson meant by his caution to Chief Justice Warren? He had meant that if there were Soviet involvement in the assassination (Oswald had spent time in the Soviet Union and married a Russian woman), then the United States would have to treat the assassination as an act of war. The result would likely have been an American nuclear attack on the Soviet Union and a 100 million people in the U.S.S.R. and the U.S. (from Soviet retaliation) would probably have died. Better to let the matter pass, and deal with the Soviets in other ways.

Over the ensuing years there has continued to be speculation about the killing of President Kennedy. Late in 2020 the matter was finally resolved by a careful study written by Josiah Thompson (*Last Second in Dallas*, University of Kansas Press) and based on the forensic work of James Barger, America's top scientist with respect to sound. Barger carefully studied the limited evidence that exists about the killing and determined that there was not a single shooter, but at least two, because Kennedy was hit by a single bullet from the front of his limousine as well as two from the rear. There had to be more than one assassin. There had to have been a conspiracy. What that conspiracy was, and who engineered it, was not addressed in Thompson's book.

The Soviets or their Cuban clients may have been involved in the killing. But President Johnson's decision to avoid discovering that at the time and thereby to avoid the consequences of the discovery — 100 million people dead — was likely the right decision. Transparency — a promise to make government decisions and actions known to the public, and now a shibboleth of American political promises — was not justified.

No sooner was it proven that President Kennedy was killed by people shooting from different directions than conspiracy theories about the assassination emerged again. Among the most interesting is the assertion by Ambassador James Woolsey director of the American Central Intelligence Agency (the CIA) 1993–1995 that the Soviet leader at the time, Nikita Khrushchev, may have personally ordered JFK's death.

A Discovery Too Awful to Contemplate

Something very similar is now happening with respect to China and COVID-19. The virus has now killed more than eight hundred thousand of Americans. There is much speculation that the virus originated in China and that China knowingly, perhaps intentionally, released it into the world. If that is so, the consequences are appalling.

The fact that Biden has continued the Republican's caution about the role of China in the pandemic demonstrates that Biden does not naively follow a campaign promise. Instead, he makes judgments about when to be transparent and when not to be.

Chapter 22

The World's Flash-Point — Taiwan

It is unfortunate that attention must be devoted to the risk of military conflict in East Asia. We and our readers would prefer a peaceful world without concerns about military conflict.

The American view is that under the American hegemony — the Pax America — of the past 75 years East Asia has benefited enormously. China, Japan, Taiwan, South Korea, Singapore, and Malaysia have made dramatic economic strides. These strides can continue under a continuing American security umbrella in East Asia.

The Chinese increasingly do not share this opinion. The Chinese are impatient with the American hegemony and want it to end. Their position is that they no longer need American intrusion into their affairs and are fully able to provide security for themselves.

The Americans continue to maintain a strong military presence in East Asia including bases and military alliances with Japan, South Korea, the Philippines, Taiwan and perhaps, in the future with Viet Nam. This American presence is increasingly a provocation to China and China is rapidly building a military force in all modern modes (conventional, nuclear, cyber, and space) to counter it.

The Americans in turn see the Chinese military build-up as a threat and are apprehensive about what it implies.

The result is a military technology race in East Asia. From the military technology race emerges the risk of warfare either accidentally or intentionally.

Today Taiwan is a major flashpoint in Asia, with China seeking to regain what it considers a renegade province, and the U.S. wishing to prevent that happening by force.

For these reasons discussion of the military situation in East Asia and the Biden Administration's reaction to it is necessary in this book.

China's Obsession with Taiwan

From the Chinese perspective Taiwan has been a province of China since the Ching Dynasty in the late seventeenth century. China ceded Taiwan to Japan in the Treaty of Shimonoseki in 1895 with subsequent approval by Teddy Roosevelt, at that time the American President. After World War II Japan chose to abandon Taiwan, and the American occupation authorities allowed Chiang Kai-shek, President of the Republic of China, to govern it. It has been practically independent since. Recently, China has been harassing the government of Taiwan with increasing military incursions.

Taiwan is the major flashpoint in the world today. This is because a Chinese attack on Taiwan is not only an attempt to reclaim a renegade province but inevitably, because of Taiwan's location, an assertion of an enormous advance in China's geo-political position and a consequent reduction in that of the United States.

There is not likely to be another Cold War-like struggle with China. But there could be a hot war, compared to which the Cold War with the U.S.S.R. will appear benign.

If China were to attack Taiwan, would Biden direct the U.S. military to intervene? Probably, though there would be strong influences urging him not to do so. Would American intervention be successful in repulsing a Chinese attack on Taiwan? Today, probably, yes. But Democrat policies in the years ahead are likely to weaken the U.S. military broadly in comparison to that of China, so that in the years ahead America may not be able to keep Taiwan out of China's grasp.

America would have the option of widening a war against China if its intervention on behalf of Taiwan were to be failing. Biden would not wish to do this, but he might be forced to do so by a combination of geo-political considerations and public opinion.

Chinese control of Taiwan would be a major threat to America's allies — Japan and South Korea. Taiwan dominates shipping lanes to those two countries which carry raw materials essential to their economies. Chinese control of Taiwan would give China a chokehold on both countries. China would thus enfeeble the United States in the Pacific. Chinese domination would replace that of the United States in the Far East — a major objective of Chinese foreign policy.

Danger exists of a direct military conflict. Its most likely cause would be a Chinese attempt to reclaim Taiwan by military force. This is especially likely if Taiwan should move toward a declaration of independence, which it may be doing. It is to be expected that the Biden Administration will oppose such an action by Taipei strongly.

Biden's working assumption seems to be that Taiwan is safe until 2030. He may be wrong. Today's increasing danger is that China will conclude that the United States will not fight for Taiwan. Biden's presidency increases the likelihood of that conclusion. If the Chinese were to be mistaken and launch an invasion of Taiwan, the results may be disastrous for East Asia and potentially for the world.

Biden's Approach

Democrats show a surprising ability to delude themselves about the international situation. For example, they are now convincing themselves that allowing China to reclaim Taiwan is nothing more than permitting China to reclaim a province that rightfully belongs to it. This has always been the American left's position. The adverse geo-political consequence for America is ignored. Biden is likely to lean increasingly to this point of view. Democrats are not alone in adopting this perspective. Many other Americans are also looking for an excuse to avoid a conflict with China over Taiwan.

People familiar with history will see a parallel in the attitude of the British government during the Munich episode. Hitler was claiming part of Czechoslovakia in which Germans resided. The British government persuaded itself that this was only Germans reuniting with Germans and was therefore permissible. Britain agreed to the German aggression in the Munich Agreement in 1938. Flushed with his diplomatic success Hitler soon overran all of Czechoslovakia and then invaded Poland. The British, furious that they had been deceived at Munich, declared war.

A similar sequence of events is possible around China's claim to Taiwan.

The most likely cause of a direct military conflict today would be a Chinese attempt to reclaim Taiwan by military force. The big question for the U.S. is will we have to fight China at some time? If so, Biden will be told by military advisors that war will be better now than later because China's strength is growing much faster than ours, and our resolve is eroding while their determination is growing. Even now we must strengthen our hard power in the Far East if we are to engage China militarily.

Most likely the Biden Administration will convince itself that we do not have to fight them — now or in the future, including the distant future. It is likely to conclude that there will be intense rivalry but no overt conflict. It will give itself many reasons why this is correct. This reasoning will allow the U.S. to avoid war with China no matter what it does in the Far East. This reasoning will permit the Biden Administration to focus on domestic spending.

China Danger

From one perspective, the danger has grown so slowly as to be imperceptible. From a different perspective, it has grown clearly and inevitably. China has reversed the positions in East Asia of the Americans and the Chinese. From its position as dominant power in the region, the United States has moved to the defensive. No longer can America dictate any action to Beijing. The initiative in the region now lies entirely with the Chinese Communist Party.

It would not be impossible for the U.S. to retake the initiative. But it is almost impossible to imagine a Biden Administration doing that.

China is now crushing efforts at democracy and freedom in Hong Kong and the West has no effective method of constraining or reversing the actions of the Chinese government. This shows that the protests and threats of the Western governments in support of human rights in China are simply posturing for domestic political consumption.

Biden's Probable Response to a Chinese Effort to Take Taiwan by Force

The key question is what will the Biden Administration do if China reaches for Taiwan by force?

In the aftermath of the American withdrawal from Afghanistan with the collapse of the Afghan government which was allied to the United States, China informed the Taiwanese government, "The U.S. is untrustworthy and unreliable." The Chinese believed that America's behavior in Afghanistan demonstrated that it would act in a similar fashion in Taiwan if a conflict occurred there. This belief made the Chinese more likely to reach for control of Taiwan. Ironically, to people who know the U.S. well, the fiasco in Afghanistan made the U.S. less likely to repeat the error in Taiwan and therefore more likely to resist a Chinese grab for Taiwan. Events in Afghanistan made a conflict over Taiwan much more likely — it made the Chinese more likely to attack and the U.S. more likely to resist.

Under the title "A Strategy to Prevent War" two authors writing for the Council on Foreign Relations proposed that if China were to isolate Taiwan the U.S. should provoke a localized war in Taiwan with China and then instead of escalating the war, if necessary, should turn to economic and diplomatic pressure on the Chinese to withdraw. A larger war would be averted. Probably the Chinese would not withdraw, Taiwan would have been forfeited, and in good time the U.S. would grow weary of the sanctions and China would possess Taiwan. (Robert D. Blackwill and Philip Zelikow, "The United States, China, and Taiwan: A Strategy to Prevent War," Council on Foreign Relations, *Council Special Report No. 90*, February 2021).

The search for a way to avoid war which American organizations have been conducting can also be perceived to concede Taiwan to China. For example, a cyber-war is suggested by some American observers (Harvard homeland security expert Juliette Kayyem '95 says we are fighting an "epic cyber battle," Jeff Neal/HLS News Staff, July 14, 2021, HARVARD LAW TODAY, July 19, 2021).

China has to import most of its raw materials. In consequence, it is vulnerable to disruption in its production of conventional weapons. The U.S. can cut it off from supply. But China has made itself very strong in non-conventional weaponry. In that aspect of power, the U.S. is falling behind.

These are likely weapons of choice for the Biden Administration even in response to a Chinese attack on Taiwan: naming and shaming in the diplomatic world and covert activities to disrupt Chinese military networks. In the meantime, it is possible that Taiwan will fall into Beijing's grasp.

Biden and Xi

Biden's first conversation with Xi was by phone and lasted some two hours. Biden reported afterward that he described for the Chinese president three pillars of American foreign policy.

First, we will invest more in science and technology in order to maintain our position of leadership in the world. Second, we will restore our system of alliances, which Biden went on to identify as the group of democracies in the world. Third, in East Asia the U.S. will work with the four countries known as the Quad.

Implicitly, therefore, Biden recognizes a quasi-ideological struggle between, as Biden describes it, the autocratic nations and those that are democratic. Biden sees the U.S. as leading the democratic bloc. He views the difference between the autocracies and the democracies as primarily one of values, in which the democratic nations value freedom and human rights. He intends to call to the world's attention — but apparently not to take other actions — China's human rights violations, in Hong Kong for example.

Finally, he believes the contest between autocracies and democracies will turn on how well each side helps its citizens to adjust to major changes that are occurring in the world, including climate change and technological developments.

In this conversation and in the diplomatic language of the Biden Administration China is likely to perceive conflicting signals. First, when Biden suggests that the U.S. champions democracy in the world, the Chinese hear an echo of the Republicans' Secretary of State's assertion that the overthrow of the present Chinese government is the objective of American foreign policy. This will not evoke a warm response from the Chinese government. Second, there has been some effort in the U.S. to escalate the Taiwan problem to sharpen American attitudes toward China generally. Finally, Biden's suggestion that the U.S. is rekindling relationships with our allies indicates an effort to better prepare an overall response to China.

The Republicans are given credit for pointing out that China is and will be our main threat economically, politically, and militarily. A good point but the U.S. may have to recognize that it will not be as easy to push China as it has been to push rivals in the Middle East and elsewhere.

"U.S. policymakers may hope that Beijing will balk at the potential costs of such aggression, but there are many reasons to think it might not.

Support for armed unification among the Chinese public and the military establishment is growing. Concern for international norms is subsiding. Many in Beijing also doubt that the United States has the military power to stop China from taking Taiwan — or the international clout to rally an effective coalition against China in the wake of Donald Trump's presidency. Although a Chinese invasion of Taiwan may not be imminent, for the first time in three decades, it is time to take seriously the possibility that China could soon use force to end its almost century-long civil war" (Oriana Skylar Mastro, "The Taiwan Temptation," *Foreign Affairs*, July/August 2021, https://outline.com/SbPWX9).

China has been building military power rapidly, and especially naval power. Probably Chinese military spending now equals or exceeds that of the United States. This is so despite official statistics on military spending that indicate that the U.S. far out-spends China. Chinese figures on military spending are greatly understated and American figures are overstated. For a discussion of this complicated and important topic see Rosefielde and Mills, *Beleaguered Superpower*.

Many Americans presume that China lacks the military power to reach Taiwan in the face of American naval force. This could be true, but it is not self-evident. It would have to be demonstrated by American resistance to an effort by China to invade Taiwan. Taiwan has its own defense capability and that adds to American resources if the situation requires. It is even possible that Japanese and South Korean forces would join in the effort to protect Taiwan. This is because Chinese control of Taiwan would alter the strategic balance in the Far East dramatically in China's favor.

It appears that China is testing Biden's fecklessness over the status of Taiwan. American Asian power is crumbling. Xi can probably pick his moment to seize Taiwan.

Chapter 23

The Initiative Lies with China

Russia, China, and Taiwan

Suppose a conflict between the United States and China over Taiwan widened enough to bring the Russians in on China's side. What then?

American military planning for many years projected the ability to fight two wars at once. Former defense secretary Ashton Carter revealed, however, in his excellent book *The Five-Sided Box* that this capability is largely imaginary. When Carter as Defense Secretary reviewed the plans for each of two wars to be waged simultaneously, he discovered that the plans for each war drew to a large degree on common Pentagon assets — that is, the two wars were to be fought with many of the same military resources — an impossibility. For this reason, among others, the United States is not able to wage major wars with China and Russia simultaneously. Yet they are now allied against us.

This is the background to the major geo-political confrontation in which the Biden Administration finds itself — the confrontation with China and its ally, Russia.

If China were to invade Taiwan, and the United States were to respond with military force, and the conflict were to escalate beyond the environs of Taiwan, as is very possible if either side were to be losing the contest over Taiwan, would Russia enter the conflict on China's side, perhaps on the other side of the world in Europe? How would the Biden regime respond?

Americans like to think in terms of compartments. Segmentation reflects the rationing mindset of American politicians — that is, each country will be allocated its share of American attention and treasure. Our politics are country specific. This mindset makes it difficult for America to respond effectively to a challenge from a group of countries. This was true before World War II as we faced a combined threat from Germany, Japan, and Italy. It is true now as we face a threat from China and Russia in almost-alliance.

Our government tends to treat China and Russia as separate matters. Relations with Russia are generally addressed without reference to China; relations with China are generally addressed without reference to Russia. In a crisis over Taiwan the Biden Administration is likely to be unable to think outside the compartments and address the threat that a combination of China and Russia presents. But if Biden perceives that the threat is from both China and Russia, as it may be, then this may make the Biden Administration much less likely to defend Taiwan in the event of a Chinese assault. And this calculation may enter the thinking of the Chinese regime as it contemplates an attack on Taiwan.

The immediate situation, therefore, is that the Chinese are preparing an attack on Taiwan, but prior to launching it are feeling out whether the Biden Administration will, in the event, defend Taiwan militarily.

Biden and the China — Russia Alliance

Thirty years ago, Russia was moribund in the wake of the collapse of the Soviet Union. Much of its empire was gone. Twenty years ago, Russia was weak. Meanwhile China was just starting on its meteoric rise to power. China is short of natural resources and land for occupation. Russia has large amounts of both. They were neighbors with as much potential rivalry as cooperation.

The United States at the start of the new millennium misunderstood them both. Most Americans viewed Russia as a collapsed superpower with little economic and military strength. China was viewed as a rising power which would soon become democratic.

Within a decade the rising threat of China was noticed by some American politicians and thought leaders. Russia was beginning to flex long-unused military muscles. It was pointed out in America that it was important to keep the two nations from an alliance against the United States. The foremost objective of the U.S. foreign policy should be, it was pointed out, to detach one from the other. This matter should have been debated between the two presidential candidates in the 2016 election.

Both candidates had given thoughtful foreign policy speeches. But in the debates, the moderators preferred to discuss whether the Republican candidate was unkind to women, and whether the Democrat candidate was a criminal. In consequence, the matter was never discussed or debated.

It was, however, very important. We have discussed it previously and return to the topic again here from a different perspective.

The Republicans seem to have been aware of the issue. When the Republican became president, he put out feelers to Putin for a possible accommodation. His purpose was to separate the Russians from the Chinese, leaving the Americans to confront China, if necessary, facing also only one Chinese ally, North Korea. The Republicans seemed to understand that the United States was far better off facing an isolated China than China with Russia as an ally.

However, the Democrats chose to use Russia as a key element of their campaign against the Republicans which continued and only gathered momentum after the Republican became president. The Republican was charged by the Democrats with collusion with Russia during the 2016 campaign, and Russia was charged with interference in the American election. When the then Republican president-elect's representatives discussed removing sanctions on the Kremlin and some Russian officials, the only reason the Democrats could imagine for such discussions was corruption. The idea of trying to work out an accommodation with Russia to avoid a Russian alliance with China apparently never occurred to them. Instead, the Democrats and some Republicans who were also strongly opposed to Russia instead of considering the possible merits of such a policy alleged that the Republican president was in Putin's pocket. Such allegations continued for the Republican's presidency. Mrs. Clinton was charging the Republican with being a pawn of Putin as recently as the winter of 2021.

In this political environment the Republican was forced to abandon any effort to reach an accommodation with the Russians, and by the third year of his administration he was declaring that no other President of the United States had ever been as tough on the Russians as he was being.

So today the Russians and Chinese have developed a relationship which is evidently close to becoming a full-scale military alliance, including joint military exercises, aimed at, of course, the United States. Its logic is easy to understand. China has masses of conventional weaponry and troops; Russia has large numbers of sophisticated nuclear weapons. China has a powerful position in the Far East; Russia has a powerful position in

Europe and the Middle East. Together each extends the other's weaponry and geographic reach. Together they are much stronger than either alone.

China's Options

Biden is extremely unlikely to make any aggressive move against China. His Administration is absorbed in domestic political issues and is content with "smoke and mirrors" international security policy. He has no ambitions for a larger American role in the world beyond sponsoring the usual color revolutions as targets of opportunity arise (e.g., Belarus). Most likely, he will try to retain American global influence and he might defend it with military power. He will not use military power in an aggressive way. He wants to preserve the status quo including America's self-declared right to sponsor color revolutions.

Commentators who are supportive of the Biden Administration insist that Biden has abandoned American ambitions to remake other societies in the democratic mode. They cite Biden's withdrawal from Afghanistan as evidence and couple it with Biden's stated purpose of focusing his attention on the American economy. These items are lumped into what is labeled the "Biden Doctrine" by which America foreswears nation-building, and implicitly color revolutions, abroad. (See, for example, Dmitri Trenin of the Carnegie Moscow Center, "Interpreting the Biden Doctrine," September 7, 2021, https://carnegiemoscow.org/commentary/85278).

The United States under Biden's leadership is seen to be uninterested in interfering in nations abroad, including China. There is a qualification to this in that the view of some members of Biden Administration of China is that U.S. advantages include that the U.S. is ally-rich while China is ally-poor and that this is an important strength of the U.S. If it is an element of strength for the U.S., it must be in diplomacy and is coupled with the idea that China is sensitive to international opinion. There's little evidence of this except that China pays some attention to propaganda directed at international opinion. Militarily, our allies are of some use, but it isn't clear how much. Influencing American allies to support diplomatic initiatives in international organizations regarding Chinese practices as for example with respect to human rights in China is therefore a likelihood of the Biden Administration. But these efforts will not reach beyond diplomacy and do not contemplate serious efforts to alter the American relationship to China.

The Biden Administration does not want to decouple our supply chains too quickly because we need the low-cost product to restrain inflation in the U.S. and because there is currently serious global supply chain disruption that is a major economic problem, and the Administration doesn't want to worsen it.

There is in the Biden Administration the notion that we can participate in changing China into something more amenable to us. This has failed for decades, but the idea persists. The Biden Administration continues to believe that China can be nudged in our direction and continues to appease it for that reason.

Yet in major areas of American interest, including the protection of American intellectual property from Chinese appropriation, the Biden Administration has been reluctant to be aggressive. When Chinese courts declared that efforts to sue Chinese companies over alleged infringement of intellectual property would be met by penalties imposed by China, the Administration was noticeably slow to respond.

American passivity means that the initiative in its relationship with the United States lies with China. Even though China believes the United States has no role in China's domestic affairs — and it considers Taiwan a domestic matter — to act on that conviction risks a major military conflict that it might not be possible to localize. It is in the nature of the American political process and its media to intrude into the human rights actions of other nations. Biden's Administration may even increase that sort of intervention in China's internal affairs.

China believes that the United States interferes in its domestic affairs regarding Taiwan and American assertions of Chinese human rights abuses. Yet China is best advised to restrain its reaction to this intervention. Restraint requires considerable self-control on the part of China and will require more in the future. This is because China's military power is growing rapidly and China may be tempted to believe, for example, that it can either intimidate the United States into acquiescence to its take-over of Taiwan, or that China can defeat the United States in a limited conflict over Taiwan. China is now testing missiles the purpose of which is to destroy American aircraft carriers which are the major conventional power than the United States deploys in the seas around Taiwan. I (Mills) have talked to the commanders of American aircraft carriers, and they are convinced that they have defensive weaponry sufficient to protect their vessels. But they could be mistaken, and the Chinese may be tempted to discover if they are.

In addition, China's long-range nuclear-armed missile capacity is growing rapidly so that it can pose a deterrence to American action in the form of a threat to the American mainland. China's cyber and space warfare capabilities are also growing, and China may be tempted to exploit them in a conflict with the U.S.

It would be best for China and the rest of the world if China can resist the temptation to try out its developing military strength in a conflict with the Americans. Peace is likely to bring the Chinese continuing major advances in a variety of areas — economic, financial, and diplomatic. Biden will even be supportive. To risk war by reaching for Taiwan, for example, is to create an uncertain and likely dangerous outcome.

China's Best Response

The actions of American governments in international relations are historically difficult to anticipate. In part this is because the American government is large and disorganized. Top American officials complain that China's authoritarian system permits China to act in a coordinated manner, while America's multiple branches of government (now four, not the three envisaged in the American Constitution — legislative, judicial, executive, and administrative) often acting independently of one another, cannot present a common face to another nation. For example, when Meng Wanzhou, chief financial officer of Huawei was arrested by Canadian officials at the request of American authorities, several major American agencies, including the Department of Defense, which have important relations with China, complained that they had not been informed of the intent to do this. It was apparent that they would not have approved of the action. There was, they said, in the United States no central authority with final review of important matters of policy, as they believe there is in China. Americans presume that coordination and oversight of this nature is the role of the president. Unless the matter is political, it doesn't work that way any longer.

America cannot today execute a common policy toward China even if Biden's White House were to develop one. America's government is too big and too decentralized, and its business sector cannot be corralled by the American government to follow a national policy.

About the Republican president early in his presidency the Chinese are said to have observed, "His strategy is very clear, but his tactics are completely unpredictable." This seems to have been — as seen from the aftermath of the Republican's Administration — a very astute assessment.

Biden may well be the opposite of the Republican. His strategy will be obtuse, but his tactics quite predictable. In this situation, China should be very cautious. The Americans have the military ability to do great harm to China, canceling out much of the progress China has made over recent decades. There is no reason for China to take that risk by, for example, reaching aggressively for Taiwan.

Part VIII

Biden's America: The Perils of Biden's Democracy

Chapter 24

The Bastion of Democracy

We will be discussing the United States and its current political, economic, and social shortcomings and controversies. This should not suggest that the United States is without great strengths. To avoid misunderstandings about America we list below a few of our nation's substantial strengths.

- What has been up to now a strong commitment to what can be called either democracy or republican government.
- Free elections scheduled years in advance and conducted on the scheduled dates.
- Peaceful transference of power. In 2021, the completion of peaceful transference of power from the Republican Administration to the Biden Administration was hailed, particularly by Biden's political party, the Democrats, as strong evidence of the continuing strength of American democracy.
- Sponsorship and support for democracy worldwide.
- A system of political governance which, with only two parties, provides great stability of government. Israel, in contrast, had about a dozen contending parties in its multiple 2020–2021 elections, with none likely to get a majority, so that the government was by coalition, and was inherently unstable.
- Freedom for social advocacy on a large basis with many advocacy groups of all political complexions.
- A rule of law enforced by an autonomous judicial system which is constituted as one of the basic branches of government.

- A wide scope of personal freedom enforced by a constitutional defense of human rights enforced by the courts.
- Freedom for citizens to gather to advocate changes of all sorts.
- An economy with considerable personal freedom of choice and action.
- A large economy, probably the world's largest.
- A strong military, probably the world's strongest.
- The third largest population in the world (China and India are larger).
- The third largest land area in the world (Russia and Canada are larger).
- Very substantial natural resources.
- A formally well-educated and resourceful population.

Having listed America's strengths we turn to the opposite perspective and point out that many of these strengths (but not all) are perishable and some are in dispute. America's political process focuses on the country's limitations. President Joe Biden is very much in that tradition.

The Not-So-Good

Dumbing down

In the 1970s, Rupert Murdock complained that Americans were always trying to improve themselves rather than just let themselves be entertained. This was a great strength of America and a problem for the acceptance in America of Murdock's brand of tabloid journalism. Today, Americans have fully turned about and ridicule efforts to improve as elitism while embracing entertainment in increasingly degraded forms. Murdock's tabloid form of journalism now dominates the American scene.

The American people now show little sense of aspiration to improvement whether in appearance, behavior, or culture. Instead, people seek to look as casual as possible — a sort of grunginess in appearance and dress. Beards, often unkept, have reappeared for men. Feminists wear long hair hanging straight and often uncombed. Most people do not dress up for anything. Popular culture is all that is of interest to most people — whether in music, video, or print. Popular culture is generally simple-minded and crude. American popular culture as people experience it all over the world is dominated by drugs, sex, violence, sports, hedonism, and cultish activism. Video and motion pictures streamed have so much replaced the written word that many people are now functionally illiterate.

They have internet, video, and other media skills, but are neither creative nor able to understand what they hear or see in depth.

For example, "an education headline that, even in 2021, demands a double take: 'Gov. Kate Brown signed a law to allow Oregon students to graduate without proving they can write or do math.' Brown, Oregon's Democratic governor, had quietly signed Senate Bill 744 into law last month, discarding the requirement that high school graduates be able to demonstrate an ability to read, write, and do math at a high school level" (*The Dispatch*, Education K-12 Schooling Leadership and Innovation, August 13, 2021).

When American football player Tom Brady was instrumental in winning the 55th Super Bowl on February 7, 2021, almost all the discussion in the media afterward was about his advanced age, 43, none about the other lessons of his victory. His experience, his skill, his self-discipline, and commitment — all these are now too elitist to be mentioned — they were politically incorrect. America is in a slough of mediocrity, and no one any longer endorses excellence. There is no striving or betterment, no concept of perfection. In time unless somehow reversed, this may end the nation's greatness.

The American education system is a bifurcated one. Some of the best secondary schools and universities in the planet are in America. They teach a small portion of the nation's young people. The vast majority are in schools the performance of whose students on world-wide standardized tests is poor. This reflects the low value given to academic education by the nation's popular culture and most of its parents. There is extensive competition among parents for entry of their children into the better schools. This does not normally reflect a desire that their children learn, but rather that the children's education ticket be punched by the best educational brand available.

Progressives are now requiring review of advanced learning programs in large city public schools and universities. They proclaim an interest in insuring equitable access. It is unclear what that means, but it seems to be that if some students get admitted to programs based on demonstrated academic performance, those who do not make it have been inequitably denied entrance. The likely remedy for this inequity is that the programs will be "canceled" or refocused to promote social coddling (expressed in a social worker-special education type mentality). The principle seems to be that if one person does better than another, her or his gains should be taken from them in the interest of leveling everyone down to the same level. Stated differently it is that if she can do more than we, then we can't let her do it. This principle will, of course, drive almost all high performance out of our society, except in athletics where the principle of all at the same low level is not yet being applied.

One school board expressed the new rule clearly. It's important to hear this statement because most school boards and state officials intentionally mislead the public about what is being done. Higher level courses were being dropped from the curriculum, it said, "to combat the effects of academic tracking" because it "ultimately separates students of different socio-economic and racial backgrounds." Academic tracking is placing students who perform at different rates into courses based on their performance. Better students get more difficult courses. But this, as the statement above says, tends to separate students by socio-economic and racial backgrounds." The higher-level courses are eliminated, and all students are driven down to the performance level of the lowest ("Mediocrity is Now Mandatory," Andy Kessler, February 7, 2021, 1:56 pm ET).

Liberals don't think this way. They would prefer to try to move heaven and earth to improve the performance of the less-well performing students. They would hope to elevate student performance to eliminate racial and socio-economic differences. Universities still adhere to this approach in core fields but provide weak students including sports majors with soft alternatives and other accommodations.

Progressives have given up on liberal approaches as failing to eliminate differences in performance among racial and ethnic groups and have moved instead to level down instead of up. Elimination of academic tracking, as announced above, is a progressive approach.

Biden has always been a liberal in his political philosophy. He is now responding to progressive demands in many areas of policy. He is proposing substantial additional spending on schools. In line with progressive demands and rejection of liberal methods, the funds may be used to level down the American education system.

Despite all this, American politicians continually promise to improve the education system. President Biden is among the group of promisers.

It is best to be cautious when viewing America from abroad and assessing its apparent weaknesses. Before World War II both the Japanese and German governments decided that Americans were a pleasure-loving people who would not fight if attacked. In consequence Japan attacked the United States and Germany followed almost immediately with a declaration of war. Both decisions turned out badly.

Will the U.S. be able to lead the world from a position of dumbed down mediocrity? China and Russia are aiming higher. Is Biden trying to reverse this trend? He should. Biden appears to believe, with his party, that social equity is far and above the most important objective of government. This is not what brought America to world leadership and is not what will keep it there.

Other elements of decadence in the West

Attitudes toward learning and performance, particularly regarding the schools, are often cited as evidence of the clear decline of the West. There are others. Economic stagnation compared to China, South Korea, Taiwan, Singapore and the countries of southeast Asia is important. So is declining population.

Democrats sometimes accept these things — even endorse them.

Economic stagnation

Until recently Democrats defended slow economic growth. Today's reversal is an attempt to justify massive government spending. The switch in attitude, which Biden has embraced, has not been clearly explained. It probably reflects a large pattern of double mindedness.

Slow economic growth had been supported and still is by progressives on the grounds that it protected the environment and provided for sustainability. Now fast economic growth is stressed on the grounds that it will fund technology to reduce climate change and so protect the environment and will also provide jobs.

If, as is possible, more rapid economic growth threatens environmental damage, as it may (wind farms for example), then conflict will arise within the Democrat coalition. Biden will be ill-positioned to deal with it. If the economy tanks, he will save face by reverting to the progressive anti-growth political line.

Failure of faith in progress

The faith that used to characterize America about the eventful progress to prosperity of all peoples has been challenged by both economic events and by the ideology of progressives disparaging "modernism." It now seems that some people are fated to live in deprivation (absolute or relative) and some in privilege. This means that there is a political question as to whom each shall be — who will be deprived and who will be privileged.

By 2016 in America the Gini Coefficient and the share of the top percentile in wealth were at highest level in over 50 years. From 2016 to 2019, during the Trump Administration, both declined. Biden has promised to continue this trend, though he gives the Republicans no praise for the progress that they made. (Edward N. Wolff, "Wealth Inequality in the United States," *NBER Reporter*, No. 2, June 2021, p. 14).

Declining population

Women of developed countries have made a choice to have fewer children. This offers a more desirable lifestyle and lessens pressure on the environment. Democrats do not oppose these choices. In the United States, they support abortion on demand without ethical qualms or discussing its impact on population.

Falling population is a result of women's decisions about maternity, unless off-setting policies are adopted. The trend is not unique. Low birth rates are prevalent in Europe and much of developing Asia. In the past, falling population led to the collapse of states when areas of rapid population growth spilled over into them. America is more adventuresome in this regard than Asia, Russia, and Europe.

Growing population elsewhere and climate change creates large-scale migration and combined with political democracy shifts power in the developed countries to immigrant-supported politicians and parties and changes culture.

Biden will seek immigration to counter population decline. Most likely Biden's choice will be made on a short-term political basis — seeking Democrat voters and cheap labor for employers. These considerations have been discussed in a previous chapter.

The collapse of traditional morality

The breakdown of traditional morality in American means that almost everyone is absorbed in personal problems — divorces, break-ups, abandonments, lawsuits, poverty, desperation — and unable to fulfill civic responsibilities.

This is an age of self-indulgence and self-love. That is so widely recognized in the public discussion that it need not be argued here. Many American politicians now assure the electorate that they themselves express only love in all they do. During his resignation speech Governor Cuomo of New York reassured the people of his state numerous times that all his actions have been based on his love for them.

Yet all this love is accompanied in today's America by what Psalm 55 of the Bible (verse 8) speaks of as "a wild storm of hatred."

In America today the storm of hatred is intense. It comes to a degree from the far right directed at minorities. It comes to a large degree from progressives directed at the white majority of which most are a part. Self-hatred is not an uncommon human trait. In the case of progressives, it is not directed at merely things they have done in the past. For many progressives, hatred is directed at themselves — at white people, at whiteness.

Unfortunate attitudes

Non-Americans are aware that Americans are often very unsophisticated in many ways. For example, Americans cannot assign responsibility without also assigning blame. This is especially true in politics where every event is an occasion for assigning praise or blame to some politicians. This prevents Americans from identifying and addressing problems because it introduces defensiveness into every discussion. It also inhibits problem-solving by causing our politicians to avoid responsibility for something bad. Rather than identify and address a problem, American politicians often prefer to continue its existence so that they can blame the other political party for it.

Chapter 25

The Paradox of American Democracy

America acclaims its democracy all over the world and sponsors democracies everywhere. No one is a louder proponent of democracy worldwide than Joe Biden.

But America is itself a peculiar form of democracy. When the Constitutional Convention had finished its work in Philadelphia in 1787 Benjamin Franklin was asked by a group of citizens what kind of government had been created for the new United States. He is said to have replied, "A republic, if you can keep it."

The story is famous in America. Speaker Nancy Pelosi, a leading Democrat, on December 18, 2019, opened the House debate on two articles of impeachment against the Republican President by quoting Franklin's remark.

Franklin did not describe America's new government as a democracy. Historians, noting the difference, pass over a potentially embarrassing distinction by referring to America's government as a "democratic republic."

Formally, America is, as Franklin understood and said, a republic, not a democracy. The two are very different. The essence of a republic is that its form is intended to provide protection for the rights of political minorities. The essence of a democracy is that the majority has unfettered authority to have its way. The two appear directly contradictory. A reconciliation of sorts is achieved by assuming as most Americans do, that the people will protect basic human rights including the right to private property, business, and entrepreneurship. If this perspective is accepted, then a democratic republic is not contradictory, but it can easily become so if the majority forgets its implied commitment to human rights including private property rights.

When Franklin made his comment he feared, as others did, that the new American republic might be lost to a monarchy — then the most common form of government worldwide. That never occurred. But today the American republic is being devoured by a different opponent — "progressive-liberal" democracy without a strong commitment to human rights including private property rights. In the pattern of current political propaganda, as described previously in this book, Democrats describe their majority-dictated democracy as for the purpose of protecting human rights.

At the forefront of the challenge which democracy is presenting to the American republic is the Democrat Party and Joe Biden. They do not seem aware of the difference between a republic and a democracy. They champion majority-dictated democracy selectively committed to the human and property rights that suit their political agenda and expect every American to be as committed as they.

In America the conflict between republic and progressive-liberal democracy threatens to come to a head at each presidential election. In 2016, for example, the Republican candidate won the election in the electoral college but lost it in the popular vote. The electoral college is a republican institution in which votes are counted by state. The popular vote is a democratic measure in which votes are counted on an individual basis. Under the American Constitution the electoral college vote determines who wins the presidency. Under a democratic system, the popular vote would be determinative. Because the United States is a republic, in the 2016 election the Republican candidate became president although millions more Americans voted for his rival — Mrs. Clinton — than for him.

Because the popular vote would have put the Democrat in office rather than the Republican, Democrats called for elimination of the electoral college and a shift to the popular vote as the determinant of who would be elected president.

In 2020, however, Biden won both the electoral and the popular vote, so calls for a shift to election by popular vote instead of electoral vote all but disappeared. Still, it is an important (albeit expedient) part of the progressive agenda.

In republics bipartisanship can usually survive because it provides a basis for accommodation over time. Progressive democracies have no such reason for bipartisanship over time.

In a democracy as Democrats today conceive it every person should vote, and every vote should count equally. It is wrong to have regions or states with smaller populations have as much power as more heavily populated regions or states. In the United States this would mean that California and New York would over time dominate the rest of the country. Rural areas would have no say. The states of the great plains would be powerless, as would be those of the mountains. States in the upper Midwest and the south would gain influence by negotiating with the most populous states. The limitations on the power of the most populous states which was the essence of the constitutional republic would disappear.

When a person or a party adopts a generic commitment to full democracy regardless of human and property rights, then accommodation and bipartisanship disappear. There is no right but the desire of the majority and it knows no limits other than those which the majority imposes on itself. As the majority becomes more radical in its expectations, as the Biden Administration's supporters are doing in America today, then there is no legitimate reason why the majority would not impose its will on the political minority to the full extent it wishes to do. In today's America the majority will now seems to demand that it remain in power indefinitely and that the law be altered to make that certain. In this way America is drifting toward a one-party state. This will be the effect of leaving the constitutionally provided republic for an intolerant progressive democracy. To Democrats this self-serving ideological conviction seems the right thing to do. In this way America can be united under Democrat control. Everyone else will become *vragy naroda*: "enemies of the people."

Biden's Concept of Democracy

President Biden promotes democracy world-wide. Democracy is intended to provide government which includes, represents, and benefits the people. It is a noble aspiration. America champions it in the world.

What does democracy mean to the Democrats and to their leader Joe Biden?

Biden retains a somewhat traditional view of democracy. Democracy in his traditional conception has three elements.

(1) Processes such as elections, the peaceful transference of power, and the rule of law. Government divided into independent branches — in America legislature, executive, and judicial.

(2) A government that expresses the will of the people.
(3) Accomplishments based on policies of government that support the well-being of the people.

The Progressive View of Democracy

To the progressive wing of the Democrat Party democracy means the agenda of progressives. If a government departs from that agenda, it is being non-democratic — an enemy of the people — and is denounced as exactly that. The clearest statement of this viewpoint was made a few years ago by an African American woman who was, of all things, a Republican, Condoleezza Rice. She defined democracy in her book entitled *Democracy* as the agenda of the American civil rights movement. Nothing else, not elections nor any other process, but simply as the agenda of the civil rights movement. With some additions, including a more equitable distribution of income, her conception of democracy is that of today's progressives. And democracy so defined is to them the supreme and only legitimate goal of political action. Anyone who supports any other agenda, such as a Republican political agenda, is undemocratic and a nuisance to the body politic. The adherents of any of other concept of democracy require re-education to be brought to understand, accept, and support democracy — that is, the progressive agenda.

Progressives have strong reservations about Biden's comparatively tolerant style of democracy. "Lawrence Lessig says voter suppression, gerrymandering, big-money politics, and the Electoral College are undermining our democracy" (*Harvard Gazette*, November 5, 2019). Apparently, the Republicans are responsible for all attacks on democracy. This is Democrat doctrine — we support democracy, and our opponents oppose it. Also, as to practical matters, this suggests that the Democrats think that all the marginal voters who are supposedly excluded from the electorate will be Democrat voters and will provide a margin of victory for the Democrats in key races everywhere.

Different Concepts of Democracy among Americans

Championing democracy all over the world, Americans do not agree on what democracy means.

"Democracy" means very different things to different people, which is a reason it can be difficult to discuss. What is a person talking about when they speak of "democracy?"

Condoleezza Rice: Democracy is the agenda of the American civil rights movement — it is human rights.

Progressives — Democracy is the progressive political agenda involving special benefits for demographic minorities and support of radical causes.

Liberals — Democracy is the rule of the majority and providing what they wish for themselves; it is fairness for all (albeit often with a willingness to transgress the human and property rights of those they disesteem).

Conservatives — Democracy is a republican form of government with protection for political (not demographic) minorities.

Populists — The groups above revere democracy, but not all populists do. Democracy is one form of government that may or may not achieve populists ends.

The U.S. is not yet a progressive democracy and never has been, progressives tell us. But they wish America to become a progressive democracy by adopting their policies. Biden is supporting this perspective.

All political persuasions agree that government should act in the interests of the people (as dictators and monarchs also say), but each defines those interests as its own program. As for economic equality — is that equality of opportunity or equality of result, or as the progressive now define it, economic equity? Social unity means that all agree on the same political program — which each political persuasion defines as its program.

Three essential components of democracy are economic equal opportunity, social unity, and a government that acts in the interest of the people. America lacks all three of those components, says Vanderbilt University Law School Professor Ganesh Sitaraman. "In study after study, political scientists have shown that our government is responsive primarily to the wealthy and interest groups, not to ordinary people," says Sitaraman. "A system of government that is mostly unresponsive to the people is not a democracy at all." Sitaraman argues that the neoliberal era is what divided America and continues to prevent the country from realizing a true democracy. In a video available under his name on the internet he explains the problem with neoliberalism and how a new agenda could create far better opportunities. This is the progressive critique of American government, and is not shared by conservatives, populists, and many liberals.

Americans Have a Glorified View of Their Own Democracy

While continually criticizing American democracy where it fails short of their own political preferences, Americans also think it so good that they should promote it as a preferred form of government for the entire world. Yet the American form of democracy has serious limitations based on excessive partisanship and corruption.

America as a Limited Democracy

A democracy is supposed to do discussion, debate, and problem-solving.

American democracy today makes very little effort to identify and resolve problems. Any problem identification is primarily used by a political party to advance its own position. Hence, American political discussion is primarily partisan assertions and denunciations, with no in-depth discussion of policy.

There is no significant discussion of national economic policy — only claims that the economy is good or bad and that the president is to be praised or blamed.

About international relations there is only partisan praise or blame. There is little discussion of what has gone right or wrong. There is no discussion of how to do better, or what can be learned.

There is no generosity by critics. There is no admission that this or that went wrong by those who did it. Any admission of responsibility is *pro-forma* only. There is what is known as the "Clinton apology" — "I take full responsibility; but of course I didn't do anything." Anything that goes wrong is blamed on the other political party.

Chapter 26

How the U.S. is Governed

It is unfortunate but the way the American government now works should probably be considered a weakness of the United States.

Edward Everett Hale, the United States Senate chaplain from 1903 to 1909 and a celebrated writer, was once asked: "Dr. Hale, do you pray for the senators?" Hale replied, "No, I look at the senators and I pray for the country."

With the Federal government and big business in charge of the U.S., conservatives charge that the U.S. will never again possess an economy which benefits its people. The government will see that the economy benefits insiders, and Wall Street will see that it benefits speculators. There will be nothing left for the middle class.

America is almost paralyzed except for politics by its plutocratic style of governance in which insiders devote themselves to peddling public services for personal and political gain at home and abroad.

Biden's America is an increasing bureaucratic and rule-driven society in which people are expected to obey the letter of regulations while many ignore them completely. The result is that many people are punished for technical infractions while others go free for major violations. For example, during pandemic restrictions a woman took a photo of her son's ball team with them spaced far apart but with their masks off. She was punished because their masks were off. The fact that she had a good reason was ignored. Meanwhile, other people went about their lives without masks, and no one objected.

The U.S. secular society and government are in process of endorsing every form of vice other than adult sex with minors and incest. This is being done under the rubric of tolerance, but it seems much more than that. It is endorsement.

The End of the American Dream

There is much discussion in America about the end of the American Dream. The American Dream is the expectation that children can expect to have a better life than their parents. Among the key elements of a better life are a better financial future based on a better career. The concern is that a better life for children can no longer be expected because of changes in the economy and society in America.

The dream was important because by it parents were fulfilled in their own lives. They found fulfillment in the progress of their children. Now, with most American children no longer expecting to do better than their parents, the children become impatient, greedy, without ambition, and hanging around their parents for financial support. A struggle ensues between parents and children over scarce finances. Parents are no longer fulfilled by their children's success but find themselves struggling and resentful. A general unhappiness results in the society.

Finally, "can-do" America seems to be almost gone. Now it's "never-ready" America. The vaccine turnout is a classic case. It was left to the states and became a total muddle. Distribution, inoculation, and testing were all in disarray. The big problem was with the software by which people registered for vaccination or got test results. It was virtually impossible for months to get the software to provide people with timely vaccinations or test results. I (Mills) got my test results verbally from a person trying to get me on the web platform so the software would provide me test results as it was supposed to do. When she couldn't make the software work right, she gave me my test results verbally. Verbal results were of no use, of course, to show to anyone else.

All this shouldn't have been left to the states, which often left it to the counties, and the counties to the towns and everything was duplicated and different and a total confusion resulted which hampered and delayed response to the virus.

But there is some reawakening of can-do. A high-speed rail line will soon connect Miami with Orlando, linking two of the fastest-growing sections of the United States — southeastern Florida and central Florida. Finally, the U.S. will have high speed rail in an area that matters.

How the Politics of Exceptions Works — An Example

The Florida Legislature passed a law providing for making public actions of the Florida government — executive, legislative, and judicial — transparent to the public. Then it began passing exceptions — by mid-2014, some one thousand exceptions had passed the Legislature. The general principle was in the law, and it was violated by a thousand exceptions. Legislators favored friends and special interests with exceptions and were rewarded by election support, campaign contributions, favorable media mention, or in other ways.

In a common practice in American government politarchs identify real social concerns and propose self-enriching programs to deal with them. A major way to do this is to pass prohibiting legislation and then grant exceptions to it. For example, the federal tax code is mostly exceptions for specific special interests and individual organizations.

Bureaucratic Thinking

Bureaucratic thinking has displaced can-do action in much of the United States. It paralyzes the government.

In a public hearing held by the Town Planning Board of a small American town (Bar Harbor, Maine) which was reported in the local newspaper (*The Islander,* January 23, 2020, p. 1) a woman described the use of some housing units on the street where she resided and asked whether they were "Employee Living Quarters" or "Shared accommodations?" She was answered by the Board spokesperson "they were neither, since neither use was allowed…" That is, they weren't there, since it was not yet legal for them to be there. Something does not exist, if it is not provided for in the regulations. This is a classic bureaucratic response. The possibility that the uses might exist though not yet recognized in the law was not admitted.

Biden is a champion of gun control legislation in the United States. Canada recently introduced new legislation that would make it possible for cities and provinces to create a buyback program for banned military-style semiautomatic weapon. This would seem a sensible proposal for the Biden Administration to make, but it doesn't. It holds out for national level prohibitions. The U.S. can't do something sensible like Canada.

The American political parties do not want to resolve problems but instead to continue them for political controversy.

The Republicans did allow states to do their own anti-COVID plans, where it made little sense. Biden doesn't allow states to act where it makes a great deal of sense. The U.S. not only can't get things done right, but it does them backwards. The Republicans' and Biden's actions both became fuel for the raging partisan political fires in the U.S.

In the U.S. government at this stage, less would seem to be more. Today's government is too large to be effective at any mission or to be affordable by the taxpayers. Overlarge government is choking economic progress in the country. Although the number of federal civilian employees has remained at about two million since the 1960s, federal power and its intrusiveness in the American economy and society has grown substantially, mainly through contracting out of federal bureaucratic activity. The best estimate of the size of the federal workforce today (direct employees and contract workers) is some seven to nine million.

Drastically downsizing government will improve all government does. Bureaucrats will be able to address their missions, not just exchange paper with each other. The poor will be assisted; veterans will get medical care without waiting indefinitely in lists; Social Security pension checks won't be stolen from the mail; tax refunds won't be stolen by IRS employees; national defense will be more effective; foreign policy will keep us out of war.

Chapter 27

Money and Power in American Politics

Making Money Out of Politics

Candidates for elective office in America raise a great deal of money for their campaigns. It is said that office holders in the federal government spend 40% of their time raising money. When Congress is in session office holders go to special rooms from which they phone potential contributors. This is jokingly called "Dialing for Dollars."

Presidential campaigns involve raising and spending large sums. Roughly 2 billion dollars were spent by the two presidential candidates in the 2020 election. Roughly equal sums were spent on their behalf by others — mostly by political action committees.

Office holders deny that they act on behalf of contributors. But there are prices that are known informally. A recent governor of California is said to have charged 50,000 dollars as a contribution to his campaign fund in return for a meeting to discuss some issue of importance to the contributor. If a person didn't pay, they didn't get a meeting. This is called "pay to play."

A person (or an organization) is generally thought to have to contribute at least 100,000 dollars to a presidential campaign in order to get an audience with the candidate or office holder. The price rises annually.

Again, office holders deny that they are responsive to contributors in their actions. This is not credible to most Americans who in poll after poll show that they believe the system is corrupt.

Fund-raising from small contributors has become more and more expert. Democrats now email small contributors messages like this:

DNC SUPPORTER
NAME   JOHN
ID   *********
2021 DONOR   NO- NOT YET
2022 DONOR $ 0

Messages like this intimidate a potential small contributor by informing him that he or she is known to political authorities who are watching whatever he or she does. The consequences of not donating, or of not donating enough, are not spelled out, but they could be imagined to be significant.

Fund-raising from small contributors has also become more and more dishonest. In the aftermath of the 2020 presidential campaign the Republican National Committee was cited by 3% of all complaints about financial fraud to the authorities, and in America there is a vast amount of financial fraud. A friend of mine (Mills) tried to contribute 100 dollars to the Republican National Committee (RNC) in response to one of their solicitations. The software took him to a contribution of 1,800 dollars. When he discovered the amount, he complained vigorously to both the RNC and the federal election authorities. He got none of his money back.

The Democrats have their own methods of fundraising. It was widely believed during Barak Obama's two presidential campaigns that large funds were sent to him by the Chinese government via hundreds of thousands of false small contributions. This has not been verified.

So much money flows into the coffers of candidates and the two political parties in America that it has created a variety of frauds which exploit contributors for personal gain.

One of the most successful tricks is to form a political action committee. The most recent widely publicized and well-documented possible fraud involved supposedly Republicans opposed to the Republican president's re election in 2020. The Project raised 90 million dollars. It spent 27 million dollars on media advertisements opposing the Republican president. It spent 63 million dollars for consulting firms connected to the sponsors. This came out after the election. How much went back to the founders for their own income is being determined by investigators. This is a common ploy in American politics: raise money for campaigning and divert it to your own or your relatives' use. It is done by members of both parties but not generally on the large scale of the Lincoln Project.

Efforts by honest citizens to reform the financing of American elections are ongoing. They are not generally successful.

In part this is because the American Supreme Court has in a series of cases essentially legalized any amount of spending on American elections. It has found that spending on campaigns is protected as free speech by the First Amendment to the American Constitution. The court, in a 5-4 ruling in 2014 said "Congress's interest in fighting corruption doesn't justify the burden on political speech posed by aggregate limits."

This seems an open invitation to financial corruption.

President Biden gives no emphasis to election reform. Biden is not likely to lead the nation that way. He is a beneficiary of the current system. His campaign was likely financed by many of the special interests that corrupt all American politics. He is unlikely to bite the hands that have fed him.

The American political system, based on money and party politics, doesn't allow a president to care much about the national good, or even if she/he cares, to act on the caring. American elected officials often show most responsiveness to the people and organizations which contribute to their campaigns and thereby put them in office.

Financing of Election Campaigns

Apparently, entities associated with a Swiss billionaire gave some 180 million dollars in dark money (unreported campaign contributions) to funds that supported Democrat presidential candidates during the 2020 presidential campaign and the years of the Republican Administration proceeding that campaign. Previously the Democrats had condemned dark money and had refused to accept it. But, consistent with the principle of the progressives that ends justify means, Democrats accepted large sums of dark money to win their campaign against the Republican president in 2020.

Each party to gain an advantage over its rival has sold itself to elements of the rich and sold out the public generally. America has two political parties each swearing allegiance to working people and acting on behalf of the wealthy.

The Presidency versus the Congress

One of the strongest criticisms of American government made by the Democrats has been that the presidency has grown too strong in comparison to the Congress. This criticism has been muted since Biden has become president and issued a plethora of executive orders.

There may be excessive presidential strength in one way. When Congress refuses to act, it often lobbies the president to do so. The flood of presidential executive orders that came in the early days of the Biden Administration was evidence of this. For example, Biden issued orders that turned American immigration policy on its head. The Congress has been dead locked for decades on a new comprehensive immigration bill, and that deadlock leaves to the president the determination of the nation's immigration policy.

Another primary example comes from the Republican Administration but persists into the Biden Administration. The United States has fought wars in Iraq and Afghanistan on a considerable scale and for many years. The Afghan war is now ended but some fighting continues in Iraq and Syria. In clear violation of the American Constitution these wars have never been declared by the Congress, which has the sole power to declare war. When the Republicans took office in 2017, the President had insisted that if Congress did not declare these wars in a short time, so that they were legal, he — the President — would end them. Congress did not declare them. The Republican President tried to end them but encountered such political opposition that he was unable to do so before losing office. Biden has now ended the war in Afghanistan.

These examples make the presidency seem to have growing power *vis-à-vis* the Congress, although it is at Congress's will that the presidency acts. At the start of Biden's Administration, Biden authorized an attack by the U.S. forces on Syria. This excited a group of Senators of both parties to express concern that the president's war powers were now excessive and to propose legislation that would return performance in American government to the Constitution's requirement that Congress alone had the power to declare war. The bill was described as limiting the president's war powers. It has not been enacted.

The Administrative State

The president does not direct most of the federal government despite his Constitutional responsibility to do so. Instead, in today's Washington, D.C., the White House tells the agency heads that they should administer their departments as they wish, subject only to direction from the White House occasionally on political matters — that is, the White House will occasionally contact them when it wants something done for political purposes, and the agency heads are to do that. Otherwise, they are responsible to the Congressional committees that control their budgets. The agency state is not a group of independent agencies at all. It is governed as we have just described. Congress is not simply a legislative body — it is an executive body which uses the control of the purse to dictate policy to the agencies. In Congress the committees are controlled by the political party that has the majority, and the committees are run by their chairpersons, who therefore are like little presidents.

A huge federal bureaucracy has grown up in Washington supplemented by an even larger bureaucracy of contract employees. Millions of people are employed in a thousand or so agencies. Formally, the president directs the agencies. Practically, Congressional committees and especially their chairpersons direct these agencies using control of their budgets and specific legislation to direct them. Most agency heads are responsive to Congressional committees with respect to policy, not to the White House. The president's actual power is limited to political considerations addressed by the top officials of agencies whom he appoints, while those same people run their agencies in response to direction from Congressional committees.

In view of these considerations, the president of the United States does not seem to possess too much power. But in 2020 and 2021 decisions of the Supreme Court ended the independence of agency heads from dismissal (when a term expires) by the president. So now the agencies may have a dual responsibility in practice — to the president and to Congressional committees. But whether the president will try and if so, can succeed in exercising actual oversight and direction of the agencies is uncertain. The federal bureaucracy is enormous and complex, and the president has little staff for such a task.

Chapter 28

The Challenge to Democracy

We have in a previous chapter discussed President Biden's endorsement of democracy as a key element of American foreign policy. We have noted that democracy has many meanings, and that it is imperfect in the United States. In this chapter, we examine the challenge to John Locke-type (featuring constitutional minority rights protection including human, civic and property rights) democracy in today's world from the authoritarian nations. This is a challenge that democracy will face regardless of who is at the helm of the American ship of state. But since Biden is now president in the world's foremost democracy — though certainly not its largest — Biden's attitude toward democracy is very important.

Biden tends to view democracy from an exclusively American perspective. He presumes that democracy is the right form of government. He presumes that the right electorate is the largest possible electorate. He damns the Republicans for supposedly trying to suppress the electorate by calling for standards for voting. He denies that fraud in voting based on opportunities provided by loose voting standards ever occurs to a significant degree. All this is standard Democrat doctrine and Biden accepts it as self-evident and challenged only by people with ulterior and improper motives. Because he denies weaknesses in democracy, he is not well-prepared to meet the challenges it is now facing.

Democracy as a system of government is now challenged as it has not been in the past three decades. Authoritarian leaders have taken control in many countries, including the Philippines, Hungary, Turkey, Poland, and Venezuela — and even in India. The Democracy Index, which rates the state of democracy in 167 countries on the basis of electoral processes, the functioning of government, political participation, democratic political culture, and civil liberties, currently gives the world a global score of 5.4 out of 10, the lowest score since the survey began in 2006.

Polls also show that satisfaction with democracy in almost all democracies has declined substantially over recent decades and is a minority almost everywhere. Nearly two-thirds of Americans aged 18–29 have more fear than hope about the future of democracy in America. In the U.S. and the U.K., only around 30% of the youngest voters feel that it is essential to live in a democracy, compared with upwards of three-quarters of voters born before World War II.

Republics versus Democracies

Today we call a republic a democracy and ignore the difference. We can think of today's republics as John Locke-type representative democracies — a bit of a contradiction in terms, but today's common usage.

An ancient democracy involves the direct decision on matters of public interest by the electorate. This is how it worked in ancient Greece where democracy began. The Greek model was supported by slaves, employed by all other classes.

Modern nations are much too populous for such a direct form of government. There can be no direct democracy at a national level in almost all modern nations. They must work on a representative basis. But there are different ways by which representatives can be chosen.

Because democracy is prone to demagoguery, and to other limitations, some political thinkers are anxious to restore the difference between republics and democracies. They seek to strengthen republics to avoid a descent into democracy.

Democracies in Today's World

Democracies in today's world are very different in many ways.

For example, the United Kingdom and democracies modeled after the U.K. are governed by a legislature (Parliament) that selects the executive. In the United States and democracies modeled on the United States the chief executive (president) is selected more directly by the people.

In the United Kingdom the House of Commons debates issues of government. In the United States the House of Representatives and the Senate work in committees. Decisions are made in party caucuses and the House and Senate floors are primarily for votes or ceremonies.

Elections are run differently in democracies all over the world. In the United States each of the 50 states runs its elections as it sees fit subject to general federal court oversight to avoid overt discrimination in how elections are conducted.

Common Elements of Democracy

Differences of the type among democracies that we have just noted are important, but they may be viewed as superficial. Rebecca Henderson of Harvard Business School has provided a list of characteristics she views as central to a free society. The United States retains them all.

- Democratic pluralism
- Voting rights
- Checks and balances in government
- Free media
- Freedom of speech and other personal rights
- An impartial judiciary

But a closer look may raise skepticism.

Democratic pluralism in the United States now is expressed poorly by two political parties that fully dominate the national scene and differ from each other mostly in their antagonism to one another.

Voting rights are extensive but provide a largely ignorant or misinformed electorate which makes poor choices for office holders and is vulnerable to all sorts of manipulation.

Checks and balances in government are now fragile when, as often, one party controls two or even three branches of the federal government. States no longer provide a significant balance on the federal government, meaning that America is now a vestigial federal system.

The media is free but linked so closely to one political party that it is almost a house organ and is more often misinforming than informing.

Freedom of speech is increasingly curtailed by censorship and what is called cancel culture (discussed in a later chapter).

An impartial judiciary is also vestigial. The form is there but judges are known for their political leanings and the decision about a case can often be predicted by the political convictions of the judge. There are Republican and Democrat judges.

All this means that America retains the forms of democracy but has sacrificed its content. Polls now show that most Americans no longer have confidence in the honesty and effectiveness of their government.

Why Don't Americans Select Better Presidents?

Most American presidents are not very impressive. We have in a previous chapter ascribed the decline of American power over the past 30 years to a succession of ineffective presidents. American politics are such that we choose poor quality presidents and suffer generation after generation for it. In addition, the U.S. swings widely in its choices for president. This is not just regarding political parties but also with respect to personalities. Trump never had any political experience before being elected president. Biden had no experience but political. Both were extremes. This would not suggest the selection of outstanding candidates. During a president's time in office political commentators often point out their limitations and errors. But many presidents have cheering sections which include historians who clean up their reputations. Hagiography may be consoling, but it doesn't help improve anything.

The recent insistence by the media and political partisans that presidential candidates and presidents themselves must be fine people in order to be suitable for the presidency is the imposition of a naïve standard which is virtually never met and leads to endless controversy.

How Democracies Degenerate

All over the world efforts at democracy tend to degenerate into either partisan deadlocks or one-party dictatorships. Successful long-term democracies can be found only in northern Europe. Biden seems unaware of this. The label "democracy" on a country's government seems to satisfy him that it meets his standard for being an American ally. Further, he seems unaware except when crises emerge of the need to strengthen democracies against their tendencies to degenerate.

Failure of Democracy in Latin America

In the past 40 years democracy had made its strongest surge in the world in Latin America. A large area that had been dominated by authoritarian regimes had shifted toward democracies. At the end of the twentieth century almost 90% of the region was countries governed as democracies. But in the twenty-first century population grew rapidly, economic growth slowed, and economic inequality grew. By the beginning of the third decade of the twenty-first century autocratic regimes were re-emerging in several large countries — sometimes of the political left and sometimes of the right.

There is a contest between democracy and autocracy in the world. In Latin America democracy has slipped badly. As the slippage occurred, people began to leave the region in droves, most going to the United States where a problem with illegal immigration became a bitter political issue which we discussed previously.

Failures of Democracy in History

Democracy has existed previously in history and has collapsed. It has been revived and collapsed again. It is now in its greatest resurgence and is again facing challenges that might lead it to collapse. Briefly, in historical perspective we note two periods of democratic collapse.

Collapse at the End of the Roman Republic

Popular rule in the form of what we would call today a quasi-democracy with a limited electorate existed in the ancient European and middle Eastern world. It struggled with monarchies and survived in a few places for a long time. The Roman republic was perhaps its greatest success. But as Rome entered upon its greatest period of empire, the Roman republic collapsed and was replaced by an authoritarian system in which an emperor held all the power.

"Democracy had failed…" concluded an eminent American historian. "It could rule a city, perhaps, but not a hundred varied states; it had carried liberty into license, and license into chaos, until its class and civil war had threatened the economic and political life of the entire Mediterranean world" (Will Durant, *The Age of Faith*, New York: Simon and Schuster, 1950, pp. 6–7).

Re-Emergence in the Late Eighteenth Century

The French Revolution established a form of democracy in which the capital, Paris, was the key electorate. But it degenerated into the Napoleonic Empire. Later France returned to a republic, and has had several republics following one another.

Sovereign Democracy

China is offering the most effective challenge to democracy in today's world. The Chinese challenge is primarily one of performance. China offers its enormous economic progress of recent decades as proof of the superiority of single party, authoritarian rule. It points to political stability and the ability of the authoritarian government to mobilize common effort among its citizens as key elements of why it out-performs the democracies.

Russia, without China's sort of economic progress to show, has offered logical arguments in defense of its governmental system. Russia, confronting in the world a period of democracy ascendant before China's recent challenge, has been reluctant to forego the label of democracy itself. Vladimir Surkov devised the concept of "sovereign democracy" to justify Putin's claim that he is a "democrat."

Sovereign democracy according to Surkov is popular consent to the leader's programs.

It is an interesting notion. We have introduced it in our chapter about Russia. Progressives might be said to be trying to convert America into a sovereign democracy. This is because key aspects of Biden's program have only limited public support, but Biden is energetically seeking to increase their popular support broadly in the country.

Americans are embarrassed that a concept of government championed by Putin should be applied to them. They are currently ignoring the Russian concept totally. No mention of it can be found in voluminous current writings in the United States about democracy and authoritarianism.

Yet it might be said with some justification that a switch to sovereign democracy is being made world-wide by political insiders and is the reality behind the attack on the Western world order. All over the world nations are trending toward more authoritarian leadership and away from a key component of democracy — the frequent and peaceful transference of power nationally.

Part IX
Too Much Partisanship

Chapter 29

The Bane of American Democracy

Joe Biden was elected president of the United States in the context of general disgust at and distrust of the political leadership of both major political parties. Polls indicated that more than 70% of the American electorate were exasperated with the political establishment.

The decay of American democracy has been most evident in the partisan controversies which occur continually over every major issue in the nation — over education, healthcare, public safety, immigration, defense, foreign relations, and government budgets.

Having only two significant political parties gives American democracy a superficial stability, but they are almost always locked in stalemate. With respect to all public issues there are straightforward advances that could be made if there were a disposition on the two sides to solve the problems. There is no such disposition. Instead, the objective of each side is to denounce and demonize the other in order to gain an advantage in the political contest. Neither side wants to improve the country; both sides want to seize control and exploit the country for private advantage.

It is this contest over the spoils of America which the people now recognize for what it is. Disgust turns them against the establishment of both political parties. Neither party seeks the public good; both posture for the purpose of private gain — and the public now recognizes it.

John Browne speaks of the U.K. as "a democratic monarchy in which the Sovereign retains great constitutional power, subtly preventing such power sliding into the hands of party politicians." The American government lacks any such brake on the politics of the country, and so all power is sliding into the hands of party politicians running the country as a personal slush fund. We have previously shown this to be contributing to the decline of American influence in the world (Newsmax Media, "HRH The Prince Philip, Duke of Edinburgh, A Tribute," John Browne, April 15, 2020).

Partisanship began as the cooperation — one can legitimately say collusion — of people who shared certain political objectives. Each party had a platform or ideology. But we cannot say whether the ideology proceeds the party organization (that is, the party was organized to pursue a certain way of thinking) or that the party organization proceeds the ideology (that is, that a party was formed to benefit its members, and to gather support the members needed to justify their actions by creating a rationale — an ideology or platform).

Partisanship developed over time into an objective of its own. In the United States, today partisanship dominates everything else, including policy objectives. Most major issues are fought out on strict party lines. A vote in the House will ordinarily have all Democrats voting on one side and all Republicans voting on the other. The same in the Senate. The few so-called "independents" in the Senate, two of them at this moment, always vote with the Democrats and so are not independent at all.

What is most important is that actual opinions of Representatives and Senators may range widely but when called upon to vote, they set aside their own views and vote with the party.

Nowhere in these party calculations do the nation's needs or the people's will enter the partisan party calculation, except tangentially. It is argued in defense of party partisanship that this or that party has in its general orientation the good of the nation. This rationale is not however taken seriously anymore. What a party has in its general orientation is the good of its constituents — and these may be the people who vote for the party or the special interests that fund it, or in the case of the Democrat Party the activist groups that comprise it.

Parties now exist for their own sake — or rather for the sake of those who compose and benefit from them. Issues which mobilize voters or donors for a party are secondary.

Partisanship has moved to a new level. A party that loses a high office moves to resistance and carries on the battle to thwart the will of the majority. This happened in the United States most dramatically with the election in 2016 of a Republican to the presidency.

It was possible for the Democrats to have made the most of it by working with him when possible — nudging him in what they considered right directions and opposing him, when necessary, from their perspective. But they chose a path they labeled "resistance," and fought him at every turn. They chose to make the worst of his presidency. The Republicans denounced the Democrats bitterly for this.

The Republicans now do the same — turn about is fair play they say — in Biden's presidency. For example, when Biden became president, he allowed much more immigration through the nation's southern border. Republicans demanded he send many illegal immigrants out of the U.S. When Biden did so upon a surge of immigrants from storm and earthquake ravaged Haiti to the U.S., Republicans could have endorsed his action and praised him for it. After all, it was what they were urging him to do. Instead, they denounced him for inconsistency in his policy. Whatever he did, they were going to criticize him. This is partisanship of the American style today.

Commenting about modern party politics George Will said, "the Founders didn't anticipate how political parties would come to exert iron-clad control over not just ideology, but self-identity and all legislative action — and inaction. Now that they think of themselves as teammates of the president — and inferior teammates, that he's the quarterback and they're interior linemen blocking and tackling for him — the whole script of the Madisonian balance is dissolved" (George Will, "What It Means to be Conservative in the Republicans Era," *Harvard Gazette*, October 25, 2019).

One of the worst failures in history of cooperation by our two political parties for the good of the nation has been occurring in the fight against the pandemic.

The War against COVID-19 — No Cooperation

Democrats frequently used the rhetoric of a "war" against the virus and pointed out that the loss of more than half a million American dead to the disease in one year exceed the four-year loss of American lives in World War II. But always in a foreign war — as the pandemic surely was, wherever its origin, it was not American — there had been a unity of political parties. But the Democrats refused any such cooperation with the Republican Administration in this war. This is a key reason why the virus was so badly mishandled in America — though, of course, the principal responsibility was that of the president.

For example, a man runs a patient home for 160 people with dementia in southern Connecticut. As part of a conversation, he was asked how many patients had contracted the virus. His answer: none. How did he do it? By following closely recommendations of the CDC including especially those which the Republican Administration had ordered CDC not to release publicly. Still the CDC was operating at that time in the context of a Republican Administration.

The Connecticut authorities were Democrats. They were not prepared to learn anything from the Republicans. The Connecticut authorities told the operator of the patient home that his success was due to luck and his methods extreme. No effort was made by the Democrat public health officials of Connecticut to extend his methods to help control the virus.

In its turn the Republican Administration muffled the CDC on many things because of the attacks by the Democrats who made the virus a major plank against the Republicans in the 2020 election battle.

The Democrats did all they could do to sabotage the Republicans efforts to end the pandemic. They then declared that the Republicans' efforts had failed, and the Democrats had the media tell the public, "See, we told you they wouldn't work."

Meanwhile the Republicans did all they could to sabotage the shut-down policies of the Democrat-run states, and when the virus spread rapidly, the Republicans said, "See, we told you shut-downs didn't work."

When Democrats — now in the White House — began to consider if vaccine passports would contribute to containing the disease, now again expanding rapidly, the Republicans seized the opportunity to make political points. A Republican email sent widely read, "Vaccine passports now required in NYC. Democrats across the country are pushing to *cut unvaccinated Americans off from regular life* — and YOUR city could be next. State GOP need your response: Do you support authoritarian COVID mandates, or do you believe in individual responsibility?"

The CDC, the American public health agency, which both political parties should have supported wholeheartedly during the pandemic, was instead attacked by both. It is now charged in the media with having made serious errors in the conduct of the response to the pandemic. Yet vaccines were developed in record time, and the nation was so largely vaccinated by the summer of 2021 that the number of cases and deaths both were dramatically reduced. The renewed epidemic of summer 2021 was due entirely to the unwillingness of political officials to accept the agency's guidelines. The agency was not dysfunctional at all. But there was continual confusion during the period of the pandemic about public policy. This was fostered by the Democrats during the Trump presidency and by the Republicans during the Biden presidency — all for partisan political advantage.

Democrats blocked in mid-June 2021, a Congressional inquiry into the causes of COVID-19 saying that the inquiry would distract attention from their continuing criticism of Trump's mishandling of the pandemic when he had been president.

Partisanship in this instance causes the U.S. to shoot itself in the foot. Failing to identify cause may hinder avoidance in the future of another pandemic; it tells the world that U.S. leadership is uncertain and flawed by domestic political considerations.

Patriotism Has Given Way to Partisanship

Partisanship deprives the nation of good service. In the past, American presidents of either party often sought members of the other party to serve in their administrations. In line with this tradition a question was raised as Joe Biden prepared to assume the presidency. Should he invite any Republican, or for that matter, any non-Democrat to serve the nation, perhaps as a member of his Cabinet. Democrat commentator Jill Lawrence responded in print: "A Republican in Joe Biden's Cabinet? The president-elect should just say no. The doors may be closing on the chances of a Republican in President-elect Joe Biden's Cabinet and, honestly, so what? There's no good reason for him to name one, and lots of reasons to give this tradition a pass" (*USA Today*, December 31, 2020).

How Politics Became More Partisan

Changes in how both parties choose their candidates for public office have caused American politics to become more partisan.

In the U.S. both parties have lost control of their nomination processes for the presidency. Parties' rules allow almost anyone who desires to run for president. Choice among candidates is made by elections held by each party. Nowhere else in the democratic world do parties have so little say in who is nominated. The result in America is that party candidates are chosen by the relatively few party members who vote in primaries and they are usually the most committed and zealous and radical of the members of a party. In partisan politics people lose all sense of fairness and moderation. For example, most zealous Republicans can stand no criticism of the former Republican president, and most zealous Democrats can stand no criticism of President Biden.

The battle between Democrats and Republicans has become one for its own sake. Issues are not the source of party conflict, but rather it is the enjoyment of the fight. One is reminded of the street fighting in ancient Byzantium by gangs of "blues" and "greens" which began as supporters of different chariot racers and expanded over the years to be quasi-political bodies. In America the parties exist to do battle with each other, and the issues are whatever falls to hand.

Damage Done by Partisanship

Because of extreme partisanship American politics is not an effort to resolve problems and move on as democratic government should be. It is instead a fight between two parties, neither of which is attempting to solve a problem. American politics has become a tug-of-war between two extremes, and has lost sight of the national interest.

Ungovernable Due to Partisanship

By the time of the pandemic of 2020 the U.S. was almost ungovernable due to partisanship. The Congress wouldn't pass a timely rescue bill. The President wouldn't lead a general response — health and economics — but was pushed by partisanship into supply chain management for development of vaccines. Everything was delayed, debated, criticized, and undone. The one exception proved the rule generally — the Republican president was able to get vaccines developed in record time. The distribution of inoculations was delayed and made chaotic by partisanship.

Rather than participate constructively in governing the nation each party now denounces the state of the country and blames the other. Possibly the Republican president — who had been a Democrat before he ran for president as a Republican — started his administration in a different direction, expecting bipartisanship. But the Democrats refused to accept his outreach and soon he was as partisan as they.

Political partisanship is not limited to the legislatures, executive offices, and courts of America. It extends to the school systems. *The Chronicle of Higher Education* reported on May 11, 2021, that the President of the University of Colorado system of campuses was stepping down after only two years because the board of regents had gone from a Republican majority to a Democrat majority, and, in the words of *The Chronicle*, "a deep partisan division among the regents … may have hindered [his] capacity to lead."

The result of current-day partisan politics is that the nation is ungovernable in any rational sense. Partisan politics is a perpetual motion machine in which issues are endlessly fought over with little progress being made on them.

Trying to Serve America and Being Ground to Pieces between the Parties

It is likely that one or two Americans just wanted to serve the government when they first worked for President Obama and then for the Republicans in the same roles. But they were attacked vigorously and forced from office by Biden's Administration on largely invented charges for being disloyal to the Democrats. They are like the footballs in a game — kicked back and forth between the two teams. There was no America to serve — there was only either a Democrat America or a Republican America — nothing to which both parties were loyal. It was impossible to keep out of the partisan fight — there was no middle or neutral ground. That is what partisan politics had evolved to in the U.S. by 2020. Non-partisan public servants are now political footballs.

A non-partisan person — even an only mildly partisan person — cannot serve America today. Only bitterly fiercely partisan people inhabit high-level government and every decision is decided on partisan terms. There is no national interest — only a Democrat or a Republican interest. There is no United States in international affairs — only a Democrat U.S. or a Republican U.S. Biden reminded the world of this when he spoke on September 21, 2021, for the first time as president to the UN. He promised the international body that he would reverse everything his predecessor had done.

Republicans who criticized the former Republican president appear to be disloyal. They are criticized as out of touch with big issues — which demand purely partisan commitment — and outdated. Democrats who criticize Biden and the Democrat Congressional leadership are in the same position. It is still possible to have a contest over the leadership of each party, but the contest is held tightly within understood boundaries and has no role in public policymaking, which is a thoroughly partisan affair. Stalinists will have no difficulty recognizing the mindset.

Chapter 30

The Democrat Party and Democracy

President Biden insists that democracy is mankind's best form of government. Winston Churchill agreed, but on the basis that democracy was not so good as that the others were worse. American democracy today may be the best form of government in the world, but it has serious limitations. We will discuss democracy and its apparent decay in this chapter. Our only purpose is to identify elements for improvement.

In doing this we explicitly reject the advice of the ancient Israelites to the prophet Isaiah, a counsel we hear often from politically conscious Americans whose political party is in favor. Isaiah tells us that the ancient Israelites didn't want to hear counsels about shortcomings. "Give us no more visions of what is right! [Instead] Tell us pleasant things. Prophesy illusions!" (*Isaiah* 30:10).

Biden endorses democracy. What does he mean by that? The topic merits a book of its own. We will only give a brief overview of the controversy that illuminates the challenge facing our president.

All Americans would like their countrypersons to agree with them about the most basic issue — what is our desired form of government? But there is no such agreement today. It follows that for progressives, people who disagree with them about issues of policy — say how much spending the federal government should do this year — are opponents of American democracy itself.

The concern is echoed on the other side of the political spectrum. Progressives are believed by conservatives to be Marxists whose purpose is to alter what conservatives believe to be the essence of the American republic.

To both progressives and conservatives America now faces strong internal political movements that threaten to undermine it entirely. To both, perhaps most of the American electorate, American democracy is in full decay from inside.

American democracy has ceased to function well, as we have seen in previous chapters, or even acceptably. It is in decay. Before we turn to the details, let us recognize that there are examples in history of nations' decay to destruction.

We have already referred to the self-destructive partisanship that emerged late in the Byzantine Empire. It collapsed in 1453 under an assault by the Turks. Six thousand fighters defended the walls of the great city, Constantinople, then the strongest bastion in the world. Only another 20,000 defenders on the walls would have repelled the Turks and saved the city. Two hundred thousand more men cowered inside the city. None of them would come to the walls to fight — they were too afraid, too pleasure-loving, too effeminate. The city fell to the Turks and those cowering in the city were enslaved or massacred.

The most dramatic modern example involves France between the two world wars. In World War I France fought Germany to victory. It took four years. In World War II France collapsed before Germany in six weeks. This is what 20 years of leftist agitation will do to a country, a French political leader said. It is what American conservatives and populists believe the Democrats are doing to America.

Democracy has always meant the right of the people to do foolish things and to be self-destructive. Athens, the first great democracy, fought a war with Sparta, the dominant autocracy of the time, and lost. In addition to losing the war Athens lost its empire and its freedom. The French democracy lost its freedom to Nazi Germany and was restored to freedom by its allies. In fact, democracy in our era is largely an extension of Anglo-Saxon governance. It will not survive the extinction of Anglo-Saxon imperial ambition that is now underway in the political life of the United States and Britain.

Democracies tend to fall into corruption or ineffectiveness. Ineffectiveness is caused excessive political partisanship.

Republics do work but are today less preferred than democracies. Republics are surviving in today's world by rebranding themselves as democracies and operating more like them.

American Media and Democracy

American media are supposed to play an important role in the effective operation of American government. They are supposed to help voters understand public issues and follow developments.

Partisanship has overtaken this important public service and undermined it. American "news" networks and newspapers are not intended now to be educational (help Americans understand correctly); they are not even intended to be informative (provide news). They are intended to entertain and by entertaining an audience to gain advertisers who pay the network for advertising time and so make a profit for the network. Espousing the political point of view of a party or part of a party is entertainment (and party line guidance) for many Americans. The American media is now largely an expression of the views of the progressive wing of the Democrat Party. There is nothing in this system that contributes to the health of American democracy.

The effectiveness of journalist ethics in counterbalancing entertainment and partisanship and thereby providing some education and information disappeared decades ago. Journalists are only employees (or in Marxist jargon "running dogs of imperialism"), and they continually see their reporting distorted to serve the objective of economic gain or of political partisanship.

It was discovered by the media a few years ago that Americans liked their information dished out in partisan terms. In consequence, media outlets have identified with one or the other of the two parties and now serve as hardly more than propaganda organs for it. When a person stumbles onto an incident which he or she has seen described in American media, he or she is normally horrified at the spin that has been placed on the news — even to disinformation or as the Republican President described it, "fake news." In return, the Democrats generally describe the Republicans' pronouncements as lies.

It is not possible to press hyperbolic partisan criticism of an incumbent president without damaging the office of the president as well. The Democrats vilified Trump for several years, and now some Republicans vilify Biden. Both did great damage to the office of president in the process and thereby damaged the American government as well. Here is one example, a commentator on Fox News declared that Biden was himself the killer of a toddler who was trampled by the crowd outside the Kabul airport in the days of chaos that accompanied evacuations from

Afghanistan in August 2021. Of course, Biden was not in Kabul and did not himself trample on the child, however much he might be held to blame for the circumstances which led to the child's death.

The Democrat Party

President Biden is a Democrat. The Democrat Party controls both houses of the American Congress. This makes the Democrat Party the most important political party in American.

What is the Democrat Party? Strangely, it's not an easy question to answer. The Republicans are currently intent on describing it as a radical leftist party. But many of its major supporters describe it as a conservative party.

It is an establishment party in the U.S. Most convincing are data provided by the Conference Board, an American business organization, that polls top executives of American-based firms about their confidence in business conditions. This poll serves as a measure of big business support for whatever Administration is in power. During the recent Republican years, the measure of confidence sunk to historic lows. It has since recovered dramatically during the Biden presidency.

What does it mean to be an establishment party? It means support for the *status quo* in many ways including government policy and the choice of people to be appointed to high positions in government.

Where then is there evidence that the Democrats are not simply a conservative party? It comes from Democrat positions with respect to social issues. Business cares about business; it is largely uninterested in social issues and will support important changes if persuaded or pressured to do so. Lenin expressed this point very trenchantly when he said that the capitalists would sell him the rope with which he would hang them.

The Democrats have for decades presented themselves to the masses of the electorate as a liberal and reforming party. They have presented themselves to the business community which finances their campaigns as an establishment party — one which will not rock the business boat in any significant way. By abandoning the economic concerns of working people in favor of big business the Democrats moved away from a socialist orientation. By championing social reform the Democrats appealed to an emerging coalition of social activist groups which became identity groups. By endorsing the establishment and becoming part of it, the

Democrats alleviated concerns about radicalism. It has been a very successful merger of opposites — *status quo* and reform.

Democrats run their party on a quota basis for positions. White male, black male, white woman, black woman, gay, lesbian, trans-sexual, etc. They follow this practice with an endorsement of rationing and quotas among their constituent groups of benefits from the public largess.

Democrats have replaced merit (rational choice) with identity icons in staffing, and they are now conflating rationing to their constituencies with rational policymaking. This perverse logic infects foreign policy and defense as well.

Even the emergence of a more radical wing of the Democrat Party, the progressives, has not yet threatened the unique combination of political forces which are the modern Democrat Party. President Biden was elected by this Democrat combination of potentially warring elements. His challenge is to keep the Party arrangement intact — so that top Democrats can present themselves simultaneously as conservative and radical.

It is remarkable that in so complex and varied a political movement political party discipline could be as effective as it is in America's Democrat Party.

Chapter 31

The Partisan Battle

Pulling Business into Partisan Politics

Until 2020 big business in America had marginally supported Republican candidates over Democrats. Political support was primarily in the form of campaign contributions. In the 2020 presidential elections big business gave a little bit more to Republicans than to Democrats. By and large except for lobbying about their own companies' interests, business executives stayed out of American presidential politics.

This changed in 2020 and even more so in 2021. Initially in the spring of 2020 Republican fundraisers on the internet had grown so aggressive that they labeled people who didn't send them money and identify themselves as Republicans as their enemies. Their fundraising emails framed the recipient by name as a "Democrat." In essence, the Republicans were insisting that if a person were not one of them by giving money and by public identification as a Republican, then that person was a Democrat. There was no other choice. One could not be independent or neutral. There was no longer any middle ground. One had to be a Democrat or a Republican. Either a person was with them or against them. Partisanship was getting ever more demanding.

By the spring of 2021 Democrats had picked up the same theme. They identified their positions as fundamental values of the United States. They asserted that business executives had a duty to the nation to support Democrat positions. One could not be neutral. To be neutral was to acquiesce in the immoral actions of the Republicans, and to acquiesce was to be complicit. There was nowhere to hide — no place in American life outside the reach and demands of the political parties.

In this as in many other ways, the U.S. is becoming more like China. During Biden's presidency leaders of large corporations have been mobilized to support government policies in the mass media. It is likely that the CEOs of the largest American companies, which do business around the world, have noticed that in authoritarian China corporations are allowed to operate and their leadership and investors become very rich. Chinese executives support the dictatorship and it supports them. The Chinese state is the sole freehold property owner in China. CEOs are disposable leaseholders. If they do not support Xi Jinping, they cannot remain CEOs. That could also happen in a more authoritarian America. American executives seemingly realize that they might do very well working with a dominant American political party. They started to do that in the first months of the Biden Administration. In this way, American executives endorse the Chinese model and move in its direction.

All this time Biden is promoting in his speeches the old American democracy of freedom of speech and corporate independence of government.

Since Democrats and Republicans now each demanded total loyalty and recognize no independence of political position, a serious limitation by virtue of partisanship began to affect all leaders in business as well as public life. A partisan is forced to defend whatever their party or its officers do or say, no matter how foolish or extreme it may be. Nothing can be acknowledged to be an error. In the effort to defend indefensible things just because someone in your political party did it, a person ruins their credibility, making a fool of themselves, and over time destroys their own good judgment. A partisan becomes a sophist — able to defend anything, no matter how absurd.

The Attitudes of the American People

The American people are aware of how partisan the nation's political process has become. They don't like it. Many believe it is rigged. Some 70% of Americans seem to say, "Our political system seems to only be working for the insiders with money and power."

Americans cannot escape partisanship because the two parties now insist that every person must join one or the other — a person is an enemy if he or she doesn't join. Many Americans are taking refuge in one party or another. Polls increasingly show that Democrats and Republicans live in different worlds. Most Americans now inhabit partisan safe spaces, rarely interacting with people from the other political party. Americans tell each other that it is now impossible to discuss politics with another person of a different persuasion, and they don't do it. Friendships, even families, are breaking up over political differences. The parties, not the issues, have done this.

How Partisanship Works

When Democrats are in power, they try to loot the federal treasury for the benefit of their supporters. At that time, as now, Republicans criticize the Democrat's legislation for its narrow partisanship and propose instead policies directed at the welfare of Americans as a whole. When Republicans are in power, they try to loot the federal treasury for the benefit of their supporters. At that time Democrats criticize the Republican's legislation for its narrow partisanship and propose instead policies directed at the welfare of Americans as a whole. This is a standard dynamic of American politics. It is unfortunate for the country that neither party when in power pays attention to the needs of the nation though each has shown clearly many times when in political opposition that it understands the good of all the people. There was a time when America prided itself on being a can-do nation. Now it has a can't-do government which is much bigger in size and effective in nothing other than throwing money to party supporters.

The Texas Storm

In February 2021, Texas was hit by a very unusual winter storm. Days of strong winds, snow, and ice followed one another. The Texas electric grid failed, and some 4 million customers were without power for days. Eighty or so people died in the cold and dark. A key element of the electric power problem was that windmill powered generating stations which provided some 10% of the state's power froze and did not operate. Storms of this severity and length are unusual in Texas and the state was not prepared for it.

Immediately political controversy began over what was responsible for the chaos. While the storm was still raging Senator Schumer of

New York, leader of the Democrats in the Senate in Washington, told media that Texas was unprepared for the consequences of climate change (to which he attributed the storm) and that the citizens of Texas were paying the price and he hoped they would learn their lessons.

Senator Cruz of Texas responded that it was the state's effort to rely on renewable energy sources (windmills) that had caused the problem, and that Schumer was an advocate of such sources as a response to the challenge of climate change.

Nothing was achieved by this exchange except a further demonstration of the uselessness of partisan bickering to which the highest legislative body in America is fully addicted.

For example, Texas windmills froze. But there are windmills in many northern states which experience severe weather regularly like that which is unusual in Texas. Do those windmills freeze? Since the power grids do not collapse regularly in the north, but do use some wind-generated power, how is that achieved? These are the sorts of questions which could enlighten Americans to the meaning of the Texas experience, but partisan politics takes precedence and immediately undercuts efforts to identify and solve a problem.

Republicans felt they had to defend the way the Republican leadership in Texas had handled the big storm in February 2021 when the electric power and the drinking water both went out. At that time people who had lived in Houston for many decades said the storm's consequences had been the worst days of their lives.

Democrats felt they had to defend the Biden Administration's opening of the nation's southern border to immigrants who were illegal under American law and brought with them COVID and criminal activity.

This is the worst position to be in — having to defend what should objectively be indefensible positions just because the leaders of one's political party have put us there. All objectivity is lost. And it is the position adopted by millions of the most politically active people on both sides in America today.

Different Attitudes Toward the World

American partisanship is more than merely a division into competing groups, like the blues and greens of Constantinople during the Byzantine Empire. American partisanship is even more than a left-versus-right political division. American partisanship rests on two segments of the population which have different zeitgeists. There are two segments which see the world so differently that they spend mental effort trying to figure each other out. For example, on March 8, 2021, in the *Harvard Gazette*, a university newsletter, a Harvard professor and a think-tank scholar are cited as having studied conservative Americans and as having answers to the question raised by the newsletter's author, Paul Massari: "Stunned by the Republicans 74 million votes?" The professor and her collaborators, Theda Skocpol and Vanessa Williamson, are cited as answering the challenge to understanding for Democrats presented by the Republicans' vote:

"Over 70 million Americans cast a ballot for President Donald Trump on November 3. Despite losing the election, Trump collected more votes than any sitting president in U.S. history — and more than he had collected for his surprising win in 2016. Democrats and many "Never Trump" Republicans were stunned by the support for Trump in a year when a global pandemic claimed the lives of nearly a quarter of a million Americans and left millions unemployed and facing economic hardship."

In essence these commentators cited by Harvard were asking, "How could more than 70 million American voters be so unlike us? How could they vote for the Republican when we found him anathema and thought only a small group of Americans who were his hard-core supporters — described by the group of whom these writers were members as racist, deplorable, ignorant, stupid and uneducated — would vote for him? But the result was very different. Who were these people who voted for the Republican? How could they be so different in their attitudes than we are?"

The Harvard article spoke to and for people who dominate the politics of the mid-Atlantic and the New England states, and who are very different not just in opinions but in almost all beliefs and attitudes from those who voted for the Republicans.

It is interesting that the people the *Harvard Gazette* spotlighted for their insight into Republican voters did not ask what might be mistaken about their own Democrat attitudes? The only question addressed was what is wrong with the Republicans? Probably, the Republicans supporters are asking the same question about them: What in the world caused some 81 million Americans to vote for Biden? What is wrong with them?

In these probing questions about political opponents lies evidence of the very deep division in American society that expresses itself in political division.

It is possible to view these deep divisions in America as evidence of regional differences. Specifically, the northeast and the west coast are Democrat; the south and the mountain states are Republican. The upper Midwest is divided and provides most of the "swing states" — the political battlegrounds between the two parties which determine who controls the presidency. In 2020, those states were counted to the Democrats and so Biden won the election.

American Presidents in this Bitterly Partisan Era

American presidents today are chosen to serve a party function — to lead a party in its division of political spoils and its effort to extend its control of government. They have no other purpose, and so they act. But they know they should have a wider role — one that pursues the advantage of the nation and so they proclaim continually that they do that.

It is interesting that a popular American television series about the presidency, "THE DESIGNATED SURVIVOR," recognized this problem and decided to avoid it. In the story, American government leadership is wiped out by a terrorist attack. The person chosen to serve as president is not a member of either political party. He is an independent. The TV show then modeled how a president should act. Because he was an independent and had no political party responsibilities, the TV show never portrayed him doing something Biden spends most of his time and effort doing — advancing as best he can the interests of the Democratic Party. For example, the passage of the stimulus spending bill in the early weeks of the Biden Administration on a party-line vote had not only the advantage of providing the Democrats with large-scale spending on projects dear to the hearts of the leaders of their party but also preventing their opponents from claiming any credit for elements of the spending package which were of general popularity. Party discipline was not only necessary to pass the bill but it was also a way to enhance the appeal of the party to the electorate as a whole. It was less a matter of policy than a matter of partisan appeal. This is what an American president now focuses attention on, and it was excluded from the television attempt to portray an effective president.

Yet the television program was useful. It portrayed the good that a president could do if he or she was liberated from the domination of party partisanship.

A new proposal named Unity2020, recently outlined by former biology professor Bret Weinstein on the Joe Rogan Experience, calls for a new format of federal governance that aims to replace cynicism and partisanship with compromise and cooperation. The American public would draft two candidates to lead the executive branch. Here's how it would work according to a Medium article: "We the people draft two candidates: one from the center-left, one from the center-right. Once elected, they agree to govern as a team. All decisions and appointments will be made jointly in the interests of the American public. Only when they cannot reach agreement, or when a decision does not allow for consultation, does the President decide independently. A coin flip determines which candidate runs at the top of the ticket." The candidates must be patriotic, highly capable, and courageous, though it is unclear who would be judging based on that criterion.

Chapter 32

The Critical Fight over Election Practices

The ongoing battle over attempts to change voting regulations in the states is the single most significant partisan political contest now underway in America. On its outcome turns the likely result of the congressional elections in 2022 and the presidential/congressional election in 2024.

Democrats now insist that it is a fundamental principle of democracy that all should vote. Any attempt to limit those who vote is said to be voter suppression. Suppression is said to be a crime against democracy.

There is little support for this view in the history of republics and democracies. According to de Tocqueville allowing the least informed and those too lazy to work to vote will result in the demise of the nation. They will, as de Tocqueville wrote, "vote their own largess." During the pandemic Americans began to do just that — vote themselves checks from the national treasury. Politicians began to bid for their support. In December 2020, Biden offered 1,600 dollars per person; the Republican President countered with 2,000 dollars. But Senator Mitch McConnell, Republican leader in the Senate, offered only 600 dollars prompting the Republican President to denounce him as "Stupid!" Biden won the contest. The Coronavirus stimulus bill which the Democrats enacted immediately after Biden took office paid most Americans 1,600 dollars a person. De Tocqueville had been right.

Thomas Jefferson said, "a well-informed electorate" is necessary to ensure the Republic. This is one of the several reasons progressives wish to cancel him. Progressives demand the vote for the least informed of all and most easily manipulated.

The battle over voting regulations is a result of the election in 2020. Republicans believed that the Democrats had manipulated voting to gain their victory. Democrats called this the "big lie," and denied any significant vote manipulation. Democrats insist that there has been no evidence showing voter fraud in the United States on a large scale. Republicans insist that Democrats have stolen elections for decades at the local level and now have extended their practices to the national level.

In the 30 or so states with Republican-controlled legislatures Republicans are in process of passing laws that attempt to restrict voting to registered voters and to one vote per person. This is labeled voter suppression by the Democrats.

The first of the Republican-sponsored voting reform bills was passed in Georgia and was denounced bitterly by Democrats. As described by a progressive Democrat publication, "The Georgia law had 'eight key provisions that Heritage recommended,' Jessica Anderson, the executive director of Heritage Action for America, a sister organization of the Heritage Foundation, told the foundation's donors at an April 22 gathering in Tucson, in a recording obtained by a watchdog group documented and shared with *Mother Jones*. Those included policies severely restricting mail ballot drop boxes, preventing election officials from sending absentee ballot request forms to voters, making it easier for partisan workers to monitor the polls, preventing the collection of mail ballots, and restricting the ability of counties to accept donations from nonprofit groups seeking to aid in election administration" ("Leaked Video: Dark Money Group Brags About Writing GOP Voter Suppression Bills Across the Country," *Mother Jones*, Politics, May 13, 2021).

Democrats have responded with legislation in watchdog Congress which would require all states to eschew requirements for voter identification and would permit mail-in-voting on a largely unregulated basis.

Republicans charge that the Biden-sponsored election reform bills, HR 1 and Senate 1, are intended to leave elections open to fraudulent manipulation. When challenged about this the Democrats respond that people won't defraud the system. Republicans answer that they did so in a big way in the 2020 election, and that progressives explicitly say the end justifies the means. With this morality, Republicans ask, how can progressive Democrats be trusted not to defraud election systems? Democrats insist that there is no evidence in American history of fraud that changed a presidential election. Republicans answer that it is widely acknowledged that Jack Kennedy's father bought a primary election for him in West Virginia in 1960 helping him to gain the Democrat nomination for president and that fraudulent votes in Chicago gained JFK the presidency later that same year. These are the most dramatic and accepted evidence of decisive voting fraud in presidential elections.

Biden's Administration has taken a leading role in Democrat efforts to alter the voting process nationally. Simultaneously, the Republicans are leading an effort to do the same at the state level. Since the Democrats were in control of Congress and the presidency, their efforts were made at the national level. Since the Republicans controlled the majority of state legislatures, their efforts were made at the state level.

The Democrats passed a bill which placed uniform electoral process requirements on all the states. Until now, elections were run at the state level. In the 2020 election some states had altered their processes without changing their laws and were arguably in violation of their own laws. Those states saw victories go to the Democrats in the presidential contest. Texas led a group of states in which the Republicans had been successful to challenge election practices in states in which the Republican president had lost. Those states appealed to the Supreme Court to hear their objections to what had happened in the other states. The Court refused to hear their objections. The actions taken in states in which Biden had won the election were allowed to stand.

Once Biden was in office, the Democrats sought by their proposed legislation to extend to all the states the devices by which they had won the 2020 presidential election. The bill became HR1 (House of Representatives 1) and S1 (Senate 1). It passed the House without Republican support but could not pass the Senate. The Republican objections were two: that the bill turned the state-by-state conduct of elections into a national system by imposing similar procedures on every state; and that the bill imposed processes which invited large-scale fraud in the conduct of elections.

The Democrats described the purpose of their bill as being to increase the suffrage. They described the purpose of the Republican bills as being to limit the suffrage. The Democrats said they wanted to increase the number of voters. The Republicans said they wished to ensure that only eligible voters participated in elections. Democrats damned the Republicans for trying to suppress the electorate. Republicans damned the Democrats for trying to corrupt the election process.

The battle over election procedure changes is a central struggle in the politics of the first years of the Biden Administration. Biden supports S1 strongly. The Republicans fear that if it becomes law, they will never again win a presidential election and will lose control of the Congress indefinitely.

Under the rules of the Senate 60 votes are required to pass S1. The Democrats have only 50 votes and so need Republican support to pass the bill. They are unable to get any Republican support for the bill and so cannot pass it unless the rules are changed. But this would alter dramatically the way the Senate functions.

The Democrats began to talk openly about changing the rules of the Senate to make S1 possible of passage. All that was needed were the votes of 50 Senators and the tie-breaking vote of the Vice President acting in her Constitutional role of President of the Senate. The Democrats had 50 votes in the Senate. But then two Democrat Senators balked at changing the rules of the Senate. In particular, Senator Joe Manchin of West Virginia announced in an article he published in the *Wall Street Journal* in mid-April 2021, that he would not vote to change the rules of the Senate (the so-called "filibuster" rule).

Unable to pass their bill in Congress, the Democrats sued to block the Republican bills at the state level citing an alleged violation of the Voting Rights Act of the 1970s. In early summer, 2021, the Supreme Court upheld the Republican bill in Arizona, eliminating the Democrats chance to stop Republican voting rights modifications in most states.

The Democrats were thereby losing the major electoral contest and with it their likelihood of retaining political control in the future. They had to find a way to pass their election regulation bill. Desperation loomed.

But even if they did, the Republicans would challenge the bill in court and the Supreme Court, in its current composition might overturn the bill. The Court had opined in its Arizona decision that the states had Constitutional authority over voting processes.

So to be sure of passing their legislation, the Democrats needed to end the filibuster and alter the composition of the Supreme Court — pack the Court. Could they do both? Would they try?

This is a very serious situation for the Democrats. If S1 cannot be passed, then the Republicans would be free to modify election rules in the majority of states. The Democrats will be put at a serious disadvantage in the 2022 and 2024 elections.

With Senator Manchin's announcement Democrats had to find some other way to hold on to their favorable position in the nation's voting procedures. Could Manchin be successfully pressured to change his position? Could the elections themselves be postponed or canceled?

The matter is that crucial. It is at the core of the partisan battle in the United States. Republicans view the efforts of the Democrats to enact S1 into law as evidence that we are living in evil times. They fear that the Democrats won't wake up until they force Republicans into such a corner that Republicans have no resort except to violence. A civil war would result. The matter is that critical.

This is a partisan controversy. The concern of each party for election reform — of Democrats to increase the number of voters, and of Republicans to be sure that voters are properly identified and limited — is not for improvement of democratic governance but instead in the case of each party for partisan electoral advantage.

Chapter 33

African Americans' Role in American Politics

Next in importance to the role of voting regulations in American politics is the role of African Americans in the disputes between the parties.

It is normally a surprise to non-Americans that African Americans are so small a proportion of the nation's population. American sports, entertainment, advertising and media discussion all suggest a much higher figure.

To an outside observer it may appear that in the United States a demographic minority, comprising about 18% of the total population are like the tail that wags the national dog. The black share of the population is officially given at 13.4%. But the 2020 census shows that roughly 4% of the Hispanic and Latino population of the United States is black. Combined, as they should be for this discussion, the African America population is near 18%.

Political spokespersons for the African American community appear to be disproportionately influential. In the last 20 years African Americans have had two presidential terms — those of Barak Obama. Now they hold the vice presidency, and their concerns appear to dominate national political discussion.

African Americans are predominately attached to the Democrat Party. Continual reference by Democrat leaders, office holders and candidates to African American grievances have made their circumstances a major partisan political issue.

In modern times the world has seen other countries in which demographic minorities have held political power for long periods of time. Those situations have all ended in political turmoil. For example, in South Africa where majority blacks overthrew a white minority government; in Iraq, where for a while Sunnis overthrew a Shia minority government leading to intervention by a foreign power (Iran) to restore the minority government; and in Rwanda, where a bloody civil war associated with genocide overthrew a minority (Tutsi) government.

In all cases minority government is associated with special benefits for the minority, and this has been developing for decades in America. It is widely argued and accepted, of course, that these benefits are justified by events in the past, even the recent past. A history of slavery in the United States that ended about 165 years ago and a history of racial discrimination since are cited to justify special benefits sponsored by government for African Americans. Whether or not a political backlash is developing against minority political influence in America is uncertain, in large part because the media reports on it only to denounce it and so its true character and dimensions are difficult to assess. But minority political influence is a continuing source of potential controversy and even conflict in the United States.

Many African Americans have prospered in American society. Many figures in the entertainment and sports worlds have become rich. Some African Americans have been very successful in business, and a few have made it to the top of the largest American firms.

From another perspective a large mass of African Americans remains segregated in inner city communities, poorly educated, low-skilled and inhabiting a violent subculture of drugs, gangs, and crime. In recent decades liberals have persuaded much of the country to view these people as victimized by the broader American body politic. Liberals promised to rescue these people by elevating their performance through public programs centering on education. With the apparent failure of these programs after decades of effort and hundreds of billions of dollars in spending, progressives are seeking to enhance the position of African Americans by leveling other people down.

If discrimination against people of color is pervasive in the United States, as liberals and progressives insist it is, then there might be expected to be some discussion of its foundations. For example, it might be asserted that discrimination does not reflect race as much as attitude, dialect, appearance (threatening, obesity) and manners. The refusal of some to assimilate their subculture, so they are not accepted to the mainstream. The core of this observation is that attitude, dialect, appearance and manners (or lack thereof) are not integral to the race. This is made obvious by contrasting the American subculture with the cultures of Africa today. There is no such public discussion. The pressure of progressives for political correctness prevents it. The cause of discrimination in America is assumed in public discussion to be race and race alone.

The significant role of African Americans in U.S. politics may be largely illusory. It is not usually African Americans who exercise power on behalf of themselves, but rather white liberals and progressives who purport to act for the benefit of African Americans. There are now strident voices that accuse Democrats of using African Americans as cover for their own agendas. The danger to the African American community is that the progressive grasp for power may generate push-back not against the progressives but against African Americans. Should this happen, the Democrats likely will deny all fault and continue behaving as expediency dictates.

Preferences for African Americans in Democrat policies is offering opportunistic propaganda advantages for American rivals abroad. The Russians, for example, denounce American racism which is said to be directed against whites. Russians further denounce Democrat favoritism that accompanies their alleged anti-white racism: "[It's important] not to switch to the other extreme which we saw during the 'BLM' (Black Lives Matter) events and the aggression against white people, white U.S. citizens," the Russian foreign minister said in early April. Lavrov also attacked political correctness and the American empire's "cultural revolution" that's causing world-wide shifts in attitudes on homosexuality, gay marriage, transgenderism, and other so-called "human rights." These are not shifts that Russia or its allies (China, Iran, and North Korea) favor. It indicates that there is more to the quasi-ideological struggle now occurring in the world than the contest between democracy and autocracy alone. There is a social contest accompanying the governance one.

It is commonly said that in a few years the United States will become a multi-racial society in which whites will be less than 50% of the population, rather than its majority as now. The implication is that African Americans will then be the dominant group in America. These demographic shifts are suggested to justify preferences for African Americans now.

This prediction depends on classifying Hispanics and Latinos — the fastest growing ethnic groups in America — as non-white. Most Hispanics and Latinos are not non-white; some are. Most Hispanics and Latinos are of European descent or mixed native American and European descent and consider themselves white. They are not a different race than American whites in their own eyes. Their rapid growth is explained by legal and illegal immigration, not natural increase.

The American census asks people for race and for ethnicity. Hispanics and Latinos made up about 18% of the American population in 2020. About 4% of them were of African descent. About 14% were of white descent. Ignoring Hispanics and Latinos, about 58% of the American population were white in 2020. Including Hispanics and Latinos about 72% were white. Including Hispanics and Latinos about 18% of the American population were African descent in 2020. Asians, who were the fastest growing component of America's population in 2020 made up almost five and a half of the population.

Political pundits make much of these demographics. Because the white population has been shrinking as a portion of the whole, progressives exaggerate the rate of change and look to a near future in which whites become a minority. Democratic Senator Dick Durbin in mid-July 2021, boasted that "the demographics of America are not on the side of the Republican Party" and predicted that an ongoing influx of "new voters" will ensure the GOP is doomed. "The new voters in this country are moving away from them, away from Donald Trump, away from their party creed that they preach," Durbin told the country.

America will be a multi-racial society in the future. Most Hispanics and Latinos are part of the white majority. African Americans and Asian Americans will be important elements of our society. They will not be a majority in the foreseeable future.

The progressive argument for special treatment for African Americans is rooted in an historical narrative. So far as it goes, it is accurate, but it leaves out much context; ignores relevant similarities in the experience of other demographic groups and ignores opportunities that have not been seized. It is a narrative intended to create a victim status for a demographic group as if other demographic groups had no analogous, if not identical, experiences. For example, Jews have suffered not slavery, but worse — large-scale extermination — yet have prospered as a group in the U.S.

There is a major difference. African Americans were enslaved in what is now the United States for centuries. "The wealth gap between

Black and white Americans has been persistent and extreme. It represents, scholars say, the accumulated effects of four centuries of institutional and systemic racism and bears major responsibility for disparities in income, health, education, and opportunity that continue to this day. Consider that right now the net wealth of a typical black family in America is around one-tenth that of a white family. A 2018 analysis of U.S. incomes and wealth written by economists Moritz Kuhn, Moritz Schularick, and Ulrike I. Steins and published by the Federal Reserve Bank of Minneapolis concluded, 'The historical data also reveal that no progress has been made in reducing income and wealth inequalities between black and white households over the past 70 years.' It's no surprise. After the end of slavery and the failed Reconstruction, Jim Crow laws, which existed till the late 1960s, virtually ensured that Black Americans in the South would not be able to accumulate or to pass on wealth. And through the Great Migration and after, African Americans faced employment, housing, and educational discrimination across the country. After World War II many white veterans were able to take advantage of programs like the GI Bill to buy homes — the largest asset held by most American families — with low-interest loans, but lenders often unfairly turned down Black applicants, shutting those vets out of the benefit. (As of the end of 2020 the homeownership rate for black families stood at about 44 percent, compared with 75 percent for white families, according to the Census Bureau.) Redlining — typically the systemic denial of loans or insurance in predominantly minority areas — held down property values and hampered African American families' ability to live where they chose" (Liz Mineo, "Racial Wealth Gap May be a Key to Other Inequities," *Harvard Gazette*, June 3, 2021).

Chapter 34

Coup and Coup Again

Partisan conflict in America has reached high levels that are not widely recognized. In fact, when they are mentioned, almost everyone dismisses the mention contemptuously as conspiracy theory. That response is likely to what is told in this chapter. Only the details of what is in this chapter can be confirmed. The overall picture of what the details mean cannot be confirmed. It is important to be aware of these matters, nonetheless, since they likely point to what may happen in the future.

This could be a long chapter. It is instead a short chapter. The material in it is very controversial in America. Almost every sentence in this chapter will be denounced as unproven — "without evidence" is the current American term of dismissal. I (Mills) lived through these events and watched them with an experienced eye and non-partisan objectivity. The narrative below is both accurate to the best of my knowledge and is very useful to understanding the background of Joe Biden's presidency and the factors that limit his freedom of action.

A most important lesson from the information which follows is that both American political parties no longer reject force as a method of gaining control of the White House. Both parties have attempted to use it. The use of force to expel an elected president is known as a coup. Yet neither Democrats nor Republicans think of their efforts to use force for such a purpose as a coup.

Both think of their efforts as legitimate attempts to avoid a disaster for the country — the other political party gaining the presidency.

Both attempts failed, primarily because of the deployment of military force by their opponents. In the events of 2017, at the Republican

President's inauguration, force repelled force. In the events of 2021, Biden's inauguration, force was one prong of a multi-prong effort that never got off the ground.

America prides itself on the peaceful transference of power from one president to the next. But lately peaceful transference has not occurred without efforts to employ force to prevent peaceful transference. The efforts were made first by the Democratic Party and later by the Republican Party. This is new in American history.

The Democrats Make an Effort

The first major effort of one political party to dislodge the other from the presidency by using force was conducted by the Democrats on the day of the Republican President's inauguration. On that day the Democrats tried a coup which failed. It was composed of the same sorts of elements that are used abroad in political coups.

A plan had been concocted to disrupt the inauguration thoroughly and in the chaos that followed, permit President Obama to remain in office. The core of the plan was to have masses of people converge on the Capitol on inauguration day and flood the grounds. On the days of Barak Obama's two inaugurations masses of people who lived in the District of Columbia came the short distance to the Capitol and poured through the security booths onto the grounds of the Capitol. They were well-behaved, celebrating Obama's election, and nothing untoward happened of significance. The plan for the day of the Republican President's inauguration was that similar masses of people would converge on the Capitol. They would not be celebrating. They would be angry and destructive. They would push through the security booths as they had years before. They would swarm over the Capitol grounds so that police security would be swamped. They would enter the Capitol and prevent the inauguration. The mass demonstration would show the nation that Trump was not acceptable to the American people — that he could not govern. In the chaos which followed, President Obama would remain in office while the future of the presidency was worked out.

Mobs of Democrats would be called to the Capitol on the morning of inauguration day by radio broadcasts. The signals would be that the broadcasters would say that mobs were predicted at the Capitol.

On Inauguration Day the plan began. The broadcasts were made. The crowds began to gather. But unexpectedly, there was deployed around the Capitol a major military presence. Tanks stood at the intersections. Violent actions by small groups of protestors were visible in the streets leading to the Capitol but were extinguished quickly by police. The first people arriving of the vast crowds that were expected looked at the tanks and personnel carriers and the many troops, and they turned around and left. They told those who were following them about the military' presence and they also turned away. The result was a smaller crowd than was expected, almost all from outside the District of Columbia, and there was no disruption of the ceremony of any significance.

When President Obama and his top aides saw that the plan had failed, one top aide was dispatched to the White House. In her office she hurried to accomplish her errand before the newly inaugurated president arrived. When he arrived, she would no longer be permitted to be in the White House. She drafted a memo to her files explaining that President Obama had instructed his aides to "do everything by the book" in introducing the president-elect to his presidency. "By the book" of course excluded a coup. The message was soon given to the national media and broadcast widely and to general support.

By this and other actions the plot was covered up and has never been revealed to the nation.

The Democrats were unpracticed in the art of the political coup. Their effort was so clumsy that it could be successfully hidden, as if it never occurred. But it did occur, and for the four years of the Republican presidency the Democrats managed to keep it a secret but pursue its objective — to keep the Republicans from successfully using power — in more conventional ways. Their efforts succeeded in 2020 when they denied the Republican president a second term.

The Republicans Make a Try

The most recent use of force to try to prevent a transference of power occurred on January 6, 2021. On that date a mob broke into the Capitol building and terrorized it for several hours.

The Democrats were genuinely shocked by the invasion of the Capitol. "We could all have been killed," Democrats complained during the Republican president's second impeachment trial. And indeed, they could have been killed, had the rioters had that intention, which they did not.

The Democrats were concerned that another mob might invade the Capitol that did intend them harm. After all, the favorability rating in the national polls of the Congress is about 13%, and the larger part of the population despises the Congress.

Mrs. Pelosi, Speaker of the House and the person in charge of the Capitol, has since had it surrounded by high fences capped with razor wire. She has tens of thousands of troops guarding the capitol. The American Capitol now resembles a fortified military camp.

What is the background to this change in the American Capitol from the open symbol of a great democracy to a fortified camp in which frightened legislators conduct their business? We tell a story here that is not told elsewhere.

When the Democrats were announced to have won the 2020 presidential election, the Republicans began to prepare their own effort to prevent the Democrat candidate from taking office. It was to come to a head on January 6, 2021, the day that the Congress certified the election results. It had several parts, all of which were to be coordinated to occur on that day. The several parts were to unite to prevent Joe Biden from taking office.

The Republican President gave publicity to the assertion that Biden had not really won the election — that it had been stolen and therefore Biden's election should not be certified by the Congress.

The incumbent President asked the governors and the legislatures in the five swing states, many of which were controlled by Republicans at the level of the state government, to re-count the votes and refuse to certify Biden's election.

Legal challenges were brought in the courts to cancel Biden's victory by setting aside Democrat electors in several states.

A hoped-for strong victory in two Senate runoff races in Georgia on January 5, 2021, was to demonstrate the Republican President's popularity with the voters. This would show that if the Democrats hadn't stolen the election, the Republican President would have won.

A mass crowd was invited to come to Washington D.C. to support the Republican President on January 6, 2021.

Republican Senators and Representatives were to challenge the delegations from several states who were certified for Biden when the Congress convened on January 6 to certify the election results.

The Vice President (Pence) who presided over the joint session of Congress that day was to reject the delegations of several states. Without the electors from those states Biden would not have 270 electoral votes (a majority) and could not be certified as elected president.

If all this occurred, Biden could not take office, but what would happen next was unclear.

Much of the plan went ahead. About 40% of Americans told pollsters they believed the Democrats had stolen the election.

Court challenges were filed.

Republican Senators and Representatives challenged the delegations of several states in the joint session of Congress on January 6.

A crowd gathered in D.C. and the Republican President harangued them.

But several elements failed. The Supreme Court rejected the petitions filed by the Republicans challenging Biden's victory.

The Democrats won the Senate run-offs in Georgia.

The Vice President refused to reject the delegations of the several key states.

On January 6, elements of the plan occurred but others did not. Only the mass demonstration occurred, and it got out of hand at the Capitol. While it was in progress the President, still in office, demanded that Republican leaders in Congress fulfill their part of the plan by opposing the certification of Biden's election victory. They refused.

The effort to block Biden's accession to the presidency failed.

The Consequence of the Failed Coup Attempts

Americans — Democrats in 2016 and Republicans in 2021 — could plan coups but they could not carry out all the complex elements and coordination necessary to make them successful. American politicians don't know how to organize and carry-out coups. The big difference between the American attempts at coups and those abroad which succeed is the role of the military. Abroad, the military almost always plays a key role in coups. The military often stages them. In the U.S. the military in both the instances described here caused the coup efforts to fail. The Americans use of force was limited to mobs — demonstrations were the force employed. This is not enough. The role of the military is key — there must be military support for the coup attempt. Presumably American politicians have learned this from their failed experience and the next efforts will seek to involve the military. This will have a very peculiar form in America since the United States has no central military command structure. Under the Goldwater–Nichols Act of 1986 the United States has a dozen or so independent commands each reporting directly to the President through the Secretary of Defense.

Goldwater–Nichols seem to have presumed that the Secretary of Defense will be a civilian, and ordinarily he or she is. The purpose of the Goldwater–Nichols Act was to strengthen civilian control of the military by eliminating any top military command and having the combat commands report directly to civilians. Biden has changed that by appointing a general to be Secretary of Defense. So today the Goldwater–Nichols Act has been largely invalidated by Biden — the commanders of the combat commands report to a military person, who is not in an officially military position.

There were two failed coups accompanying the past two presidential elections. They have left little mark on American politics. Most people know nothing about them, and many who have heard of them dismiss what they heard as fiction — yet another conspiracy theory. But the efforts to mount coups did occur, and they were critical to the direction taken by the American republic. They may be repeated.

Had either coup succeeded it would have been at the cost of the essence of American democracy — the peaceful transference of power.

Part X

The Progressives

Chapter 35

The Challenge of Progressivism

Joe Biden has been a liberal all his political life. He has been a liberal and a Democrat — the two terms were almost synonymous for many years. But he is governing as a progressive. It would be a difficult challenge for him were he not, like so many professional politicians, adept at changing positions as politics requires.

Biden has his hands full trying to work with progressives. He sacrifices his liberal instincts to advocate their policies. They know that his liberalism and his liberal political allies are not their friends. No sooner had Biden entered the White House than in late-January 2021 there were riots by progressives in West Coast cities against the new Biden Administration.

The Biden Administration is composed of Democratic moderates, as he styles himself, and progressives who are radical reorganizers — not reformers — of American society. Moderates are reformers. The progressives are attempting to lead America into a system of radical statism. They are not socialists as their opponents like to charge. They do not place the working class at the center of their agenda. Instead, they are radical cultural revolutionary statists.

The basic approach of progressives is to identify a significant national "social justice" problem and to offer impractical but idealistic solutions which they then champion as practical. Gun violence is an example. Climate change is another. This is a very difficult approach for Biden to resist.

To protect his political flank from the progressive attack Biden is leading America in the direction that the progressives advocate. It is the agenda of the Black Lives Matter movement — a combination of pseudo-Marxism and radical statism. It has gained wide support. All over America one passes homes of people of almost all economic classes which have signs in front which proclaim, "Black Lives Matter." This is the cutting edge of the progressive movement.

It is very important not to underestimate the vigor of the progressive movement. Liberals — or "moderates" as President Biden now prefers to label himself — outnumber progressives. Liberals are disheartened and have failed at altering American society dramatically by reform. In contrast, progressives are excited and energetic and confident. Biden has no choice but to lean the progressives' way if he is to lead the Democrat Party successfully.

Although progressives reject religion in all its forms, their movement has the flavor of a religious awakening. Jeffrey Sonnenfeld mobilized corporate support behind the Democrat effort to block state-level, Republican-sponsored election laws in 2021 which Democrats saw as a form of voter suppression (we have discussed this in a previous chapter). Sonnenfeld, a dean at Yale's School of Management, is the most knowledgeable academic in America about the American big business community. In an article published on April 15, 2021, in the *Wall Street Journal*, Sonnenfeld referred directly to the religious fervor — zealotry — of progressivism: "American religious history produced four Great Awakenings — and now American business is sparking a fifth spiritual awakening." This sentence has the flavor of religious conviction which drove the abolition movement about 155 years ago.

The Failure of Liberalism

Contemporary progressivism has Marxist roots. It is the antithesis of Golden Age American progressivism (1870-1940) epitomized by Theodore and Franklin Roosevelt. Both called themselves progressives, but were Biden reformist liberals in contemporary parlance. The Roosevelts spoke for ordinary people, workers and the nation. They did not pit races, ethnicities and genders against one another. Today's progressives are against ordinary people, workers and the nation and for special interest street justice agendas. Their program is a complex blending of class struggle, Leninist, WWI radical syndicalism, iconoclastic feminism, anti-slavery, internationalism, anti-war and civil rights activism, extreme environmentalism, and neo-Marxist ideological commitments. It has grown to great influence in America out of liberal fatigue. A sequence of liberal presidents and their trade-mark programs had led America. Jack Kennedy's New Frontier, Lyndon Johnson's Great Society, Jimmy Carter's effort at a European style social democracy which he called "The National Accord," Bill Clinton's hopefulness which substituted for any ideological conviction, and most importantly Barak Obama's African American presidency, left America in the first quarter of the twenty-first century with increasing socio-economic distances among people, and poverty and racial animosity at greater levels than before. Liberalism had failed to keep its idealist promises. It still held a grip on the thinking of many Americans, but it had lost its appeal to many others. A more radical political approach emerged, and the name it has embraced is progressivism. The label is a misnomer. The left wing of the Democratic Party is anti-democratic. It is against ordinary people, workers and the nation and for its own tyrannical power. The faction is more accurately described as revolutionary progressive. Its strategy for seizing power mimics revolutionary Marxist-Leninism.

Liberalism's tepid performance caused it to erode as the central ideology of the Democrat Party. Liberalism has declined because of its failure to deliver on many promises made to the electorate, and because an alternative political orientation has emerged. The alternative addresses the same issues with the same promises of progress as does liberalism but offers a different diagnosis of the origin of the problems and a very different prescription for their solution. The alternative is revolutionary progressivism.

The Appeal of Progressivism

Revolutionary progressivism espouses noble goals. This is the essence of its appeal to most people. It promises:

An end to racial distinctions, discrimination and racism.
Restorative justice.
An improved life for women.
A better life for the poor.
Inclusion fully in society for gays, trans-people, and other groups.
Fair treatment for immigrants and inclusion in American society.
A less unequal distribution of wealth and income.

Equity for all.
A major improvement of the natural environment.
Progress against climate change.
Peace in the world.

Revolutionary progressivism finds modern society to be woefully lacking in each of the areas above. It diagnoses the roots of each of these shortcomings and ascribes them to racism and colonialism. It holds white men responsible for racism and colonialism. It seeks to rectify centuries of mistreatment by white men via political actions in current times. It sees its goals as so important that they justify any means taken toward their accomplishment. Revolutionary progressives reject traditional personal morality as a white male pretension and advance instead a morality that is political in nature. That is, moral action means supporting the advancement of non-whites and women in all aspects of life.

For revolutionary progressives, politics takes precedence over all other aspects of life. A columnist for the *Los Angeles Times* in February 2021, reported that her neighbors had done a favor for her family. However, she wrote, her neighbors had voted for the Republican President's reelection. The columnist wrote that she owed them no thanks until they admitted that the Republican was awful and that they had made a mistake in voting for him. She could not accept an act of kindness from a neighbor until they had accepted her political views.

In traditional morality deception is normally not accepted. Ethicists write books condemning lying. But in progressive politics deception is a usual tactic because society is still dominated by white males. In order to be able to advance the progressive cause without getting identified and disrupted by a society dominated by white men, deception is necessary.

Sometimes the deception seems somewhat innocent. The people of the United States have become aware that the nation's physical infrastructure has deteriorated badly and needs repair and extension. In consequence, both political parties support major spending on infrastructure. The Biden Administration has proposed a large infrastructure spending bill.

Included in that bill due to progressive demands are many items that are not what is traditionally meant by the term "infrastructure." For example, paid leave for workers, childcare, and caregiving are all defined as infrastructure by progressives. In one perspective they are right. These items are the infrastructure — a social infrastructure — that support the ability of women who are caught in traditional roles as mothers and housekeepers to be able to join the workforce. From another perspective, these things are not highways, bridges, airports, ports, and the internet, which are the normal reference of the term "infrastructure." For progressives to label social welfare purposes as infrastructure is perceived as deception.

Thinking that their priorities should take precedence and that it is useful to define them in any way that might advance their funding is a characteristic of the tactics of revolutionary progressives.

Revolutionary progressives hold that their purposes justify any means they use to accomplish them. Yet they insist that they can be believed in whatever they say to the electorate. It is surprising how many Americans accept this sophistry. A friend asked me (Mills) about Mrs. Clinton, "do you think she would really lie to us?" The questioner was a Democrat, and like many of the rank and file, wanted to believe the best of his political leaders. He believed about them what he wished to believe. It is on naive popular confidence like this that a modern political party, which is exploiting propaganda techniques, counts on to make its appeal to the masses — no matter how disingenuous — believed.

Are Today's Revolutionary Progressives Socialists?

During the 2020 presidential campaign the Republicans continually referred to the Democrats as "socialists." The Republicans would add, "America will never be socialist!"

The Democrats now have control of the presidency and the Congress. Is American socialist? Are the Democrats socialists?

No, not as a political party. Is their revolutionary progressive wing socialist? It certainly speaks in terms that have a long history in Soviet and social democratic lingo in Europe.

But strictly speaking, the revolutionary progressive are not socialists. Socialists have a clearly thought-out ideology. American revolutionary progressives have lots of opinions but no ideology. Socialists focus on supporting the working class. Revolutionary progressives are leery of most workers, especially whites who they perceive to be anti-revolutionaries concerned primarily with their own material welfare.

Radicals claim that revolutionary progressive goals can be achieved best with (1) government "directed" markets, (2) stakeholder ownership and control, and (3) confiscatory egalitarian taxation. They contend that neither central planning and *laissez-faire* are necessary nor desirable. Some revolutionary progressives understand that notions they have pulled from socialism such as government-controlled markets, stakeholder ownership corporate management, and confiscatory taxation will impair economic efficiency, productivity and growth, but do not care because they insist that satisfying revolutionary progressive needs is the highest good.

Socialists are strongly pro-working class. Revolutionary progressives are not. Their commitments are to demographic and social groups — African Americans, Hispanics, and Latinos, women, gays, and others. The Democrat Party complains that it has lost the main body of the America working class to the Republicans.

Revolutionary progressives are single-cause leftists. They do endorse some socialist goals, and there are some nineteenth echoes in what they advocate. Revolutionary progressives at this point are primarily leftist social reformers rather than anarchist radicals.

Today's American progressives have little affinity to the progressive movement associated in the early years of the twentieth century with the Presidency of Theodore Roosevelt. Progressives then were religious, and their anti-capitalism was limited to Teddy Roosevelt-style "trust busting." That is, it was aimed at breaking up monopolies. Progressives then sought to reform the "system" rather than replace it. The "system" included abiding by democratic majority rule and protecting the rights of political (rather than demographic) minorities.

Socialists (democratic socialists, but not revolutionary Marxist-Leninists) then shared aspects of the progressive package, but not all. They paid no attention to temperance. More importantly, socialists, especially revolutionary Marxist–Leninists, sought to destroy the "system" (that is, religious tolerance, democratic majority rule, the rule of constitutional law and imperfectly competitive markets) insisting that the righteousness of the working-class cause compelled them to impose their will on others.

The situation today is more subtle.

Revolutionary Marxist–Leninist socialists remain hostile to religion (see, for example, *bezbozhniki*, the League of Militant Atheists) all markets, and democracy. They seek to overthrow the American political, economic, and social system, replacing it with a secular, planned society governed by a communist-like party.

Other socialists including non-revolutionary Marxist democratic socialists claiming to serve the proletariat have shifted their ground. They no longer insist on strict secularism, economic planning, and authoritarianism. They tolerate religion if it stays out of politics. They tolerate markets and social privilege (including labor exploitation) if socialist parties are in command. They tolerate democracy and the rule of law if they control them.

Bernie Sanders and Elizabeth Warren, two Senators who speak for today's revolutionary progressive Democrats, exemplify this strain of non-Leninist pink socialist principle to such a degree that they no longer focus their concern on the working class. They are best understood as Nordic-style corporatists willing to use democratic capitalist institutions to improve the people's lot without prioritizing the proletariat (wage labor).

Golden age progressive reformers have never had any qualms about using democratic capitalist tools, but today's cohort is more amenable to bending the rules of civilized democratic process. They have moved toward the revolutionary Marxist–Leninist position on religion, markets, and democracy, but continue to pay only lip service to the working class. They prioritize diverse radical causes over labor, and do not hesitate to harm workers (for example, advocating open immigration) in achieving their ends. This explains why they are competitors of revolutionary Marxist–Leninists and democratic socialists, even though many are intensely hostile to capitalism — for example, see the speeches of Democrat Representative Alexandra Ocasio Cortez (AOC) from New York.

The Democratic Party's policies today are anti-worker and anti-socialist, despite its pro-revolutionary progressive, anti-religious, anti-market, and authoritarian proclivities. Revolutionary progressives are mostly anti-socialists, nonetheless they loudly proclaim and endorse cultural Marxism.

Republicans proclaimed repeatedly during the 2020 election campaign that "America will never be socialist!" They thought they were stating a fact. It appears though that they were only making a political appeal. The revolutionary progressives are not socialist in doctrine, but they are Leninist in methods (Leninism is Marx's late insurrectionism of the early 1870s), and America seems to be headed that way. The American electorate has empowered revolutionary progressives, though it did not know that at the time. The electorate thought they were voting for a moderate as Biden styled himself. But Biden has turned out to be a facilitator for the revolutionary progressives' radical agenda.

Americans have been conditioned to believe that "it cannot happen here."

It should not be happening here.

But it seems to be here, is embedded and metastasizing.

Revolutionary progressives today are an authoritarian-minded coalition in the process of orchestrating an internal take-over of control within the Democrat Party. Although, they are not revolutionary Marxist–Leninist socialists, their radical statism has many similar features and will have much the same results.

Revolutionary progressivism is a practical means of capturing power and a rival ideology to liberalism or socialism. If one searches the scholarly political science literature, as we have done, one finds that there is none on contemporary revolutionary progressivism. This implies that the left is coy about promoting revolutionary progressivism. as an ideological alternative to liberalism and socialism. There is a tactical advantage to this — not picking fights with one's political allies — but it is still surprising because contemporary progressivism emerges out of a very ideologically oriented base.

Chapter 36

The Danger of Revolutionary Progressivism

Published in 2007, Walter Russell Mead of the Council on Foreign Relations saw the United States as trying to create a world of order, law, and justice. He saw America puzzled as other nations did not endorse the American effort. He recognized three sorts of challenges to the U.S. effort: people who seek a world government; people who advocate a religion-driven world (radical Islamists); and devotees of various sorts of cultural and identity dominance, sorts of fascism (Walter Russell Mead, *God and Gold*, New York: Knopf, 2007, pp. 404–406). What is most interesting about this list is what it doesn't include — what has emerged as the greatest danger to the American-sponsored order: a revolutionary progressive Marxist — Leninist-style movement that has attained great power within the Biden Administration. It describes itself benignly as the progressive political movement.

There are a multitude of progressive activist groups, all of whom recognize each other, support each other, and link with the Democrat Party. In Boston alone there are these groups: Trans Resistance, The Transgender Emergency Fund, Boston Black Pride, Mass Equality, the LGBTQIA+ Partnership, Pride 4 the People, Mass NOW (National Organization for Women), Love Your Menses, and MME Coalition. The emergence of activist groups has been a key element of the renewed political power of the Democrats.

Revolutionary Progressives as People

Revolutionary progressives are without a sense of humor and almost without common sense. They are busy trying to right all the wrongs of the world and take themselves very seriously. For example, *The Chronicle of Higher Education* — a strongly revolutionary progressive newsletter — reported as fact that York University was going to confer an honorary doctorate on a duck which dwells on its campus. It should have been obvious to anyone with common sense that this story was a spoof. It was not obvious to these progressives because they will believe anything of their opponents in the world of politics. York University was to them an at least partly conventional, conservative institution and so they would believe it capable of any foolishness. Soon thereafter the Chronicle admitted that the story had been an April Fool's joke which it had taken seriously (Megan Zahneis, newsletter@newsletter.chronicle.com, May 3, 2021).

Revolutionary Progressives in Higher Education

All progressives say and do is summed up by writers for *The Chronicle of Higher Education* as "higher ed's efforts to improve racial diversity and inclusion" (June 29, 2021). This is the ultimate rationale for all the cancelling, group pressure, incitement, criticism, dishonestly, special pleading, and exclusion that has characterized the major universities in America in the past 20 years.

If that were all or even most of what there is to it, then many people would support contemporary progressivism who instead are scared to death of it. In fact, in addition to attempting to improve racial diversity and inclusion revolutionary progressives are trying to regiment American society to their own notion of what is right, and to change fundamentally the nature of American economic and political systems. This is a lot more than improving racial diversity and inclusion.

Revolutionary progressives denounce voter suppression, but they endorse thought and speech suppression. They are not defending freedom when they attack what they call voter suppression, but only suppression which injures their political aspirations — in America voting without identification supports progressives; freedom of thought and speech imperils them.

Revolutionary progressives (but not Roosevelt era progressives) are strongly anti-white. Professor Jane Mansbridge, a political scientist at Harvard, in telling us how to restore civil dialogue in America, cannot resist a slap at white people — "…you have to have good representation from everyone, not just the white retirees who don't have much to do and would love to come to this sort of thing." Apparently African American, Asian American, Hispanic and Latino Americans who are retired have no interest in improving civil dialogue in America. Professor Mansbridge finds it appropriate to attack the one racial group in America — according to her — who would support her proposal by willingly participating in it. A revolutionary progressive must appear to hold white people in contempt even if they are supportive of revolutionary progressives proposals.

("How Can We Restore Civil Dialogue in the Nation?"
Jane Mansbridge, *Harvard Gazette,* May 6, 2021).

A new analysis by the Foundation for Individual Rights in Education — a nonprofit group that advocates for free speech on campus — details a rise in what it calls "targeting" incidents of scholars. Such an incident is a "campus controversy involving efforts to investigate, penalize, or otherwise professionally sanction a scholar for engaging in constitutionally protected forms of speech," according to the analysis, which defines a scholar as "any individual who engages in acts of scholarship within the academic domain and has an official affiliation with a college." Researchers at the group, known as FIRE, chronicled 426 such incidents that occurred from January 2015 to July 2021. They examined and logged contextual details, like what type of speech had provoked the backlash, in what environment the speech had occurred, what sort of people had objected to it, and if any action had been taken against the scholar.

FIRE found some "worrying trends." The annual number of incidents has "risen dramatically," from 24 in 2015 to 113 in 2020. Targeting is increasingly "coming from within academia itself," specifically from undergraduates, other scholars, and/or administrators. Nearly 75% of those 426 incidents resulted in some form of sanction, including a formal investigation, a demotion, or termination. The incidents were spurred by people and groups that are to the political left of the subject more often than to the political right. When on-campus targeting incidents come from people who are more conservative than the scholar, they "tend to be initiated by administrators," the report says, not students or peers. As for subject matter, scholars were most often singled out for speech involving race, the report says. (Read FIRE's full report, and examine its database.)

Responding to all this and much more a North Korean defector says "even North Korea was not this nuts" after attending an Ivy League school. Yeonmi Park escaped the oppressive regime in 2007 at the age of 13. Yeonmi Park was shocked by the oppressive culture within the university, reminding her of the country she had fled. One of the several hundred North Korean defectors settled in the United States, Park, 27, transferred to Columbia University from a South Korean university in 2016 and was deeply disturbed by what she found (Teny Sahakian, "America's Future is as Bleak as North Korea' Says Defector after Attending Columbia," By Teny Sahakian, Fox News).

In this environment people who do not wish to get involved in political battles and wish not to be identified as an enemy of progressives, or of refusing to commit to the progressive agenda, find themselves trying to keep out-of-sight by keeping quiet, working in secret, outwardly conforming to political correctness, and keeping their thoughts to themselves. With their opponents silenced progressives dominate the landscape of opinion.

Progressives and Revolutionary Leninist Tactics

Many observers studying progressivism today worry at how close its tactics seem to revolutionary Marxist–Leninism. Although Bolsheviks and revolutionary progressives seek different ends, they share the conviction that there is no middle way. It is their way, or the highway. The progressive credo is less coherent than Bolshevik ideology, but the political imperative is the same. Both insist on obtaining power by hook or crook and canceling naysayers.

The Bolsheviks seek revenge for capitalist exploitation.

Revolutionary progressives do the same on behalf of blacks, minorities, and women.

Women were not given a fair shake. Minorities, blacks, native Americans and the obese suffer the emotional trauma of discrimination.

The emotional charge of revolutionary progressives is relatively weak, although the progressives are becoming ever shriller. Basing political righteousness as revolutionary Leninists do on exploitation is more compelling than basing it on white male oppression.

Revolutionary progressives chances of succeeding in their tyrannical quest are substantially less than the Bolsheviks had in 1917 because contemporary revolutionary progressives are divided. Each faction cares little about the others. They are likely to devour each other over the spoils and will have greater difficulty sustaining power. Nonetheless, they seem determined to impose their unilateral rule.

With such an assessment, the difficult issue for revolutionary progressive opponents is whether the menace they present will provoke fierce resistance.

At this point the conclusion of the Republican Party seems to be that the American political system is sufficiently decentralized to absorb progressive assaults, and robust enough to thwart a revolutionary progressive *coup d'etat*.

Revolutionary Progressives — Plans

Revolutionary progressive leadership is knowledgeable and sophisticated. They know what they are doing, including how to deny it convincingly.

They support a rapid rise in inflation. This will impoverish those with savings, who tend to vote conservative. It will also disorder the financial markets, which seek political stability, even though the financial community has been pressured into supporting the Democrats. Revolutionary progressives welcome another 2008 scale global financial crisis because it will undermine the capitalist class and provide an excuse for expand government spending and power.

Revolutionary progressive leadership seeks the elimination of police — not because of unfair treatment of minorities — the mantra of Black Lives Matter — but because police are defenders of law and therefore of the *status quo*. The first people to be liquidated during the Russian Revolution were the Constituent Assembly's police (November 7, 1917– January 19, 1918). Removing them in the United States is a key to a successful radical reorganization of the country.

Biden is not yet knowingly supportive of progressive radicalism. He doesn't seem to fully understand it. But he wants to be a "transformative" president and the revolutionary progressives are the only element of the

Democrat Party that is offering him a transformative agenda. So, he is adopting it.

Revolutionary Progressives Are Lethal, Not Just Bizarrely Conceited

Revolutionary progressives will impoverish the people in order to retain power. For them privilege is a crime. The privileged should be "liquidated." Both revolutionary Russia and China attempted their extermination. The result was tens of millions killed in one way or another. It is possible that the progressives have the same intention for the U.S.

Perhaps, they will be less bloodthirsty.

Chapter 37

Biden is a Liberal Who Struggles with Revolutionary Progressivism

Joe Biden's first speech to the nation as President was given to a joint session of Congress on April 28, 2021. It was an indication that he will talk as a moderate and govern as a revolutionary progressive.

This appears to be an excellent tactic for dealing with the division in the Democrat Party. The liberals (many of whom now refer to themselves as moderates to distinguish themselves from revolutionary progressives) have known him as one of their own for five decades. When Biden speaks, it is as one of them. The moderates assume Biden speaks as the real Biden and believe it is the revolutionary progressives, not them, who are being fooled. They are wrong.

The moderates are older and tired. They are anxious to believe Biden is on their side and that in consequence they have nothing to fear from the progressives.

Radical progressives are younger, energetic, and active. They care little for words, including those of President Biden. They want to see action. Biden is giving them that.

By giving the moderates words, and the radical progressives actions, Biden satisfies both wings of his party and avoids an open clash. It is an excellent tactic for keeping peace in the Democrat Party. It is not good for the nation.

The Advance of Revolutionary Progressivism

Critics charge progressives are willing to change the system to get their agenda through. Not exactly. Their agenda is to change the system.

Progressives are gaining influence because they are successfully manipulating public perceptions and tapping thwarted idealism. As we have observed frequently in previous chapters, American society is replete with injustices and inequalities which call for attention. Radical progressives are much aware of these. They use injustices, inequalities and what they term "inequities" to suggest that their opponents are foot dragging and to foist their promised solutions on the public.

Revolutionary progressives will make times worse because their economic policies are destructive. Cuba and Venezuela are today's dramatic evidence. Both are revolutionary progressive-like economies. Radical progressive will also extend sufferings of some to others — leveling down. This seems to be a solution which many people accept — in Venezuela, for example. Misery loves company. Others do not, and since they resist strongly, revolutionary progressive government requires a forceful police presence to allow them to remain in power. It is ironic, therefore, that revolutionary progressives call for reduction or elimination of police when they are not in power, but if they are to hold power will be compelled to increase police presence. A similar irony appends itself to Speaker of the House Nancy Pelosi whose political party, the Democrats, calls for defunding or eliminating the police while she builds a fortress full of police around the Capitol.

Revolutionary Progressives and the Working Class

President Biden asserts strongly and frequently his commitment to the working class. In America not long ago the working class was becoming a middle class. People owned homes, had savings accounts, sent their children to college, and had reliable health insurance and retirement accounts. Some people still have those things. Most do not.

Radical progressives are not in any way friends of a middle class, even though their parents are "blue-collar bourgeoisie." As the American working class prospered after World War II and began to achieve a modicum of security in the form of health insurance and pensions and assets such as homes that they owned, and so became a real middle class, the progressives lost interest in them. They became "Joe Six Pack" and "Archie Bunker." Security and assets made the middle-class increasingly conservative politically. Some workers continued to vote Democratic, but many turned Republicans. Revolutionary progressives were not happy with this. As the American economy ceased to support a vibrant middle class and as economic inequality expanded in the twenty-first century, revolutionary progressives grew more numerous and more energetic, until today they wrestle with liberals for control of the Democrat Party and the presidency. Progressives have moved from Golden age liberal reformers sympathetic to the working class to political radicals uninterested in working people except as they fall into demographic groups which progressives favor.

Throwing out the Baby with the Bathwater

Revolutionary progressives are determined to end racism in American society and around the world. To accomplish this, they are committed to ending Western civilization, which in their view is the primary sponsor of racism in the world. That racism was part of Western civilization most of its existence is certainly true. But racism was also part of almost all human societies and is still part of many today. Except for instances of genocide, the worst aspect of racism in Western civilization was slavery. But slavery was part of almost all human societies and is still part of some today. Yet Western civilization is identified by revolutionary progressives as especially guilty.

From a perspective that is increasingly prominent in American society radical progressives are thought to be throwing out the baby with the bathwater. The bathwater is racism which is real and continues and needs to be discarded. The baby is Western civilization (classicism, renaissance, and Enlightenment) which used to be taught in the liberal arts colleges and the secondary schools and is among the highest achievements of humanity. When the baby is thrown out with the bathwater, it should be understandable that many people are more concerned with saving the baby than they are with throwing out the bathwater. It is characteristic of revolutionary progressives that they are willing to let the baby die in order to discharge the bathwater.

Liberalism versus Revolutionary Progressivism — An Example with Indigenous Americans

A few years ago, a small business owner who had too little work to keep his few employees fully employed, recommended one of them to a woman to do some work for her. She hired him for a day a week. He came to work. He was a full-blooded native American who looked the part — short, strong, with long black hair that hung down his back. He was very friendly and a hard worker. His employer took to him immediately. She paid him on time, full amounts as agreed, and gave him lunch and coffee. He seemed to like working for her. Soon he began to tell her about his life. His mother and his grandmother had told him from his earliest years that he was mentally disabled. He couldn't do schoolwork, they said. On the ground of his disablement, they collected generous sums from the federal government and spent them on themselves. He said he wanted to find a better life than yard work. He wanted to go to college. He wanted to move out of this parent's shack and be able to afford a home with his girlfriend.

His employer told him that his mother and grandmother had treated him badly. She said he was not mentally disabled. She would help get him into college.

After a few weeks the boy ceased to come to work. A few weeks later she received a letter from him. He said he didn't want to work for her anymore. He wrote that what she had told him about his mother and grandmother had made him uncomfortable. He didn't feel comfortable working with her anymore.

The letter was clearly the result of his talking with his family, and they applying their expertise in appealing for money from the federal government. It was a set-up for a complaint of job discrimination and legal action against her.

Thereafter she found him working bagging groceries in a supermarket.

This was a good example of the difference between liberals and progressives. Liberals would have applauded the woman's efforts to help the young man better himself. They would have tried to supply more assistance to him.

Revolutionary progressives pushed him to find a way to extort money from her before moving on to the next victim.

Liberalism is about self-improvement. Revolutionary progressivism is about false accusations and extortion.

The lesson to generation after generation of indigenous Americans — don't try to be successful by bettering yourself with education and effort — make yourself a more deserving victim and seek money to be given to you because of your mistreatment and need.

Above is evidence of that by an example.

Liberal versus Radical Progressive

Biden is a liberal. He does not instinctively pursue revolutionary progressive policies. Classic liberalism as defined by *The Economist* magazine includes "The belief in freedom as the underpinning of civilization, in the state as the servant of the individual rather than vice versa, and in the open exchange of goods, services and opinions." ("Into the Unknown," *The Economist,* February 1, 2020, p. 10).

Biden accepts this except for giving more significance to the state as the source of social and economic improvement in society. Political social liberalism of the sort that Biden has espoused all his political life involves:

Opportunity for all
Internationalism
U.S. global hegemony
Focus on law
None of this is accepted by revolutionary progressives.

Biden's Democratic Party claims to be America's best option. It proclaims that it offers the electorate a judicious balance of revolutionary progressive and liberal programs. The mix is supposed to satisfy the demands of victim rights and welfare advocates without abridging democrat freedoms and stifling economic competition. There is an intra-party debate among moderates, revolutionary progressives, and socialists about priorities. Moderates tilt toward prioritizing welfare programs, tolerance, and competition. Revolutionary progressives advocate shifting resources from the rich and working class to their clients. Socialists favor soaking the rich and curbing markets, primarily for the proletariat's benefit. Revolutionary progressives and Marxist–Leninists seek totalitarian control.

Revolutionary Progressives Champion Diversity and Inclusiveness

Diversity and inclusiveness, key slogans of progressives, are not about individuals, but about groups. They are concerned with how many whites, how many men, how many African Americans, how many women are in various positions and circumstances. It doesn't matter who a person is, it matters what group that person is in.

In the wide diversity of humans, revolutionary progressives see only discrimination and exploitation. They never acknowledge the potential of differences among equals. They prefer that everyone feel themselves victimized by others or be ashamed of themselves as oppressors. They acknowledge no other categories than victim and oppressor.

This also is very different from the perspective of liberals. Liberals champion diversity not as a response to exploitation but as a source of improved performance for all organizations (Adam Smith's division of labor). As a liberal Biden starts from this position but is compelled by political reality to accept revolutionary progressive leveling down.

Under pressure from revolutionary progressives many organizations and the federal government have instituted diversity training. Ostensibly to encourage people to see the value of diversity in life, the training programs debase white males. For example, it is taught that whites are oppressive, arrogant, offensive, ignorant, and solidly against non-whites. Horrified by both the content and the implications of the government sponsoring such training the Republican Administration ordered these programs to shut down. Biden immediately reinstated them upon taking office. Biden rejected his liberal convictions and adopted the very different approach of the revolutionary progressives.

Liberals and revolutionary progressives take very different approaches to rectify demographic imbalances. There are many examples of this. For example, for decades liberals have pushed colleges to increase the number of African American senior faculty on their rosters.

As reported by the *Chronicle of Higher Education* on February 23, 2021, "…over all these years faculty-diversity efforts have stagnated. Between 2010 and 2019, the share of Black PhD recipients increased less than one percentage point, according to the annual "Survey of Earned Doctorates." That's bad news for colleges that want to diversify their faculty — as many student activists have demanded. Under pressure, many colleges have announced high-profile efforts to create a more representative professoriate.

"But until higher education can expand its share of doctoral recipients of color, faculty diversity remains a zero-sum game, favoring the institutions that have the money and prestige to pick off the relatively small pool of Black and Hispanic doctoral recipients on the market, or from other institutions."

This is a liberal analysis that lays the responsibility for the failure of colleges and universities to add more African Americans to their faculty squarely on the back of African Americans who do not earn PhDs in sufficient numbers. Liberals accept this point of view and address the problem by trying to get more African Americans into the PhD programs.

Radical progressives reject this approach and accuse the colleges of using an unnecessary criterion — having a PhD — as a basis for discrimination against African Americans. Their solution is for the colleges to abandon a false and discriminatory meritocracy — the PhD requirement — and add African Americans to their faculties who do not have the degree and the academic training which it signifies.

Biden is a liberal, and by nature will agree with the liberals on this matter, but under the political pressure of the revolutionary progressives: he is likely to support their interpretation and their solution.

Revolutionary Progressives and Their Opponents

The core of revolutionary progressivism when it achieves power is thought and speech control, and therefore censorship, repression, and resistance to challenge by political opponents. Progressives do not cooperate with non-revolutionary progressives; they try to silence and then eliminate them. Before gaining power, radical progressives focus on reputation destruction of their opponents. There is no attempt by progressives at serious debate with opponents; they only issue propaganda.

What Will Happen in the Long Term from Revolutionary Progressive Policies?

Revolutionary progressives policies dry up economic resources. The more the state leans on the masses for increased taxation; and the more police, national guard and the military are used to spy on and oppress the population the more people will flee from the country. At first it will be the rich, but soon the upper middle class will follow. Revolutionary progressives will welcome their departure. As people desert the country the U.S. will become for the first time in its history an exporter of people instead of a target for immigration.

Dependency on Government

For minorities, including the poor, dependency on government is nothing more than being exploited by the people who run the government.

Revolutionary progressives like the Bolsheviks promise wonderful benefits for the poor and minorities but run the government primarily for their own advantage.

Revolutionary Progressives and Political Conspiracies

Revolutionary progressives deny participating in political conspiracies. Revolutionary progressives TV anchors ask if the Republicans have fallen into conspiracy wormholes — that is, do they get lost from reality when imagining conspiracies? Revolutionary progressive deny any involvement in trying to steal the 2020 presidential election on the grounds that "We don't do that. We don't participate in conspiracies to steal elections."

But revolutionary progressives proclaim with conviction that their political and social ends justify any means. People who will do anything for political success might steal an election. Radical progressive denials based on their supposed honesty are not to be taken seriously.

In the end in America's 2020 election, the Republican President complained that the Democrats had stolen the election from him. The Democrats left it to him to prove that this had happened. He was not able to do so. The reasons are contested. But since the Republicans failed to prove in some court that the election was stolen, the Democrats insist that it has been proved that it was not stolen. This is not so.

Revolutionary Progressives Sponsor Equity Not Equality

On his first day as president, Joe Biden issued an "Executive Order on Advancing Racial Equity and Support for Underserved Communities." Radical progressives had persuaded the new president to champion a concept they had just brought to national attention. In place of equality, they now champion equity (and additionally "restorative justice"). The difference appears to be that equality implies opportunity while equity implies outcomes. Revolutionary progressives demand that demographic minorities should have all that success provides for other Americans and more until restorative justice is achieved. When that can be achieved only by pulling the top down rather than lifting the bottom up — that is by leveling down — progressives advocate that. One sees the consequences of that policy in Cuba and Venezuela. But not, importantly, in China, yet.

Chapter 38

Canceling in the Name of Justice

Canceling is a very potent political weapon. It intimidates opponents and squashes opposition. Revolutionary progressives have grasped the weapon and are using it effectively. It is recognized immediately by citizens of countries that are dictatorships of right or left. It may be less familiar to residents of democracies. It was unknown in the United States until recently except in blacklisting during the communist scares of the 1950s.

Canceling is a term used to describe the removal of books, signs, and statues depicting historical figures unacceptable to Revolutionary progressives, and defunding "offensive" government activities. It is also a practice of denouncing and imposing severe penalties on people who intentionally or accidently transgress the sensitivities of progressives. Revolutionary progressive-initiated canceling is done in the name of perfecting American democracy. Lenin said that Soviet democracy (totalitarianism) was 1 million times more democratic than Parliamentary democracy in England! Canceling is said to be motivated by the effort to remove from our society references which are hurtful to the feelings of demographic minorities.

"Cancel culture" is journalist slang for denunciations backed by threats of radical violence. It is an aspect of leftist revolutionary action and is akin to nihilist terrorism and WWI style revolutionary syndicalism. It is used interchangeably with the term "call out" (*J'accuse*).

Currently, denunciations leading to canceling are accompanied by demands for defunding and boycotting organizations, as well as dismissing and ostracizing offending individuals, all done in the name of "fair play" and "justice."

Cancel culture is the epitome of revolutionary progressive tactics It is draconian; it is vicious. Radical progressives are without humor, and they are without mercy.

Canceling originated in America in the best universities. Research or writing conflicting with the dominant narratives in the field are not answered. They are repressed — as evidenced by their code of silence and publication censorship — or simply ignored. It is as if the work has not been done. Every field becomes a sort of club of the initiated — those who share the same or similar opinions. Those who differ are ostracized, no matter how much work they have done or its objective value. Like so much in radical progressive tactics, university-born canceling has moved out of the schools and into the mainstream of American politics, following the nineteenth century revolutionary socialist pattern.

As we saw in the previous chapter, revolutionary progressives respond to police violence and opposing opinions in the same way — by canceling police enforcement of laws and by censoring opposing expressions of opinion.

Cancel culture is best explained via examples, and there are several types of canceling — the Soviets preferred the term "liquidating." The different types are mainly of what gets canceled. The motivations are always the same. The methods are much alike.

Last summer journalists at a supposedly independent large city newspaper summarized their feelings about their profession in this way, "We are tired of being told to show both sides of issues there are no two sides of" (Christine Rosen, "Getting the Hell Out of Dodge," *Commentary*, March 2021, p. 16). They were speaking for many more journalists than just themselves. Probably they were expressing the views of most journalists in America today. The matter they were referencing was a political opinion. The journalists agreed that they already knew the truth of the matter, so they asked why they should have to show an alternative opinion. They would prefer just to cancel the other side of each issue — and there were many such issues — about which they thought they already knew the truth. The American Constitution's guarantee of freedom of speech means little in such an environment of opinion.

There are not two sides of everything, of course. Facts are facts. But political opinions are very different. There are almost always two sides. Sometimes one side is more convincing than the other. But not always. There are two sides of many more things than many journalists will admit or than they find convenient.

USA Today's Hemal Jhaveri, for example, wrote a piece titled "Oral Roberts University isn't the feel-good March Madness story we need." She says that the evangelical Christianity of the University is "wholly incompatible with values of diversity and inclusion."

"Founded by televangelist Oral Roberts in 1963, the Christian school upholds the values and beliefs of its fundamentalist namesake, making it not just a relic of the past, but wholly incompatible with the NCAA's own stated values of equality and inclusion," Jhaveri says. "While the school has been soundly mocked on social media for its archaic standards of behavior and code of conduct that bans profanity, 'social dancing,' and shorts in classrooms, it is the school's discriminatory and hateful anti-LGBTQ+ policy that fans should protest…"

Later on Jhaveri writes that the team should be banned from National Collegiate Athletic Association (NCAA) competition altogether because of their "anti-LGBTQ+ policies" and general "bigotry and exclusionary fundamentalism." She was very serious and completely consistent. "The fact is," she continued, "any and all anti-LGBTQ+ language in any school's polices should ban them from NCAA competition." She was trying to cancel many universities from participation in national athletic contests. If this were done, it would punish the student athletes as much or more that it would punish the schools. She would apparently welcome that. In her progressive America only students who attend politically correct schools would be allowed to compete with other schools.

Howard Bauchner, editor in chief of the *Journal of the American Medical Association*, was placed on administrative leave after a deputy editor — not Bauchner — made controversial comments about race and medicine on a podcast. Ed Livingston, the deputy editor, said on the podcast that structural racism no longer existed in the United States, and as a result of expressing that opinion later resigned. Bauchner is now the subject of an independent investigation. Not only the offending speaker but his superiors are canceled when an offending comment is made. The fear inspired by political correctness in America is widespread, not just specific to the speaker or writer who makes the offending comments.

Canceling in the Form of Censorship

Canceling is not just of people who offend the progressives. It extends to censoring their publications. Nor is censorship exercised only by the government; it is done by private organizations as well.

"Amazon Won't Sell Books Framing LGBTQ+ as Illnesses" (*Wall Street Journal*, March 12, 2012). "The company said it recently removed a three-year-old book about transgender issues from its platforms because it decided not to sell books that frame transgender and other sexual identities as mental illnesses. Amazon has taken upon itself in the interests of progressive doctrine to determine how a writer has framed issues. Did the book involved in this example frame transgender as a mental illness, or simply raise the possibility? We don't know because the book has been denied to us by the major book retailer in America. Presumably Amazon now has staffed itself with unchallenged expertise in medical matters of many kinds. There could be offensive publications about COVID-19 for example. Surely Amazon would protect the American people by censoring any such publications. The social networks are also censors with no better qualifications to do so than Amazon."

Revolutionary progressives and President Biden argue that the social networks are privately owned (proprietary) and should be allowed to censor their sites as they desire, even if the censorship has a political bias, as it has been shown to have.

But Amazon is not a social network, and Microsoft also censors, and it is not a social network. For instance, attempting to go to a newsletter site with an article about a court decision favorable to the Republican Administration brings this pop-up from Microsoft and a complete blocking of the site:

"Microsoft recommends you don't continue to this site. It has been reported to Microsoft for containing misleading content that could lead you to lose personal info, financial data, and even money."

Microsoft expects people to accept its assertion that the censorship is being done by Microsoft on its customers' behalf. And possibly it is, but it is Microsoft's conception of the political (not privacy or financial) welfare of their customers.

It is ironical to see revolutionary progressives defending large capitalist-owned companies since they denounce them in other contexts. This is an example of how broad the reach of the Democrat coalition in American politics is. It includes both the most valuable capitalist firms and their sworn ideological enemies. In a nation which it damns for systematic racism revolutionary progressives support the political judgment of white-run corporations (when they do the radicals' bidding).

Another form of canceling takes the form of renaming building and streets. For example, James Madison University renamed three campus buildings for prominent black people with ties to the university. All three buildings were previously named for Confederate leaders.

Canceling isn't only about correcting our memories of the past. It is also about revolutionary progressive concerns in the moment. Valparaiso University retired its Crusader mascot, which its interim president said promotes "aggressive religious oppression and violence." The offense of the mascot is that it references the Christianity of soldiers a thousand years ago. Revolutionary progressives are attempting to refashion all human history in ways which they consider more appropriate. Only the communists in Soviet Russia and in China have ever before undertaken such an ambitious task.

Rebalancing history by correcting past errors or biases is a good thing. But trying to eliminate from human memory the errors which are corrected is a dangerous extension.

Confederates and Nazis are both being canceled. That they deserve condemnation for certain of their deeds is certain. But consider the consequences of canceling them entirely.

Erich von Manstein was a German field marshal engaged in an aggressive invasion by the Nazis of the Soviet Union. At one point in the war, in the winter of 1943, "Manstein was faced with strategic problems of a magnitude and complexity seldom paralleled in history. He handled the situation with masterly coolness and judgment ... To find another example of defensive strategy of this caliber we must go back to Lee's campaign in Virginia in the summer of 1864." (F. W. von Mellethin, *Panzer Battles,* Norman: University of Oklahoma Press, 1955, p. 203).

A person facing a crisis in military strategy would turn to these two campaigns (von Manstein in southern Russia in 1943 and Lee in Virginia in 1864) for guidance.

Cancel culture would deprive students of strategy of the lessons to be learned. Manstein was a German field marshal serving Hitler, and possibly himself a Nazi. Lee was a Southerner who had left the service of the United States to serve the Confederacy. He could be considered a traitor. He was also a slave owner. Both these men would be canceled in today's revolutionary progressive United States.

Canceling Moves Mainstream

For years Revolutionary progressives had the canceling tactic to themselves. As we said above, it is effective and intimidating. Conservatives took notice. By 2021 state legislatures were adopting the tactic.

For example, a bill proposed in Idaho would make it illegal for the state's colleges to teach "divisive concepts," which the bill defines as those that make students "feel discomfort, guilt, anguish, or any other form of psychological distress on account of their race or sex." According to the bill, "the Idaho legislature finds that social-justice concepts such as critical race theory represent a class of divisive concepts that exacerbate and inflame divisions on the basis of race, gender, or other sectarian criteria." The bill also says that some of these concepts might be discussed in class, but students can't be compelled "to espouse or adhere" to them (*Chronicle of Higher Education*, April 19, 2021).

Canceling in the Future of the Revolutionary Progressive Movement

Although conservatives have begun to adopt canceling, it remains primarily a weapon of Revolutionary progressives. Its future direction can be ascertained from experience.

Canceling has deep roots in Soviet Russia. The phrase in the socialist literature borrowed from Danton's famous remark at his Jacobin trial in 1789 is "the revolution devouring its own."

Alexandra Kollontai was the only original member of Lenin's inner circle who survived Stalin's purges. Soviet wags are fond of quipping that Kollontai survived because Stalin was chivalrous.

Today American revolutionary progressivism's canceling is widespread and is bound to be destructive of its own. The extremism will intensify until, as in Danton's France and Stalin's Russia, canceling is turned on its own. Progressives will begin to cancel other revolutionary progressives who are their rivals or with whom they have disputes of one kind or another.

Canceling by Democrats has reached what may seem to non-Americans a surprising height. On January 7, 2021, following the mob invasion of the Capitol building in Washington, D.C., Facebook removed the Republican president from its platform. This was to deny him access to the people who follow the social media platform. On May 5, 2021, a panel chosen by Facebook decided to continue the former president's exclusion from its platform. This was a political act by a private company. It was intended to silence the ex-president. It made him a martyr in the eyes of his supporters and encouraged him to find other means of communicating with masses of people.

Chapter 39

Radical Progressivism in the Democratic Party

There are things that all Democrats agree on. The most important, probably, is that government is the best solution to many societal problems. In consequence the Democrat Congress and President Biden set out in 2021 to spend money on many social matters and simultaneously began a publicity effort to convince Americans that any progress on these matters was a result of Democrat-initiated government efforts. This Democrat effort took place in a context of deep public mistrust of the federal government. It was an effort to reverse the Reagan-era legacy of the conservative insistence that government was the problem in American life, not its solution. Democrats all agree also on the efficacy of federal spending, and of the importance of federal regulation limiting the discretion of state governments. For example, the 2021 Democrat-passed stimulus bill explicitly prevented state governments from using any federal funds to reduce state taxes.

How Revolutionary Progressives View Their Political Enemies

Michael Gerson laid out in a newspaper column the revolutionary progressive view of how their opponents think and speak. When Republicans say "The Democratic Party," Gerson tells us, it "means liberals, which translates into Jews. They are importing 'new people' from the 'Third World' means with black and brown skin. These kinds of people, in the racist trope, are 'obedient' meaning docile, backward and stupid. Their votes do not constitute real democracy because they are replacing the 'current electorate' — presumably whiter and less docile. These paler, truer Americans are thus deprived of their birthright or political dominance. And fighting back — making sure the Third World people have less power — becomes a defense of the American way" (Michael Gerson, "Carlson's Rhetoric Gives Life to The Republicanism," *The Washington Post*, April 15, 2021).

There is some truth in this portrayal, but it is also exaggerated and incorrect. People who oppose the Democrat Party are condemned as racist and anti-democratic. America is portrayed as the Global Nation — everyone in the world by inference has a right to come to America and be accepted immediately and fully into its political life. Hispanics and Latinos are described as non-white, a different race which is colored brown.

It is understandable that conservative Americans believe that they are being maligned.

As is consistent with modern propaganda technique the revolutionary progressives accuse their opponents with hatred and hate crimes, thereby implying that they do neither. It appears, however, from their rhetoric, that revolutionary progressives are the strongest haters in American politics today.

A radical progressive is a person who says that if another person is insane — meaning that person doesn't accept as true what revolutionary progressives believe to be true — revolutionary progressive people shouldn't just accept their insanity. An insane — misguided — person needs (Maoist) re-education. Re-education should have begun in the 1970s when the Viet Nam War divided the country. If re-education had been started at that time, then the battles between progressives and others would have been settled by now with revolutionary progressives everywhere victorious. It's definitional — if someone insists the world is flat, we don't have to give them a license to drive a cruise ship. That is, if a person disagrees with you, re-educate (brain wash) them to revolutionary progressive opinions or expel them from society.

As for the Republicans, revolutionary progressives insist that they are complicit in spreading disinformation. Now that they've lost in 2020 and the White House is in Democrat hands, the Republicans want to be absolved of the responsibility for having challenged the result of the election. That is unacceptable. Reality needs to be faced. They need to be punished. Such people should be sent before a revolutionary tribunal as "vrag naroda" (enemies of the people) in Soviet Russian terminology. The term is applicable because the progressive insurrectionary tactics are identical to that of revolutionary Marxist–Leninist–Stalinists.

The New York Times speaks of the Biden Administration's plans to combat domestic terrorism. If the identification of domestic terrorism were limited to actions by suspects of crimes or planning criminal acts, this would be in principle okay. But since progressives define terrorists as people who disagree with them, this becomes a program to persecute political opponents. "Domestic terrorist" is becoming a Democrat synonym for Republican.

Progressive Tactics

The core of revolutionary progressive tactics is thought and speech control, and therefore censorship, repression, and resistance to challenge by political opponents. They do not cooperate with non-revolutionary progressives; they focus on their destruction.

Denouncing people or companies as racist in the mass media is very effective. Shaming and tabooing is effective. Shouting racism, genderism, homophobia, etc., at public figures or companies is especially effective. It is *ad hominem* reputation destruction.

Revolutionary progressives do not limit their attacks to Republicans. They also attack Biden. Below is a transcript of a revolutionary progressives speaker blasting the Biden Administration on April 15, 2021, during demonstrations against the killing of an African American man by a police officer in a suburb of Minneapolis. "Joe Biden did nothing for our g*****n community. We're going to boycott that f***ing vote," said the speaker during the demonstration. "That's why we did it (voted) to get his a** in office. He said he wasn't going to leave us behind. He said he was going to build from the bottom up, middle out. That's what he promised to the American people," the speaker continued. Towards the end of the speech, the speaker called out the U.S. government for being a "racist, fascist, and Nazi government" which was met with applause from the crowd (news=patriotsignal.com@mail.patriotsignal.come).

Americans generally are aware of the vehemence of revolutionary progressives hatred and progressive willingness to punish opponents and they wish to avoid both if possible. Therefore, only two Democrat Senators and almost no Democrat Representatives have the courage to oppose the revolutionary progressives in the Congress directly. But the failure of many revolutionary revolutionary progressive initiatives to gain passage among Democrats indicates that there is much broader moderate (liberal) support than is vocal. Biden seems to share the aversion of his fellow moderates to alienating revolutionary progressives. It is joked in the United States that if Biden lacked the courage to confront the Taliban in Afghanistan, then how could he be expected to confront the revolutionary progressives in America? Implicitly in this joke is the notion that the American revolutionary progressives are of the same sort of people as the Afghan Taliban — rigid, hard, unfeeling, and violent — even though they are on the other side of the political spectrum.

Revolutionary progressives-inspired or condoned mob violence and looting is very effective in intimidating people and local authorities. Canceling of people is also very effective.

Boycotts are not effective in affecting the behavior of their targets. They are primarily symbolic. Boycotts hurt the rank and file seriously but rarely change any actions by bosses. This is just like sanctions applied in international relations. Boycotts are for the purpose of making a show of action when nothing is expected to be achieved. The boycott of Georgia demanded by the Democrats and endorsed by President Biden to protest Georgia's election rules did considerable damage to businesses in Georgia including African American-owned businesses. Protests from African Americans against the boycotts in Georgia were largely ignored by the national Democratic Party. The Party affirmed that pursuing the interests of the Party nationally were more important than suffering caused in Georgia to Democrats.

Feminists

On Sunday, January 3, 2021, the new Congress convened and Nancy Pelosi was elected to a fourth term as Speaker of the House of Representatives. The rules of the House were changed to prohibit the use of the terms "mother" and "father" on the grounds that they are gender-specific. Some Members shouted "awoman" after "amen" was said. They were apparently unaware that amen is a Latin term for "so be it." Radical feminism had made it into the House of Representatives.

Feminists are among the more radical elements of the progressive movement. They are humorless, committed, and tireless in their efforts.

Most Americans do not know them well. They are most visible to the public in their advocacy for an unlimited right for women to choose to have abortions. Their reach is much further than that.

The National Organization for Women (NOW) is their most widespread organization, but by no means the only one. At a statewide meeting of a feminist organization in the spring of 2021, the program was introduced as follows: "Congresswoman Pressley will be moderating a panel discussion on period policy as feminist policy with Tre'Andre Valentine from the Massachusetts Trans Political Coalition, Bria Gadsden of Love Your Menses, and Diya Khullar of the Massachusetts Menstrual Equity Coalition."

The newsletter of a state-level NOW chapter wrote toward the end of the 2020 presidential campaign: "Now, more than ever, the feminist community needs to be proactive in helping candidates running for office work towards NOW's priority areas: reproductive rights, LGBTQ equality, economic justice, violence against women, civil and constitutional rights, and racial justice."

The focus of NOW on the LBGTQ community is politically wise. Public opinion polls report that 5.6% of American adults identify as LGBTQ. This is a high percentage and is led by younger people. In close presidential elections like those in recent years this percentage is enough to have provided a winning margin for the Democrats.

Polls indicate that racism and gender inequity were the top two most important social changes issues across all generations of employees, according to recent research from The Conference Board. Similarly, among women and men, racism was ranked as the top social change issue. Women, however, were more likely than men to cite gender inequity as one of the three most important issues to them personally; gender inequity showed the largest gap between women and men — a 32% difference. The second largest gap was for unemployment, with men placing a higher importance on unemployment than women (a 12% difference) (Rebecca Ray, PhD Executive Vice President, Human Capital, The Conference Board MemberEngagement@conference-board.org January 28, 2021).

Most American women do not consider themselves feminists in the sense of the political activist groups. Nor do they participate in those groups. They may even despise the members of those groups as personalities. But most American women support the issues of gender inequity, or the perceptions of gender inequity which the feminist groups identify and purport to seek to resolve.

The Biden Administration is aware of these feelings of American women. It couples them with racism, as do many American women, as major political issues.

Susan Rice, Biden's top advisor, in her first major speech — given on January 26, 2021, the first day of the Biden's Administration — said that the new Administration's top priority was equity — not equality, certainly not efficiency or effectiveness. What does equity mean people asked? It was not a common term in American political discourse. It would appear to refer to addressing the grievances of women and African Americans about their treatment in American society.

The Emergence of Revolutionary Progressives into the Mainstream of American Politics

In America both the left and right have had radical extremes which were not part of the mainstream.

On the right were neo-Nazis. They remain on the fringe.

On the left have been socialists and for a while in the 1930s communists. They remain on the fringe.

In recent years new far left organizations have emerged which have made it to the mainstream in the revolutionary progressive wing of the Democrat Party and now play a major role in American politics. Black Lives Matter (BLM) is dramatically effective in mobilizing public opinion. Anti-fa brings physical intimidation to revolutionary progressive politics.

How this happened — how it was managed — is one of the most important topics to be addressed in American politics. Perhaps the long stagnation of the middle class and the widening of income and wealth differentials provided the setting for this.

Black Lives Matter and Anti-Fa

In the country at large the revolutionary progressives supported groups which had, during the Republican's Administration, rioted in many cities. The most threatening of these groups were supporters of BLM and anti-fa.

BLM has a large following in the United States and many people gather at its rallies. Generally, BLM has no para-military organization, but only individuals who assemble for demonstrations which sometimes turn into riots. There are, of course, people who join the demonstrations in order to loot with or without political objectives.

Anti-Fa

On May 1, 2021, anti-fa staged a march in Seattle to honor May Day, the Marxist holiday. The group was about 40 people, all dressed in black. A few assaulted a woman and child who were videoing the march, and others damaged buildings along the route. Fourteen were arrested. This is pretty good evidence that despite Speaker Pelosi's effort to deny its existence, anti-fa does exist.

Anti-fa is an unusual organization. It is a network of people who share a common political philosophy. They are willing to use violence against people that they consider fascists, but it has been limited to beatings and property destruction. They have not appeared, for the most part, in public armed with guns.

They are committed to keeping people they consider fascists out of their communities. Violence is a preferred method of persuasion. They beat people they consider fascists to drive them away. To an interviewer sent by Fox News an anti-fa activist explained that his objective was to make it so uncomfortable personally, economically, and socially for fascists that they would flee his community. His method was to beat the crap out of the fascists — so he said.

Anti-fa appears to have no central authority or command. It puzzled pro-Republican journalists and Republican Administration lawyers (both of whom anti-fa considers fascists) that anti-fa did not seem to have a traditional organization with headquarters, budgets, and officers. But anti-fa is rather more like the groups that were assembled spontaneously for parties or small-scale riots in the early years of social media. They are also akin to the nineteenth century Russian socialist revolutionary circles and *ad hoc* worker councils (soviets) which played a key role in the Bolshevik insurrection. Anti-fa has taken the same "soviet" method and applied it to a contemporary political objective. Anti-fa assembles its adherents by reaching out on social media or by phone. Anti-fa partisans understand one another and join, whomever can attend, for their activities.

Members of anti-fa wear black including black face masks, less because of concern about avoiding the virus than to conceal their identities. The mask mandate because of COVID-19 is a useful cover. They, like Bolshevik "soviets", sometimes assemble for training in riot tactics. The tactics are for the purpose of provoking police and military personnel to over-react to their actions, wishing that demonstrators would be harmed, even killed, so that a political point can be made against the authorities, controlled as anti-fa insist by fascists.

Anti-fa members are recognizable by their black clothing, sometimes with anti-fa identification or slogans on their shirts or sweaters. They stand out in gatherings of protestors, most of whom are not anti-fa. When demonstrators turn to riots, anti-fa members are often leading the transition.

Anti-fa and its police and military opponents have operated with a strict but informal set of understandings. There has been very little use of lethal weapons and few deaths associated with anti-fa activities.

Anti-fa has been most active in Portland, Oregon, where it says it has waged a three-year war against fascism. There have been demonstrations and riots almost every night over these years. It was presumed that when Biden was elected, the nightly riots would cease. They have not ceased. There has been some indication that anti-fa considers the Biden Administration too moderate and is demonstrating for its replacement by a more progressive set of leaders.

It is important to note that not all cities had the sorts of riots that BLM and anti-fa staged in most large cities during 2020. Miami generally avoided them because a Republican mayor worked with community groups and deployed police to prevent widespread violence. The defense of the Democrat mayors of large cities that experienced extensive riot damage was that not deploying police prevented an escalation of violence and quieted the streets more effectively than attempted suppression would have. Miami gave a different answer.

Memphis also avoided violence. One window is said to have been broken by a demonstrator and he is said to have paid to replace it. This happened because protestors remained peaceful. The city's Democrat mayor met with the pastors of African American churches and together agreed to actions to protect the city from rioting and damage. The pastors then pressed this approach on their congregations, and it was accepted. BLM was present in Memphis and remained peaceful. It is unclear if anti-fa was there, and probably it was not. Its absence was likely a major reason why violence was avoided. It's as if Gandhi's peaceful resistance trumped revolutionary insurrection.

Deceit of Social Policy

A chasm exists between symbolic gestures and true social progress.

Revolutionary progressives — exactly like Marxist–Leninist–Stalinists — claim that they are democrats. They maintain that their goals reflect the will of the people. Their political tactics suggest that they are dishonest; that winning is more important to them than the people's will. Radicals know that their excessive demands alienate the working class, middle class and wealthy; that is, most Americans, but refuse to accommodate their demands to the people's will. This makes their social policy unwise. Moreover, many radicals are corrupt opportunists. They are more interested in using revolutionary progressivism as a tool for acquiring personal power and wealth than in improving the lot of their constituents.

A few months before the presidential election of 2020 the Democrat mayor of New York City told America that at this time in history Black Lives Matter supersedes all other concerns. (Mayor DeBlasio of New York City, Shown on Fox TV, August 13, 2020). A comment like this from a leading Democrat attempts to justify the riots, the breaking of laws, the ignoring of all legal requirements, the destruction of property, and soon will likely attempt to justify the killing of those who do not go along. The Biden Administration will surely support the agenda of Black Lives Matter, which reaches far beyond racial justice. It will be silent about antifa or deny that it exists (since it lacks a traditional organizational structure), or ultimately, if political conditions permit, endorse it.

Progressives are right in identifying many of the problems of the United States but are incompetent to fix them. They can only highlight them and make promises they can't or won't keep in order to get power. Revolutionary progressivism would seem therefore to be about power, not policies and not solutions or even progress. Liberals nibbled away at problems but made little progress; progressives promise solutions and fail to deliver.

Revolutionary progressives are gaining influence in American politics because times are difficult for many. Revolutionary progressives will satisfy the desperate by making things worse for all. They will not make them better for the poor. But they will promise to. Instead, they will level down the better-off to the level of the poor. This pattern is evident in Cuba and Venezuela.

Today's revolutionary progressivism lacks an ideology, but it has antecedents. From 1820 to 1871 socialism meant assisting workers better their lives. Few people could object to the objective. In 1871, Marx altered his prior view by insisting that helping workers necessitated destroying non-workers and seizing the state with insurrectionary violence. This is where revolutionary socialism began.

Until 1920 most socialists were traditional libertarians. They prioritized workers but workers made their own choices, and the concept left room for everyone else. After the Bolshevik revolution succeeded, libertarian socialism was forgotten. Revolutionary Marxist–Leninism became the only valid form of socialism making it seem that there were no other viable ways. They gulled a generation into believing that libertarian democratic socialism and democratic free enterprise were inferior to despotic Marxist–Leninist totalitarianism.

Precisely, the same process of radical capture is happening with progressivism. Initially progressivism was about reform. Teddy Roosevelt's progressivism was directed at reforming monopolies. FDR's progressivism was a package of social reforms labeled the New Deal.

With the rise of the Civil Rights movement in the 1960s, progressivism gradually morphed into revolutionary progressivism, borrowing all its tactics and zealotry from revolutionary Marxist–Leninism. The progressive agenda has merit as an element in a national dialogue of mutual accommodation and consensus building. It becomes dangerous when progressive issues become platforms for repression and extremist violence.

Biden's approach to building the Democrat Party relies on reconciling irreconcilables. Biden willy-nilly has become an opponent and acolyte of George Sorel, an approach echoing Sorel's advocacy of myth, lies and street violence while enriching political insiders and compelling everyone else to applaud. Progressives' abandonment of the working class, meaning productive people, contributes to today's anti-productive extremism.

Biden's complicity with revolutionary "progressivism" is novel because it does not promise a new and superior economic system. Such a promise was a selling point for Marx, Owen, Saint Simon, Cabet, and G.D. H. Cole. Biden promises instead to right all wrongs by using governing powers and political confrontation. Biden's expedient accommodation of revolutionary "progressivism" unlike Sorel's revolutionary syndicalism, is not tied to empowering workers.

Sorel devised this prescription first for revolutionary syndicalism circa 1900. Radicals will use violent revolutionary tactics for any purpose.

The ideal is secondary. Revolutionary tactics may be viewed as a form of political extortion.

Can the Democrat Party Remain United?

Biden's strategy for electoral victory in 2022 is to indoctrinate the electorate with radical progressive attitudes and then intimidate everyone into compliance. Intimidation will be accomplished by enforcement of laws, mandates, and judicial rulings Biden has sponsored and the Democrat Congress has enacted. Biden does not care how revolutionary progressives and liberals in the Democrat Party sort out the details.

Biden's strategy has helter-skelter consequences. His support for very expensive legislation proposed by revolutionary progressives led to a conflict with moderates in the Democrat Party. He was unable to heal the breach in a quick and efficient matter despite his own personal intervention. The battle in the fall of 2021 embittered relations between revolutionary progressives and moderates. It has raised the question whether the Democrat Party will split?

Biden is on the wrong track. He is taking America where it shouldn't go and doesn't want to go. He is taking America down an ever-more partisan path.

Part XI
How Biden Might Save America

Chapter 40

Putting America Back Together: What Our President Should Do

Biden has a grand opportunity. He can rise above the partisan bickering which is immobilizing the American government domestically and weakening it internationally. Thereby, he can set America on a better path. Polls in the late spring of 2021 showed that 82% of Americans believe the country is deeply divided. Biden can rectify this by trying to lead America away from debilitating partisanship.

His mistake would be to lean too far in the direction the progressives are pushing him to go. The worst thing he could do is drive the country further into the extreme partisanship of revolutionary progressives. Once again, the needs and desires of the mass of the American people would be ignored in partisan battling.

Yet that is what Biden is doing. Biden is endorsing for American policy proposals that are partisan at their core. For example, he proposes hyper deficit spending. If enacted there is a danger of fiscal collapse for this country. It is much more serious now with China aspiring to an international payments system which does not depend on the United States currency.

Biden endorses subsides and preferences for non-whites that rest on the assertion of white guilt. This is a dramatic change from the American tradition of individual responsibility because it indicts a whole race. The result is an increasing bitterness between the races that make up the American population. Biden endorses improvements in the national safety net that are not well-designed to preserve labor force participation and productivity. Biden endorses Soviet style economic stagnation rather than investment-drive competitive growth.

It is almost as if in pursuit of partisan gains Biden is sponsoring utopia-like notions that are most likely to result in dystopic results.

Bipartisanship as a Route to Unity

Joe Biden declared at the outset of his Administration his intention to reunify America politicly after the divisiveness of previous years. Many people interpreted this as a promise to pursue a bipartisan course in governing. But he is hampered continually by his need to promote the political party he heads, and by the pressure of dealing with the conflicts within that party.

As president he moved immediately to pass major legislation in the Democrat-controlled Congress on a party-line vote. No Republican supported the major economic stimulus bill which had passed both houses of Congress by March 7, 2021. Biden was immediately condemned as insincere about unification by those who saw unity as evidenced by bipartisanship in Congress.

Suppose Biden shifted course and sought bipartisanship as a route to unification of America politically. The best chance for choosing statesmanship over politics is an accommodation between moderate Democrats and conservative Republicans. It is made possible because both look back to a period in which compromise and accommodation were common and served the interest of both Democrats and Republicans and more importantly of the nation. It is possible because Biden's own political background is more statesman than partisan politician.

But bipartisanship can go only so far. Even its advocates imagine it applying only to certain national issues.

Currently both moderates and conservatives vote party-line and often against measures they would be willing to accept or even support if free of party discipline.

Each party has a wing which is not in favor of reunification on any grounds except its own dominance. The progressives prevent accommodation within the Democrat Party, the populists within the Republican Party.

The big barrier to unity on a bipartisan basis is the political party system by which America is currently governed. Both Democrat moderates and Republican conservatives would have to ditch their more radical wings in order to reach an accommodation. This is unlikely to happen and even more unlikely for Biden to lead the nation there. The roots of party ambition go too deep in America for partisanship to be uprooted. Americans know this. Alternatives are being sought, but without chance of being adopted at this time. A proposal calls for the American public to draft two candidates to lead the executive branch: one from the center-left, the other from the center-right. (*BIG THINK*, July 9, 2020, #Unity2020, "The Unity Proposal In The Election Of 2020 To End Partisan Politics").

Unity in a One-Party Nation

There are other ways to unite the country than bipartisanship. One is for the Democrats to eliminate the Republicans and unify the country behind one party — the Democrats. Biden is not adopting bipartisanship. Instead, reaching for one party unity. Every move he makes is in pursuit of replacing two parties with only one — a Democrat party.

The revolutionary progressives are pushing Biden in the direction of their conception of America as a Putin-style "sovereign" democracy subject to their polar opposite social agenda. The elements of the American Constitution that create a republic would either be changed or ignored. The electoral college would have to be abolished so that the winner of the popular majority nationally would be chosen president.

Revolutionary progressives recognize that a more authoritarian system would be required to accomplish and sustain such a transition in American government. Political parties would have to be abolished in favor of a single party which would have no legal opponents, or Putin-style rigged to assure one party rule. The presidency would have to be greatly strengthened. In effect, the revolutionary progressives envision, though they don't acknowledge it publicly yet, a system of governance much like that of Communist China's one-party rule, serving very different purposes. Xi Jinping's system like Putin's is pro-meritocratic and militarist; American revolutionary progressives are anti-meritocratic and pacifist. In America, if revolutionary progressives co-opt the liberals, there would be a single party which controls all the formal elements of government, including the Congress, the presidency and the courts. It would rule. The media would be formally, not informally as today, subject to the guidance and censorship of the single party.

At this point Biden is moving slowly in the direction favored by the revolutionary progressives without acknowledging it. He still gives lip-service to the division of power between the three branches of American government while toying with increasing the size of the Supreme Court so that it can be made of the same political leaning as the Congress and the presidency. This would be a key step in moving toward one-party control of the government. Democrats in Congress have drafted legislation to pack the Supreme Court but have not yet gained the power to pass the legislation in the Senate.

Biden is leading the Democrat Party by small steps toward the revolutionary progressives' large ambition to control the government of the United States in the form of a one-party anti-meritocratic, pacifist system. The road is difficult and uncertain. It is likely to provoke increasingly desperate backlash.

Biden has an alternative.

Chapter 41

Statesmanship as a Route to Unity

The American political system as it stands is at a dead end. It is presiding over the decay of American democracy and the decline of our position in the world. At the core of the problem is the excessive partisanship of our political process.

To improve American government, we need statesmanship to harmonize rival parties. Biden faces a critical choice involving the elections. Biden is continuing the U.S. on a destructive anti-democratic partisan path by working with the progressives on their anti-consensus program. The nation would be much better served if he would point us in the direction of non-partisan consensus to resolve the nation's major problems. Biden's popularity has declined greatly with the public since he took office. He is being encouraged by his revolutionary progressive supporters to press their agenda as a way of regaining popularity. That is not likely to succeed because the nation wants consensus more than a partisan agenda. He should rise above partisanship to do his job for his poll support numbers to rise.

There is yet another route to national unity and it is available to the president. It is to unite the country behind efforts to resolve some of the issues facing the nation's masses. The consensus would be to address great issues and small. It would strengthen the nation and assist people in their own lives. The president would develop a course of action and bring a coalition of willing legislators behind it. The coalition would be of Democrats and Republicans. Moderate progressives could join. Coalitions might change membership with each issue. The president would permit neither party to claim credit for any legislation he has sponsored.

The effort would be to pass legislation on a non-partisan basis and simultaneously undermine the present excessively partisan party system.

It might seem that so evenly divided is the American political spectrum that some deeply significant forces cause there to be such a division — demographics, or cultural, or educational, or religious. Yet it seems this is not so. In fact, there are things about which Americans are almost unanimous, and they are things that can be labeled political or cultural or social. For example, at the end of August 2021, as the American military evacuation of Afghanistan neared its conclusion, a poll sponsored by ABC network news asked Americans if the U.S. military should ignore President Biden's deadline of August 31 for full withdrawal from Afghanistan under certain conditions. The question was to the effect: Should U.S. forces stay in Afghanistan until all U.S. citizens are out of the country? The result was Yes: Republicans 87%; Democrats 86%; and Independents 86%. President Biden's position was in direct opposition to this. He was too stubborn to change, and so he became very anxious to change the subject of national discussion and did.

An effort at non-partisan governing requires a president who can get out of the bubble of his distance from ordinary people and become knowledgeable of their experiences and concerns. America hasn't had such a president since the first days of Bill Clinton, who then entered the bubble and has stayed there since. Many American presidents rise from the ranks and are pleased to forget they were ever there. This was true of Bill Clinton and Barak Obama. It may turn out to be true of Joe Biden. That isn't yet evident for Biden. He can get in touch with the people above the heads of the political activists and govern in a non-partisan way.

Consensus Reform Not Revolution

Most Americans, whatever their political leanings, would prefer to keep our system and simply reform it to their better liking. But this may not be possible. We don't have a clean slate on which to make reforms. We can't reach an ideal arrangement. We increasingly have a choice between not-very-good options. We have a choice between an increasingly Lenin-style pro-insurrectionary, stealthy, and overt left and a more authoritarian right which exists to contain them. A search for alternatives is necessary, no matter how distasteful it may seem to people who don't yet recognize the unpleasant choice that is looming before us.

As we have indicated above, Biden has a mode of operation that focuses on putting more money into any problem. His initial months as president show the pattern clearly. He has signed a massive spending bill and proposed several others. To a large degree the spending is not to redress problems but only to provide funds to Democrat activist groups. To govern effectively Biden needs to change this pattern of behavior.

IF IT DOESN'T WORK, DO MORE OF IT.

At the policy level new solutions for festering problems are badly needed. To govern effectively in a non-partisan manner Biden must be able to commission a search for new solutions, choose the better ones, persuade Congress and the administrative agencies of their value, and implement them successfully. This is a much greater challenge than proposing spending bills.

A basic prescription of the Democrat Party (and not only the Democrat Party but of many other people as well) is this: IF IT ISN'T WORKING, DO MORE OF IT.

Since the average American student is not doing well on international tests, extend the school day and the school year. What will improve performance in a poorly functioning school system? Doing more of it!

If lockdowns haven't tamed the virus, then extend lockdowns and tighten them.

Since massive spending has not created sustained economic growth, pursue more spending until fiscal policy stimulus is the most excessive in history, and then call for more. In the process, undermine the finances of the nation.

Since government responsibilities are being done poorly — for example, maintaining and improving the nation's infrastructure — what should be done? Let the government spend vastly more on doing it.

It is crucial that the president abandon this mind-set. Instead, in addressing problems that have festered for decades, he must abandon the usual approaches and commission new ones. They need not always involve heavy new spending.

Defanging Political Party Opposition

There is likely to be massive opposition from both political parties to any effort of a president to govern on a non-partisan basis as a pragmatic, consensus-building statesman. To defang the opposition, the president should try to deprive the parties of financial strength. The best way to do this is by campaign finance limitations. Financing should be restricted to a period within a month or so of an election. Today, fundraising for the next election to Congress begins immediately after the preceding election. There used to be at least a year's interval before the next election campaign began. Fundraising was set aside for that year. In Washington the campaigning period was referred to as the "silly season" and it was presumed no serious legislation would get done. Still, there was one year in which serious work was done in Washington. Now one silly season follows on the heels of another; one campaign season follows immediately on the other; one fundraising season follows immediately on the other. Congresspersons spend about 40% of their time, say polls of the Congress, on campaign fund raising; they spend more time on campaigning. The season of serious legislative work has disappeared.

America's national leadership is well-aware of this and champions it. Vice President Kamala Harris sent an email to Democrats on September 30, 2021, explaining how the Democrat Party now campaigns without interruption:

> If we learned anything last election cycle, it's that we must start building the infrastructure Democrats will rely on to win as early as we possibly can. The same is true of next year's midterms ... Our Democratic majorities are too slim and our progress too important to leave up to chance. We've got to roll up our sleeves now and get to work if we have any hope of defending and building on our majorities in 2021 and 2022. Luckily, the DNC is already hiring organizers, running its largest-ever voter protection program, and making historic investments in state parties and the grassroots — all because they know just how important it is for Democrats to win in these upcoming elections.

All this is fatal to an attempt to govern by addressing and resolving the problems of the nation — large and small. It means that our political parties never stop campaigning against each other. Since the partisan battle takes precedence of the nation's needs, all legislation is caught up continually in partisan controversy.

At the core of this situation is the issue of financing our political parties and their campaigns. Vice President Harris's email which is presented in full above is, of course, an appeal for funds to finance the activities of the Democrat National Committee (DNC) which Mrs. Harris describes. Billions of dollars will be raised by both political parties and spent on the coming campaigns.

Resolution of the campaign financing crisis — it is a crisis for effective government in America — will confront a major obstacle in decisions of the Supreme Court. But the court sometimes reverses its mistaken decisions and a major challenge to the president lies in persuading it to do so in the matter of campaign financing.

The Party out of Power

Parties cannot be eliminated, even though they can be formally repressed. They couldn't be avoided at the start of the republic though key leaders among our founding fathers wanted to avoid them because of the dangers they posed to the republic. We now have harvested those dangers to the upmost. What can be done to mitigate predatory partisanship?

The solution begins with the President and the party in power. More presidential leadership can be on a non-partisan basis. Biden's policy program does not have to be exclusively Democrat Party driven.

The Republicans, though out of power, have a responsibility a well. As is common in American politics, the party out of power (now the Republicans) is counting on the mistakes and failures of the party in power, the Democrats, for Republican victory in the campaigns of 2022 and 2024. In consequence, the Republicans are running on negatives — against the party in power. What is hard to know is what is the positive program of the Republican party?

Democrats and Republicans govern much alike in that they both are preoccupied by partisanship. Each failed with respect to the pandemic and Afghanistan. They took different routes, and each had some success, but the routes and outcomes were both far less positive than the nation had a right to expect and both limitations were rooted in partisanship. Ineffective government is not just a result of one party or the other — it is an American problem. There can be no partisan solution. And since the parties will not work together to any great degree, a solution must be non-partisan — protecting both minority and majority core interests.

There is an opportunity for Biden to go non-partisan because to a large part both working people and the business community are wondering where is their political home today?

Embracing Statesmanship

Our President should concentrate on a simple program that changes the subject of politics from partisan victory to what can be achieved by non-partisanship statesmanship.

What can be done is a pro-growth strategy that generates resources for advancement. All barriers to pro-growth — including the government itself — should be reduced.

The resources saved and new income from growth should go to modernization, strengthening, and defense of the nation.

This program is non-partisan. It also justifies compromise.

All other issues raised in this book should then be open for discussion on a basis that does not torpedo the primary agenda.

Economic Growth

The American economy has been stuck in a sluggish growth rate for more than a decade. The economic collapse associated with the pandemic has generated a rapid recovery that the Democrats are trying to pretend is a new era of high growth for America. It is not so. We will soon return to the almost stagnant economy that we were experiencing before the pandemic. The American dream will continue its disappearance for many. The dream is the idea that a person's children will do much better financially in life than they did. The dream is a great motivator for parents to work hard for their children's futures.

For the moment, the pandemic has changed the economic landscape dramatically. The U.S. growth rate rose significantly for 2021 (a partial recovery from the adverse effects of the pandemic). This is a result of the massive spending that is said to be justified by the pandemic. The Biden Administration is insisting that high spending will push the American economy into a new era of rapid growth. Specifically, spending on a new infrastructure to combat climate change is asserted to provide years of rapid growth. New jobs in the millions are forecast to grow annually for years.

This is unlikely. Underneath the rapid government spending of today we are still in a slow growth/stagnation mode. The underlying causes remain. Slow population growth, regulatory delays, environmental concerns, the satisfaction of the wealthy with the economic situation as it has been now for decades, domination of the economy by anti-competitive forces and partisan political paralysis. Nothing has changed except the pandemic and the unusual financial effort to counter it. The economic system is still stuck in a slow growth mode, not only in the U.S. but in Europe as well. This will become evident when the spending splurge of the moment is ended by either a financial crisis or a reversion to efforts to avoid a crisis.

China has done a great job of both benefiting from globalization and yet preserving independence from it. China has preserved a high growth rate and yet been subject to the risks of financial crises which accompany the global economy. The United States hasn't done anywhere near as well. Biden has returned the United States to globalization, both diplomatically and economically. The U.S. needs to plan for financial crises that will certainly occur, even originating in the U.S. as happened in 2007–2008. Biden's insistence that the U.S. is embarking on a new era of rapid growth driven by domestic spending pretends that global financial risks are negligible.

To counter long-term economic stagnation structural reform of the U.S. economy is necessary. It isn't occurring — though anti-trust action is beginning to be talked about. The American economy is oligopolized and monopsonized. This results in low domestic business investment and slow growth as a means for large corporations to maximize profitability. And the global supply chain is now so firmly established that it cannot be quickly replicated in the U.S. American firms have foreign suppliers which perform better than American alternatives and American buyers can only be dislodged from those suppliers by very strong government action — "Buy American" doesn't do it — neither do limited tariffs, though they are effective to a limited degree.

It is a mistake to view the American economy in isolation. With very few exceptions (e.g., Israel), all the major economies of the world suffered growth retardation in the wake of the global financial crisis. These countries included: America, the European Union, Russia, Iran, Japan, and India. This growth retardation preceded Biden's spending spree. Europe has had zero growth for a decade.

The West is over-leveraged and cannot accelerate growth by endlessly piling on debt — which the U.S. is trying to do. From one perspective which is rejected by the current administration the largest single cause of growth retardation is the diversion of funds directly to government spending and indirectly through outsourcing into lesser- or non-productive activities. The hidden inflation associated with this phenomenon masks the negative effect. The only thing that makes America seem to be doing well is information technology. Smartphone addicts are so intoxicated sending messages to each other that they fail to appreciate that other aspects of their living standard are declining.

Chapter 42

A Program for America's President

The American president has numerous important choices to make. Among the most important is one about America's role in the world — to continue to assert hegemony without investing in the hard power to support it, or to lessen America's footprint in the world. Biden seems to be unable to make a choice at this point and is simply flailing about. We urge him to invest vigorously in the power needed to make America's voice in the world persuasive.

American Hegemony

The American president must decide whether to attempt to reassert American global hegemony or to abandon it for a multi-polar world. In April 2021, Chairman Xi suggested cautiously that it is time for the United States to accept other super-powers as America's equal in the world.

This is the big foreign policy issue: Whether the U.S. tries to enforce the Western world order globally or to accept growing spheres of influence for China and Russia as superpowers and Iran as a regional power? It is possible to pretend that this choice need not be made. It is possible instead to lose oneself in the day-to-day challenges of foreign policy — coping with daily crises. This is the course the Biden Administration seems to be taken. But it is like an ostrich burying its head in the sand, and reality will at some point overtake it.

Going day-to-day, the U.S. continues to play "let us pretend" hegemon, but it is not following Obama's "rule of law approach." Biden has reverted to older tactics. There is an element of arrogance in this. Upon the collapse of the Soviet Union and America's emergence as sole superpower, Americans became arrogant. American political leaders began to presume that they had a right to lead the globe. This had not been the American attitude before the U.S.S.R. dissolved. Before that Americans had taken pride in their victory in World War II but had then been humbled by the fiasco in Viet Nam. Arrogance has returned. Relinquishing hegemony now is made difficult by arrogance.

America can no longer lead the global order whatever approach is taken. Russia and China preclude this possibility, and domestic politics takes precedence over defense and foreign affairs. Biden is not willing to cut domestic programs to revive America's global authority. This story may change after the United States suffers some grievous blows, but Washington for the moment cannot get beyond doublethink to a serious choice.

Partnership with Russia to break up the alliance of Russia, China, and Iran is possible in principle, but America won't be able to do this with its head in the clouds. Washington suffers from acute attention deficit disorder. It can adhere to an established pattern of behavior — such as acting as global hegemon — but it cannot discipline itself to follow a strategy that makes hegemony possible.

An inability to make a different choice forces America to rebuff Russia, China, and Iran as strongly as it can, even if the U.S. is no longer *primus inter pares*. If America cannot rebuff the authoritarians, then it has no appealing foreign policy options.

In fact, we are entering a multi-polar world and must recognize it. But we must continue to push back on the authoritarians. It is especially necessary to push back because democracy itself confronts its most direct challenge since World War II.

We need to avoid the trap of over-reaching abroad while being unable to take the necessary steps at home to support our ambitions abroad. There is room for compromise. President Biden will have to give up some domestic programs to achieve foreign objectives.

This is not at all where U.S. policy is now. Biden and his advisors are still in the American global domination mindset of the immediate aftermath of the collapse of the U.S.S.R. It is how Biden behaves. It will be best if he changes this attitude voluntarily and in favor of a well-thought-out alternative, rather than being forced to change by some disaster.

Biden's speech at the UN General Assembly in late September 2021, was a speech directed as much at a domestic audience as a foreign one. It stressed partisan themes. It avoided the major challenges the U.S. faces globally. Biden managed to not mention China or Russia by name. Partisanship will mire the U.S. in indecision about international issues. If Biden wishes to pursue an effective foreign policy, he will have to do so as a statesman, without purblind partisanship.

The Immigration Risk

Biden has been entangled in the immigration issue since he arrived in office. There is much more to the immigration issue than the domestic concerns that receive so much attention in the media. An open border means agents of foreign governments and quasi-governments like crime cartels pour into the U.S.

We are entering a period of intense confrontation with powerful rivals abroad. We must protect ourselves from their intelligence and sabotage operations much more than we have been doing. Biden is not doing so, yet. He will likely move that way. As we tighten our border and other security, we should seize the opportunity to strengthen America through our immigration policies.

Left to itself, immigration will continue until later immigrants face no better a future in the United States than they do in the places from which they have come.

The Administration has proposed a legal path to citizenship for some 11–30 million people believed to be in the United States without proper documentation, many for many years. These people are *de facto* citizens of the United States, and the argument is strong that they should be allowed citizenship after a period of years. To do this properly, the path for these people should be somewhat longer than that for people who have entered the United States legally. The path for legal immigrants should be made shorter than for illegal immigrants and should be somewhat less difficult and/or less expensive.

Engaged in conflict with strong foreign opponents, we need to strengthen the United States. We should consider using immigration as an opportunity to do several things:

Inoculate all immigrants against COVID before they enter the country from its borders. Teach them English. Expand their knowledge of the basis of American democracy, how it should work, and how immigrants can participate in it. Suggest to them a mission of bringing our principles of democracy to their home countries. Make it easy for them to return to their families and their countries with this fresh point of view, sharing our values with them after they fully understand and can pass tests on English, history, and philosophy (Suzanne McDonough, draft of a letter to *The New York Times,* April 16, 2021).

Crush the Drug Cartels

Drug cartels are as dangerous to the U.S. as Islamic terrorists. They have killed more Americans in the U.S. than the terrorists did in the 9/11 attack.

They have branches in the U.S. but are headquartered on foreign soil, where they won't be protected by an army of lawyers like they would be in the U.S. The President should do something final, not just let a bleeding wound fester. The President should authorize a military campaign in Mexico against the cartels and support efforts by the Columbian and Salvadoran governments to destroy the cartels based in their countries. Accompanying the campaign abroad should be an intense effort to eliminate the cartels in the U.S. Where there is insufficient space in American prisons for the new inmates, let there be construction of new prisons for them. Publicize the construction so that the cartel members can leave the U.S. if they wish to do so.

The U.S. has had to intervene in Mexico several times to stop cross border crime. The most important of such efforts involved a U.S. military incursion led by John J. Pershing — who would later command American forces in France during World War I — chasing guerrillas under Poncho Villa.

The cartels now so dominate illegal immigration to the United States that they must be dealt with before a reasonable solution can be found to the American immigration problem.

The United States should join Mexico in a military campaign which destroys the cartels' bases in Mexico.

The Republican Administration ignored an opportunity to intervene on a large scale against the cartels when one of them executed an American family in northern Mexico. The Biden Administration has been reluctant to intervene against the cartels. In pursuit of its political purposes with respect to immigration Biden largely ignores the existence of the cartels. It is hard to imagine that anything done to discourage people from trying to get into the United States will be effective when the cartels make a large and profitable business out of bringing them here.

The Republican's policy was to treat illegal immigrants through our southern border harshly to discourage them from coming. Biden's policy is to encourage them to come and try to treat them decently when they do. But with his policy goes entrance to the U.S. of people ill with the virus, of members of drug gangs and foreign espionage agents. Neither U.S. president got it right — a circumstance common in American government in all sorts of areas.

Getting it right means to destroy the cartels.

John Wayne was a Hollywood actor who in one movie was leading American paratroopers in the Allied invasion of France late in World War II. About the Nazi enemy Wayne told his troops, "Send 'em to Hell!"

The drug cartels are an independent force driving illegal immigration and corrupting the United States. They have advanced from a focus on drugs to other profitable endeavors including sending migrants to the United States and human trafficking.

The United States cannot prepare effectively for global confrontation without closing the open sore that the cartels present.

The American President should send 'em to hell.

Addressing Hacking Vulnerability

Our cyber vulnerability is severe. Government regulation should lessen it. The technological devices which the quasi-monopoly tech companies have sold to American consumers and businesses are seriously flawed in the degree to which they are vulnerable to hacking — from the U.S. or from abroad. There is repeated and continuing evidence of this. Our devices are like unsafe cars. The manufacturers should be forced to recall and fix them and should be prohibited from selling unsafe devices. Anti-hacking legislation should require manufacturers to fix these products as decades ago we required seat belts in cars and other safety measures. The companies should pay for these improvements.

A Bill to Require Cooperation between the Public and Private Sector

The United States is ill-prepared for the challenges it will face in the global contests which are now emerging. Because it is a mixed economy of government and private organizations, it must be able to ensure cooperation between them on issues of national concern. It is surprisingly unable to do so on the needed scale.

In areas of national concern, both domestic and foreign, the United States needs to provide a legal structure which causes government and industry to work together pro-competitively, not for politicians and monopolists personal enrichment. Too often the government ignores the private sector, or when it tries to work with private organizations the government it does so incompetently.

Chapter 43

Biden Persists in Partisanship

George Washington feared the impact of political parties on the United States. In his farewell address he said that the spirit of faction (of political parties) "agitates the community with ill-founded jealousies and false alarms, kindles the animosity of one part against another, foments occasionally riot and insurrection." This is exactly what has happened in the more than two centuries since.

In 2022, the White House embarked on a major press campaign to blame Republicans for an economy the White House says is in excellent shape, and the national public health agency, the Center for Disease Control (CDC) for continuing problems with the efforts to control the pandemic. None of this makes any sense except in American partisan politics. None of it is constructive as part of an effort to improve the economy or control the pandemic. But partisan politics is now the essence of American government.

For several decades American businesspersons advising foreign persons about entering the American marketplace have cautioned them that America is a very hostile legal environment. They could expect many legal challenges and actions in the courts. They would be surprised by the dishonesty involved in the claims. Many claims would seem to them to be nothing other than extortion.

Today, it must be added to this warning, which is now more apt than earlier, that America is a very hostile political environment. American politicians and the American government will condemn with the help of a complicit media, businesspeople, and professionals for whatever errors they, the politicians, have made. American public policy and discussion have become graveyards for the reputations of professionals and companies.

President Biden

Joe Biden has been President of the United States for more than a year. He is not a popular president. This is because of several factors. Among them is that he is president of one of America's two bitterly contesting political parties. The party which is out of power, the Republicans and their supporters in the media attack Biden continually. They attack him for whatever he does — including actions they support and actions they should support. This is the new pattern in American politics. Democrats attacked Republican President Donald Trump with the same lack of restraint. Unrestrained attacks limit a president's popularity and his ability to accomplish important public objectives.

A democracy can't succeed if each president fails. This is how modern partisan democracies fail. They destroy themselves by vilifying each president. It is easier to tear down than to build up. Each party in opposition tears down the president who comes from the other party. Every action of the incumbent is damned. The government fails along with its president. The nation fails along with the government. This is how French democracy was made impotent between the two world wars so that it defeated Imperial Germany in the First and collapsed before Nazi Germany in the Second. This is how the British abandoned their empire after the Second World War. They no longer had the stomach for the sacrifices necessary to maintain it; nor for the breadth of vision necessary to govern it. This is what is now happening in the United States and to its leadership role in the world. America now lacks the stomach for the sacrifices necessary to maintain the democratic world and it lacks the breadth of vision necessary to maintain its leadership role in the world. American democracy is eviscerating itself in partisan controversies and dishonesties.

The United States is now decaying in many ways. This is so dramatic that it is common to hear Americans complain among themselves that the U.S. is increasingly like a Third World country. Among the list of changes are these:

- Increasing violence
- Increasing crime

- Increasing gang activity
- Increasing drug addiction
- Increasing homelessness
- Deteriorating healthcare system
- Inept crisis management systems (Covid)
- Deteriorating infrastructure
- Ineffective policing
- Corruption as a way to get things done
- Unreliable and poor quality service
- No aspiration to personal improvement
- No hope of a better life (The end of the American dream)
- Arbitrary, intrusive, overbearing, ineffectual and non-protecting government
- Huge differences between rich and poor
- Rich separated into defended isolated communities away from poor
- A depreciating currency.

Because he is president many Americans blame Biden for all these elements of decay. While each find its way into political controversy, some take precedence. The position of revolutionary progressives is drawing Biden into serious unpopularity with two of the list.

Inflation is a problem which revolutionary progressives sponsor but will not acknowledge doing so. Inflation destroys the middle class. It eats away their savings. It reduces the value of their wages. It reduces the middle class to what the communists call a lumpenproletariat — people who live from day to day on what they can earn from work or receive from the government. Since the middle class leans conservative politically, revolutionary progressives endorse inflation secretly in order to disempower the middle class. This revolutionary progressive policy is the opposite of Nikolai Bukharin and Evgeny Preobrazhensky's pro-working class Bolshevik War Communist strategy. "Inflation is the machine gun of the proletariat mowing down the monied classes" (Sokolnikov, Soviet Minister of Finance in the early 1920s, quoted in Robert W. Davis, *The Development of the Soviet Budgetary Process,* Chapter 2 (1958)). Preobrazhensky said "paper money is a machine gun for the Finance Commissariat to fire at the bourgeoisie, enabling the monetary laws of that regime to be used in order to destroy it."

President Biden sent me (Mills) on December 13, 2021, an email circulated to millions of Americans. It read, "Quinn, I ran for president on a simple promise: To restore the soul of America and to rebuild the backbone of the nation — the middle class" (President Joseph R. Biden, Jr., wide distribution email, December 13, 2021). This was Biden's promise as a presidential candidate. Yet it is not the program of the revolutionary progressive wing of his party. In fact, it is the opposite of the program of the radical progressives.

Crime is the problem for which revolutionary progressives have no solution. Crime is charged disproportionately to the African American population, so revolutionary progressives simply quit addressing it. When challenged, they say that redistributed income and increased social benefits will indirectly act to eliminate crime. They don't, though they may help. Unaddressed directly by revolutionary progressives crime rises wherever they have political control. Some liberal Democrats address it — including the new mayor of New York City. But revolutionary progressives politically and in the courts hamstring the liberals' efforts.

Revolutionary progressives move to cease enforcing law because blacks are often disproportionately affected. For example, legal historian Sarah Seo traced back police officer bias against blacks in traffic law enforcement in much of the United States for about 100 years. Probably it extended further back. Because of this she called for removing police from traffic law enforcement — presumably there would be no traffic law enforcement (*Harvard Gazette*, November 23, 2021).

There are numerous crimes for which African Americans are disproportionately arrested, charged, convicted, and penalized. To revolutionary progressives this is evidence of discrimination in American society which is ongoing. Liberals seek to eliminate the discrimination. Revolutionary progressives despair of eliminating discrimination and seek instead to avoid it. Revolutionary progressives propose to cease enforcing many of laws, or to make them unenforceable (by defunding the police, for example). This effort is now under way in many of America's largest cities (including New York, Los Angeles, Chicago, Houston, and San Francisco).

In the midst of this effort led by the revolutionary progressives crime is rising rapidly in American cities, including crimes which progressives do not publicly propose to cease enforcing — especially violence and murder. But shootings and murders are rising rapidly. The public is concerned and Biden is blamed, despite the White Houses' insistence that it is opposed to violent crime and is acting to restrain its increase.

Violence is increasing in the United States in the political arena as well as on the streets. Biden will be blamed for that as well. On October 4, 2021, revolutionary progressive students angered by the failure of a Democrat Senator to support one of the Biden Administration's bills attacked her while she was visiting a state university and drove her for security into a bathroom stall (bigleaguepolitics, a video posted by libsoftiktok Twitter on October 4, 2021).

The most recent presidential elections are charged to have been accompanied by efforts to overturn their results by force, as we have seen in a previous chapter. In other countries these efforts would have been labeled coups, and they are sometimes so labeled in the United States. It is likely that efforts of this nature will continue in the future in America and become more blatant. At this point, those involved in these efforts continue to deny they occurred, and if elements can be demonstrated to have occurred, the perpetrators insist they are isolated and not part of an overall coordinated effort.

The most recent effort involved President Trump's effort to prevent President Biden from taking office. Millions of Americans who are Republican voters believe that the 2020 election was stolen. The assertions of the Democrats and the media that it is a "big lie" are of no significance to them. They believe the media is simply an expression of the establishment and offers misinformation continually, so they disregard whatever the media says. The revolutionary progressive Democrats openly proclaim their position that the end justifies the means. When Democrats assert that there was no theft of the election because they — the Democrats — always obey the election laws, Republicans scoff. In this environment, where he and his supporters believe the election was stolen, and where Trump is aware of the Democrats attempted coup in 2017 against his own inauguration, Trump had to attempt to prevent Biden's certification as president or Trump would have appeared a weakling.

Against this background, it is to be expected that the militant wing of the Democrat Party, which is revolutionary progressive, would be preparing itself to violently oppose Republican successes in future elections. In mid-December, 2021, prosecutors in San Diego, California, charged seven people identified as self-identified anti-fascists and members of *antifa* with assaults that occurred in January, 2021 directed at participants in a march organized by supporters of then-President Donald Trump. Those charged with a crime are said to have organized themselves by use of social media and were charged with conspiracy to commit riot (Alex Riggins, "DA charges California 'Antifa' groups," San Diego Union, December 9, 2021).

In his presidential campaign Biden promised to bring the American nation together. America perceived itself to be bitterly divided at the time of the election. Polls show that after Biden has been more than a year in office much of the public does not believe he has fulfilled this promise. The issue most contributing to that perception is the Biden Administration's management of the southern border of the United States. The border is essentially open. Millions of people have streamed through it without permits and continue to do so. Because this is so difficult for non-Americans to believe, I quote here from a letter to me (Mills) from a rancher in south Texas near the border with Mexico. The letter was written on November 18, 2021.

"Encroachment of our ranch via loads of illegals using heavy trucks to ram through fences continues unabated and with increasing frequency as time passes. Two such loads of illegals/smugglers rammed through our high fence on highway 97 early today with the law in pursuit. Such has become so frequent that our 4 miles of highway frontage is a shambles. Repair seems futile.

"Local law, Border Patrol and Immigration and Naturalization Service, plus State Police chase and capture some but most cross the ranch and exit though fence out back to evade capture."

"Ranch security is a joke and any livestock is scattered about the range. Fortunately, unlike illegal entry of years past when ranch assets were at risk of theft or damage, today's entry is just passing through heading to better hunting ground heading north to the cities."

It is believed by about half of Americans that the White House refuses to enforce national immigration law because illegal immigrants are perceived as a large addition to Democrat voters. President Biden makes his promise to unite Americans empty by appearing to violate national law in a major way in order to gain partisan advantage for his political party.

Biden is Being Carried along by the Shift in the American Democrat Party as the Democrats Move from Liberal to Revolutionary Progressive

One of the most dramatic transformations in the history of American politics has taken place within the Democrat Party since 2010. It is measured by a poll of the attitude of Democrats toward a single question. The Pew Research Center asked a sample of Americans whether they agreed with the statement "Racial discrimination is the main reason why many Black people can't get ahead these days."

In 2010, 28% of Democrats agreed with this statement. In 2017, 64% agreed. (These data are cited in Mark Harper, "Why is Critical Race Theory so Divisive?" *Palm Beach Post*, November 21, 2021, p. 26A.) This shift in attitude brought with it a major change in how Democrats approach American politics. African Americans are a key element of the Democrat Party and perhaps as much as half its composition. How they are to be bettered in American life is a key question for Democrat leaders. If racial discrimination is a minor element of their difficulties, then the liberal approach is the more likely successful one. If as liberal policies suggest black people obtain education, apply themselves to master skills, and work hard, they will get ahead in American life. But if racial discrimination denies advancement to African Americans no matter what efforts they make in their own behalf, then liberalism is advice without value and the revolutionary progressive approach is the valid one. The radical progressive approach is a revolutionary remaking of American society to rid it of racial discrimination. The Pew data point to the shift in the conviction of the Democrat Party from liberal to progressive. The numbers suggest that a majority of Democrats may now be progressives (64% hold the Progressive attitude toward the key question about policy toward the nation's major minority).

How did this transformation in attitude come about, how so completely, and in so short a time?

It likely was initiated and achieved during the presidency of Barak Obama and with the support of his administration. It may be considered to have been the long-delayed recognition by most Democrats of the strong role that racial discrimination continues to play in American life. It may conversely be thought to reflect a politically motivated propaganda campaign that exaggerates the significance of racial discrimination in American life.

The revolutionary progressive attitude carries with it implications whose full impact is yet to be seen. Biden is being carried along with this political logic without expecting or understanding the consequences for himself or the nation. For example, revolutionary progressives are preparing to abandon the Constitution. They are now voicing their arguments for it. But Biden has sworn to uphold and defend the Constitution. He will have to choose.

The revolutionary progressive argument is that the Constitution now and in the past has sometimes conflicted with political morality. When that occurs, progressives argue, the Constitution must give way.

The argument is made in "The Broken Constitution: Lincoln, Slavery, and the Refounding of America," by Harvard Law Professor Noah Feldman, published in 2021. In his book he "argues that the charter, originally drafted in 1787, was repeatedly violated and ultimately remade by America's 16th president Abraham Lincoln. Winning the Civil War, he says, required an initially reluctant Lincoln to ultimately shred and replace the antiquated agreement, which was fatally infected by its animating compromise to preserve and extend the institution of slavery, a practice even most framers admitted at the time was morally repugnant." (In a conflict between justice and the Constitution, "why should the Constitution prevail?" Jeff Neal, *Harvard Gazette*, November 16, 2021.) So it is that revolutionary progressives now assert that the Constitution can be ignored if necessary to advance a moral political agenda — such as the progressives believe their voting rights bill to be.

This is a remarkable reach of political ambition. Abandoning the Constitution effectively abandons the rule of law and the independence of the courts. Unable to dominate the courts now, the progressives wish to make them unfree and subject to the legislative and executive power.

Faced with revolutionary progressive ambition and political overreach Biden is being pulled in ever more radical directions. He is moving that way, despite rhetoric in the opposite direction.

The Danger of Partisanship in the International Sphere

The dangers of Biden's increasing ties to the progressives are not limited to the domestic sphere. They extend internationally as well.

It is customary to discuss foreign policy separately from domestic politics, but in the United States the two are intertwined. Foreign policy is an offshoot of domestic politics. The most embarrassing surrender of American arms in history, the Afghanistan pull-out in summer, 2021, was nothing other than a contest between Republicans and Democrats for who could claim to the American people to have ended what was being called in the media "America's longest war."

Again, partisan politics led America into a policy disaster. It was particularly embarrassing because it could not have been carried out as well as it was without the assistance of a tiny ally. Today the U.S. needs allies because of its incompetence. The best recent evidence was the fiasco in the Afghan withdrawal. Without assistance from the tiny country of Qatar the U.S. could not have managed its exit from Afghanistan. To the extent the U.S. was able to avoid a total disaster in Afghanistan it was due to Qatar. Qatar had the resources, will, and administrative capability to handle tens of thousands of people being taken out of Afghanistan — flying many in Qatari planes and receiving them and many more in an organized manner in Qatar.

Against this background of strategic incompetence, the Pentagon released its 2021 Report on China. The 2021 report explicitly describes China's goals as seeking to "match or surpass U.S. global influence and power, displace U.S. alliances and security partnerships in the Indo-Pacific region, and revise the international order to be more advantageous to Beijing's authoritarian system and national interests."

Evidence of China's ambitions was given immediately. In November 2021, China asserted leadership equality with the U.S. on the world stage. The absence of China and Russia and other authoritarian powers from the G20 session in Rome and the Climate Conference in Scotland in the first week of November 2021, was an assertion of independence from the American-led world order. Thus, while the attendees asserted a claim to represent the world (there were 200 countries represented said the media), a significant portion of the world did not participate. The two conferences represented not the world, but a portion of it. The conferences indicated that the world is again divided, as during the Cold War, though with significant differences. We are in a state of cold war, but it is being temporarily downplayed by all sides, and China leads the non-Western bloc, not the Soviet Union. Russia is leading the on-again-off-again cold war in Europe and the Middle East. The democracies face a clear challenge.

Soon after the meetings it did not attend Xi met Biden in a virtual summit. China had let the U.S. lead a Western-dominated portion of the world, then asserted itself as the leader of the rest of the world by meeting with Biden not about China's role but about the world agenda. It is possible that the summit was Biden's face-saving gesture, analogous to Munich.

Russia is key. So long as China has an alliance with Russia, it has the power to assert equality with the U.S. on the world stage. This the Biden team vehemently denies. But without the Russian alliance, China cannot equal American power and influence. Without the Russian alliance China is merely a large Asian nation which must defend itself from its neighbors and accept the American peace in Asia. With the Russian alliance it is able to aspire to equality of leadership on the global stage with the U.S.

Russia holds the balance of power between China and the U.S. It holds the balance of power in the world. The U.S. has been determinedly unwilling to recognize this. The result is that Russia is leaning toward China, allowing China to assert equality with the U.S. in the quest for world leadership.

Maybe this is the reason Biden withdrew from Afghanistan and he was unwilling to tell the world the truth about his reason. "In the past decade, Russia has made a number of breakthroughs in the development of nuclear weapons and their delivery vehicles, significantly outstripping Washington in several areas. Russia and the U.S. maintain quantitative parity in strategic weapons, whilst having different structures. However, the U.S. leadership is extremely concerned that it lags behind Russia in the field of advanced missile defense systems. This stems from having underestimated Russian military potential and spent too heavily on armed conflicts (primarily in Afghanistan and Iraq), which ate up about 100 billion dollar annually. After the withdrawal of U.S. troops from Afghanistan and the significant drawdown in Iraq, the situation is starting to change. The U.S. defense budget for 2022 will see substantial funds allocated for development of new weapons, including strategic ones" ("Russia Beyond November 23, 2021, "In what ways are Russia's nuclear forces superior to America's?" Vladimir Evseev, head of the CIS Institute Department of Eurasian Integration and SCO Development. https://www.rbth.com/science-and-tech/334437-russian-american-nuclear-arsenals).

The Democrats, in their quest for political advantage in the U.S. pushed Russia into its alliance with China and thereby undermined U.S. leadership in the world. The significance of the Democrat-led American hostility to Russia (which takes many forms) is enormous — it is the most important influence on the sliding of American influence world-wide. It also stands in stark contrast to Bill and Hilary Clinton's "normal Russia" transition line 1992–2014. It enables China to assert world-level leadership. The American decline is not in our stars, but in American politics, that we are allowing ourselves to be led by underlings.

In the distant future China may not require an alliance with Russia to assert leadership of the world. According to Henry Kissinger China will achieve dominance in its own right by hard power preeminence based on development of artificial intelligence applied to both military and economic spheres.

China versus Democracy

In the second week of December 2021, President Biden sponsored a dialogue on democracy to which many countries were invited, but several were not, including China.

According to China–U.S. Focus (chinausfocus+cusef.org.hk@ccsend.com, December 10, 2021), "China held its own dialogue on democracy last week promoting the concept that 'China's political system is, in fact, a high-functioning form of democracy of a different sort.' China's State Council also released a white paper entitled, 'China: Democracy That Works,' while the Foreign Ministry released its own report criticizing the state of democracy in the U.S."

"At a high-level press conference the following day [early November 2021], Chinese officials voiced rare, public criticism of Western democracies that impose their ideas of democracy on the world, specifically China. 'The electoral democracy of Western countries are actually democracy rules by the capital, and they are a game of the rich, not real democracy,' said Jiang Jinquan, the director of the policy research office for the CCP" (China–US Focus, December 11, 2021).

In early November, 2021, Western media reported that the CCP had adopted resolutions placing Xi on the same level as Mao and establishing his claim to be leader of China for his lifetime. We sought to obtain the resolutions to read them. They do not exist. Nothing could be found in Chinese sources of the nature described in the Western press. Several years ago the two-term limitation on Xi's role in the Chinese leadership was removed. Nothing else has been done. It is unclear even today if Xi will seek another term.

With such reporting in the Western media, uncorrected by the Western governments, it is very difficult for a citizen to understand what is occurring in the world. We are merely passive observers being manipulated by all sides.

The conviction, born of fear that holds the politics of China together is that so long as the leaders of the Communist Party of China hold the reins of government securely, the community strives and moves forward. But when their hold weakens, China will sink into anarchist confusion and decline.

Most Americans now know little history and they learn nothing more than what they can look up on the search engines. If Google's or Bing's or Wikipedia's researchers don't include it for search, this generation won't find it.

There is between China and the United States an economic contest, a trade contest, an investment contest, a soft power propaganda contest, and a hard power contest. But there is also an incomprehension problem. Neither Wall Street nor Foggy Bottom grasps the extent to which Xi controls China's economic and military systems. They are befuddled by "Market Communism" into believing that the market is king in China. This blinds them to the fact that Xi at his discretion can "terminate" all foreign participation leaseholds (*de facto* nationalization) at his discretion leaving no recourse through the rule of contract law.

"The U.S. interest is that whatever arrangement is worked out between China and Taiwan is done peacefully." So spoke the American Chief of Staff at the end of 2021. (Mark Milley, Chief of Staff, U.S. Military, at the Yale CEO Summit, December 15, 2021.) This is wrong. The American interest is to protect Japan and South Korea from domination by China via their control of Taiwan.

Secretary of State Blinken said on CNN on October 31, 2021, "We will see that Taiwan has whatever is necessary to defend itself." Asked repeatedly whether the US would defend Taiwan from a Chinese attack, Blinken replied each time with the sentence above. The answer sounds like "No. Taiwan must defend itself." This can be interpreted as similar to Biden's assertion that Afghanistan would not defend itself, so the U.S. abandoned it.

It is also reminiscent of Secretary of State Acheson's indication that Korea was not in the U.S. defense line in Asia in the early 1950s, which the U.S.S.R. interpreted as an invitation for North Korea to invade South Korea and start the Korean War.

Blinken's response may be interpreted by the Chinese as an invitation to overwhelm Taiwan.

American commentators and politicians frequently deride Russia as nothing more than an oil and gas exporter with an economy less than the size of that of Texas. This is largely true. What is ignored is that oil and gas are the most strategic products in the world and that Russia leverages its ability to supply oil and gas to other countries for political advantage. The United States could do the same, but under progressive leadership chooses instead to try to eliminate its own oil and gas industry.

In mid-December, 2021, Putin traveled to India and signed some 28 energy-related deals with Indian leadership. Military arrangements were included also. The strategic partnership emerging between Russia and India undercut America's reliance on India as a bulwark against Chinese influence in south Asia and the Middle-east.

Biden's pursuit of a domestic political victory for revolutionary progressives in America will lead to a disaster for America abroad. To focus on remolding the United States revolutionary progressives will reduce the American footprint in the world and will cede to China and Russia the areas we abandon. This policy has already led to a minor disaster — in Afghanistan — with significant consequences — for India. It will likely soon lead to a somewhat larger disaster — in Taiwan — with larger consequences — for Japan and South Korea.

What Biden Should Do

It is clear that Biden, in his effort to keep his promise to support the American middle class — who are our working people — thought he could partner with people who call themselves socialists. But today's revolutionary progressives are not socialists. Socialism is about giving precedence to working people. Revolutionary progressives do not do that. In partnering with revolutionary progressives Biden has abandoned the American working (middle) class, and so has the Democrat Party for the most part. Biden's Democrats have abandoned them except for a few rhetorical flourishes. In place of working people Biden's Democrats stress gains for racial and gender minorities. Biden has embraced revolutionary progressivism which prioritizes privilege reversal. Settling scores (in particular redressing racial injustice) is more important than prosperity, growth, national security, and working class wellbeing. The interests of working people have been abandoned. Biden could embellish his legacy and the popularity of his political party by embracing a modern socialism which provides workers with their notion of a high quality of existence, while shielding them from the exploitation by other actors. At this point Biden is embracing the exploitation of working people by the racial and gender favorites of revolutionary progressivism. It is the abandonment by Biden Democrats of working people which has stimulated the rise of populism in America. The reunification of the nation politically awaits Biden's embracing of the preferences and interests of working people. Biden proclaims that he does this. He doesn't. He should.

Biden Did It Once and It Worked

To pass the infrastructure bill which had been devised on a bipartisan basis in the Senate Biden broke with the revolutionary progressives in the House of Representatives. The circumstances were unusual. Three days before the break the Democrats had taken serious setbacks in local elections. The most serious had been the failure of a former chairman of the national Democrat party to gain election to a second term as governor of Virginia. Polls only a couple of days before the election had shown him well ahead of his Republican challenger. His defeat was a shock!

President Biden and other top Democrats, including the Speaker of the House Nancy Pelosi, decided that the Democrats had to show significant legislative accomplishments to the national electorate quickly. The revolutionary progressive caucus in the House had some 90 Democrat members. For several months they had blocked passage of the infrastructure bill — some 1.3 trillion dollars in spending — insisting that a vote on infrastructure must be accompanied by a vote on their social spending bill. But three days after the local elections, on Friday night, November 5, 2021, more than 70 members of the revolutionary progressive caucus abandoned the leadership of the caucus and voted for the infrastructure bill without an accompanying vote on the social spending bill. Biden had demonstrated that he was a practical politician rather than a revolutionary progressive ideologue. The apparent political power of the revolutionary progressive leadership had been shown to be shallow in this instance. Revolutionary progressive leaders complained to the media that they had been double-crossed by the President.

The President gave himself great credit for passage of the infrastructure financing bill. Below is the text of an email sent out by the White House on November 23, 2021, several weeks after enactment of the legislation:

"**FIRST:** Joe Biden ran on building our nation back better than before. This team believed in that mission and helped elect him to the Oval Office so that he could deliver on his campaign promises.

THEN: President Biden got straight to work negotiating a bipartisan deal to create good-paying jobs, modernize our infrastructure, and turn the climate crisis into an opportunity.
NOW: Democratic leadership got the bill through Congress, and President Biden signed it into law just last week! ..."

It was important for the United States that the infrastructure bill was passed. Unfortunately, in the House of Representatives virtually all Republicans voted against the bill in order that the Democrats not be able to claim a political victory by its passage, as they proceeded to do.

A Republican should want Biden to succeed as president not for the Democrat Party but as the leader of the United States. Republicans need to make this distinction. Biden needs to allow them to do it by separating the two roles himself. At this point he is not doing that.

Chapter 44

Progress and Biden's Destiny

"The means by which Providence raises a nation to greatness are the virtues infused into its leaders." This was Edmund Burke's insight, and it bears the test of history. Joe Biden aspires to greatness.

Early in his administration Biden met with several historians and told them that he aspired to be thought of as a transformational president like Franklin Roosevelt. But FDR was also famed for saving America from political radicalism, at that time threatened by the Communist Party of the United States. Biden's closest similarity to FDR is in having to confront radicalism. Then it was FDR or the Communists; today it could be Biden or the revolutionary progressives.

Biden has the opportunity for greatness. But one doesn't see virtues infused into the personnel of the Biden Administration. Greatness is unlikely for America if she slips into the grasp of the revolutionary progressives.

The danger is that in America the social forces now released by efforts at reform may be free of all restraint. The result will be, as it has always been in history, conflict, and bloodshed on an enormous scale. To people who know history, the American Congress appears more and more like the National Assembly in the early days of the French Revolution. The genius of the American Republic was that its government was originally small and its territory broad and growing so that people who wished to ignore the government could do so. They could go about doing imaginative and important things. The limited knowledge, intelligence, and pervasive corruption of the government could be avoided and relegated to a back space in the minds and lives of citizens.

No longer. Now the government is almost all-pervasive and getting more so and cannot be ignored. The most bitter of the cultural battles is about this — a fight between those who are willing to be sheep for the government shepherd and those who are not. It comes up in unexpected places — like the issue of mask mandates to fight the pandemic.

Biden will not earn the approbation of history if he turns out to be a modern-day Robespierre (counter-Enlightenment despot). The revolutionary progressives will make him that. They will seek to get him to purge the Democrat Party and the government of "deviants," non-progressives.

Biden has great opportunity to emulate Franklin Roosevelt in both of FDR's achievements. Biden as statesman can nudge America toward a consensus-building harmonious democracy. He can be a transformational leader in moving America toward non-partisanship. He can also follow FDR in turning back a surge of radicalism — rejecting revolutionary progressivism as Roosevelt rejected communism.

Biden is mistaken if he presumes that he can implement a revolutionary progressive agenda smoothly. America finds itself in a difficult situation that defies radical progressive recommendations in numerous ways.

The U.S. is falling into an unresolvable domestic political conflict which, if one party begins to lose, is likely to end in violence of some sort. On August 22, 2021, in Portland, Oregon, fighting broke out between the Proud Boys and Anti-Fa. Violence was coming to American politics.

The fiscal situation of the government will undercut American economic prosperity and result in a bitter battle over who will pay the bills as the debt level becomes unmanageable.

Militarist, pro-productive, authoritarian states abroad are providing increasingly aggressive challenges which may result in open conflict. America's ability to defend itself and its allies is increasingly tested.

The American people do not trust their government. In 2019, just 17% of Americans said they trusted the federal government to do the right thing. The pandemic appears to be eroding their faith even further (*The New York Times*, May 23, 2020). This is what government of the people, for the people, and by the people has come to. The more transformational in a revolutionary progressives direction Biden tries to be, the less trusted he will be. Already most of the population pay little attention to him. Polls early in his administration showed some 60% popular support for him. They were simply people pleased to have received cash from the government as part of the initial stimulus package enacted as he came into office. There are no more checks on the way, and gratitude plays little part in American politics. Biden was at the peak of his popularity at the outset of his administration. He is now far down.

This is not a political environment in which transformation of the nation according to the revolutionary progressive agenda is possible without serious internal conflict. Biden's reputation in history will depend on his ability to transcend these difficulties. This is best done by becoming a statesman advocate for non-partisanship in addressing the nation's difficulties.

Resurgent Liberalism (Democrat Moderation)

If Biden lacks the personal and political courage to lead toward non-partisanship, then his best option is to return to the liberal orientation which until now has dominated his political career — what he now refers to as being a "moderate" Democrat. He should lead the Democrat Party as a liberal, which is his natural inclination built on fifty years of political experience.

Liberal democracy may have now begun to succeed in America. Racial equality is becoming real with strong white support. The social safety net is being strengthened because of the pandemic. This is happening because most of the American electorate is now accepting the leadership of liberals, but not of revolutionary progressives.

The irony is that as liberalism begins to pay off after decades of waiting and disappointments, revolutionary progressivism is pushing liberalism aside. Progressives claim credit for the reformist achievements that Democrat moderates are now achieving. revolutionary progressives attribute liberal success to very non-liberal tactics. According to revolutionary progressives, liberal policies are being accepted by the American electorate because of violence — because of riots, intimidation, and threats made by supporters of Black Lives Matter and anti-fa. For a small demographic minority with only limited support among the demographic majority to adopt violence as the principal way to press their policy agenda is to invite disaster. The majority will cease to tolerate violence which is directed at it after it has experimented for a period with appeasement. In the U.S. the demographic majority is now beginning to tire of appeasement. If Biden throws his weight behind violence as an engine of political persuasion, he will accomplish nothing in his pursuit of FDR's mantle.

The Challenge Abroad

America must prepare itself for the burgeoning challenge posed by the autocracies abroad. It no longer has the luxury of focusing solely on domestic issues. Liberal Democrats recognize this and are prepared to try to negotiate a path that defends American abroad while improving it at home. Revolutionary progressives will not agree to this. They will delude themselves about the rising threat abroad while continuing to focus on domestic matters. Abroad they will continue to act as a global hegemon despite the decreasing possibility of success and the increasing risk of overt conflict. Biden should resist being drawn into the revolutionary progressives' illusions.

The Biden Administration acts as if accommodating radicalism, mega-welfare programs, promoting color revolutions, hamstringing hard power, and leveraging soft power are compatible with prosperity, global democratization, and security. Its strategy is inadequate to parry the Chinese and other authoritarian challenges. The revolutionary progressives recommend to Biden a fast track to Cubanizing (Castro-style) America's political and social order, secular stagnation, and global marginalization.

Revolutionary progressive America gallops toward empowering a China-centric totalitarian regime — most likely under strong Chinese influence or tacit control. America will experience economic decline and financial chaos. Already, we are experiencing massive censorship, revenge, and selective individual punishment (starting with job blacklisting) for political non-correctness.

Biden disingenuously espouses unity, equality, and equity — revolutionary progressive goals that attract many people. But is the only way that the U.S. can get there under a despotic regime such as the progressives advocate? America's national interest (purpose) should be maximizing its citizen's quality of existence within a democratic framework that reconciles political differences and protects minority rights (including property holders). This is the "reasonable" thing to do. Biden's Democrats, particularly the radical progressive wing, prioritize power over reason, and in doing so foment civil strife.

Defending Democracy

How did American leaders in the past defend democracy as the best system? They stressed:

Economic growth for the people. This was based on the experience of the U.S. But since the 1970s the authoritarians in China have far outperformed the U.S. and other democracies (except South Korea and Japan which were modeled on the U.S. as it was organized and governed in the period of World War II).

Liberty for the people. But it has seemed in recent decades that there is a trade-off between liberty and economic advance. In the democracies one got dependency and anti-productive liberty and economic stagnation; in China, one got rapid economic advance driven by pro-productive entrepreneurial liberty. Now Biden will have a period of rapid massive deficit spending growth in America. It is unlikely that modern American democracy will be able to extend it beyond a year or two.

Military prowess. That democracies were military adept was rarely said — it was thought untoward — but the United States fielded dominant hard power in and after World War II. Today Democrat influence in the U.S. may have limited U.S. hard power to a place where democracy around the world is endangered. U.S. power increasingly appears insufficient to its role as sponsor and defender of democracy globally.

Democracy is not working well. Authoritarian countries are expanding and explicitly challenging the effectiveness of democracy. *Democracy and Its Elected Enemies* (Rosefielde and Mills, 2013) showed that modern democracies are falling short of ideal results for their people. This is a result of imperfections that are difficult to eliminate. The transformational challenge to the American president is to work toward their elimination.

Establishing a Common Basis of Fact

If one considers politics to be an expression of a civilization, then one might hope that it would represent the highest element of a civilization. Instead, it appears to represent the lowest elements of American civilization.

In the Soviet Union decades ago, I (Mills) would sit with Soviet officials in a closed room listening to the Voice of America. It was illegal to do so, so we had to be careful. From the Americans we got facts about what was happening in the world. The Russians also read the Communist

Party newspapers — *Pravda* and *Izvestia* — but only to discover what the Party line was about how events were to be perceived — rather like Democrats read *The New York Times* or *Atlantic* magazine today. That is, the house media tells them what to think and say. But as to world events as honestly reported by the Voice of America, the Russians and I saw events identically, but were on the opposite sides of each.

That used to be the political situation in America. Democrats and Republicans saw the facts the same way but took different approaches to what should be done in response to them. There was disagreement, but it was based on a common comprehension of events.

This has now changed. Democrats and Republicans perceive facts to be different, and each has a derogatory label for what the other calls "truth." The Republicans coined the term "fake news" for reporting by Democrat-oriented media. "Disinformation" is a term favored by the Democrats for reporting by Republican-oriented media.

Biden finds himself in this situation — that many, probably most, Americans accept information offered by their political side and reject as false that offered by the others. Since he is a Democrat, Republicans by and large reject out-of-hand what Biden says and what is reported by his adherents. How then does he reach people who do not listen to what he says with any acceptance? His great advantage is that the mass media in the U.S. parrot his line, true or false as it may be. That helps him greatly, but it does not solve the problem.

In this situation of a very divided nation, even as to basic facts of what is happening, many Democrats argue that Republicans, and any non-aligned or independent Americans should be reeducated — forcefully if necessary. The minds of those targeted for reeducation go immediately to the brutal (psychologically and physically) reeducation camps of Mao's cultural revolution in 1960s China.

Biden can exercise transformational leadership by moving toward a non-partisan America. He can lean against the prevailing wind of partisan orthodoxy on each side of the mass media. Since his side is by far the dominant force in media, he is able to exercise effective leadership. At this time the media present narratives designed to carry a partisan message. Americans end up disagreeing about basic facts of our social life. We need not disagree about the facts, no matter how preposterous the views of others strike us. It is enough for democracy if we disagree about their implications.

American government is not thoroughly dysfunctional, but it is far less effective than is possible or expected by American citizens. In large part this is because of political interference which has its roots in partisanship. Dysfunction due to partisanship is a key topic of this book, but the ineffectiveness of government is not due solely to partisanship — it is also due to over-bureaucratization. There is a meaningless institutionalization of past practices on auto-drive across administrations and through the decades regardless of the changed circumstances. And there is the dumbing down of people which is occurring because of a general lowering of educational ambition and expectations.

We have proposed a transformational program for Biden that is key to America's future — Presidential statesmanship. If he implements it, then moderate Democrats should support him. Republicans should also support him. If the Republicans gain control of Congress in the 2022 elections, then the Republicans should adopt and continue this program working together with Biden who would still be in the White House. This is America's chance to break out of the spiral of ever-increasingly bitter partisanship that is undermining effective government in the United States.

www.ingramcontent.com/pod-product-compliance
Lightning Source LLC
Chambersburg PA
CBHW070307230426
43664CB00015B/2659